An Archaeology of Educational Evaluation

An Archaeology of Educational Evaluation: Epistemological Spaces and Political Paradoxes outlines the epistemology of the theories and models that are currently employed to evaluate educational systems, education policy, educational professionals and students learning. It discusses how those theories and models find their epistemological conditions of possibility in a specific set of conceptual transferences from mathematics and statistics, political economy, biology and the study of language.

The book critically engages with the epistemic dimension of contemporary educational evaluation and is of theoretical and methodological interest. It uses Foucauldian archaeology as a problematising method of inquiry within the wider framework of governmentality studies. It goes beyond a mere critique of the contemporary obsession for evaluation and attempts to replace it with the opening of a free space where the search for a mode of being, acting and thinking in education is not over-determined by the tyranny of improvement.

This book will appeal to academics, researchers and postgraduate students in the fields of educational philosophy, education policy and social science.

Emiliano Grimaldi is Associate Professor of Sociology of Education at the Department of Social Sciences, University of Naples Federico II, Naples, Italy.

An Archaeology of Educational Evaluation

Epistemological Spaces
and Political Paradoxes

Emiliano Grimaldi

LONDON AND NEW YORK

First published 2020
by Routledge
2 Park Square, Milton Park, Abingdon, Oxon, OX14 4RN

and by Routledge
52 Vanderbilt Avenue, New York, NY 10017

Routledge is an imprint of the Taylor & Francis Group, an informa business

© 2020 Emiliano Grimaldi

The right of Emiliano Grimaldi to be identified as author of this work has been asserted by him in accordance with sections 77 and 78 of the Copyright, Designs and Patents Act 1988.

All rights reserved. No part of this book may be reprinted or reproduced or utilised in any form or by any electronic, mechanical, or other means, now known or hereafter invented, including photocopying and recording, or in any information storage or retrieval system, without permission in writing from the publishers.

Trademark notice: Product or corporate names may be trademarks or registered trademarks, and are used only for identification and explanation without intent to infringe.

British Library Cataloguing-in-Publication Data
A catalogue record for this book is available from the British Library

Library of Congress Cataloging-in-Publication Data
A catalog record has been requested for this book

ISBN: 978-1-138-56918-8 (hbk)
ISBN: 978-0-203-70436-3 (ebk)

Typeset in Bembo
by Cenveo® Publisher Services

To Elena, Sveva and Bianca

My other space

Contents

List of figures x
List of tables xi
List of boxes xii
Acknowledgements xiii
Foreword by Stephen J. Ball xiv

Introduction: Of other evaluations in education 1

Questioning educational evaluation as a critical ontology of ourselves 3
Inhabiting other evaluative spaces 8
Book overview 11

1 Governmentality, evaluation and education: An archaeological gaze 14

Educational evaluation as a governmental practice 14
Government, evaluation and truth 20
Genealogy and archaeology: Two complementary gazes on regimes of government 22
The archaeological method within an analytics of government 25
The archaeological description of discursive formations 32
Trees of derivation, interdiscursive configurations and forms of articulation 42
Conclusion 45

2 Educational evaluation as an enunciative field 53

Suspending educational evaluation 53
A long-standing and globalised social experiment to make education governable 54
Educational evaluation as a form of rationality 61

Educational evaluation as a way of seeing and perceiving 64
Educational evaluation as a governmental techne 66
Education evaluation as identity formation 68
Conclusion 70

3 The epistemic space of educational evaluation — 72

Educational evaluation and the project of a mathematical formalisation 73
Locating educational evaluation in a tridimensional epistemic space 78
The formation of educational evaluation as an enunciative field through transferences 80
Conclusion 84

4 Living systems — 86

System as a grid of specification 86
Biology, organisational theory and educational evaluation as fields of concomitance 97
Conclusion 102

5 Forms of production — 105

Production as a grid of specification 105
Political economy, management and educational evaluation as fields of concomitance 118
Conclusion 122

6 Meanings — 126

System of meanings as a grid of specification 127
The study of language, sociology and educational evaluation as fields of concomitance 136
Conclusion 141

7 Educational evaluation and its epistemic and political paradoxes — 145

The homo *of educational evaluation* 145
Epistemic and ethical paradoxes 149
Political paradoxes 152
A reflexive government of performance 159

8 **Epistemological ruptures and the invention
   of other evaluations in education**   163

   Epistemological ruptures: Space, time and norm 164
   *Other evaluations in education: Contesting the anthropological
      postulate 172*

   References   175
   Index   187

Figures

2.1	The globalised space of educational evaluation	59
3.1	The tridimensional epistemic space of educational evaluation	81
4.1	Living system as a grid of specification	87
4.2	Biology, organisational theory and educational evaluation as fields of concomitance	98
4.3	The archaeological quadrilateral of educational evaluation, organisational theory and biology	102
5.1	Production as a grid of specification. The *Context-Input-Process-Product* evaluation model	106
5.2	Measuring, monitoring and intervening on the mechanics of the educational process as production	116
5.3	Political economy, management theory and educational evaluation as fields of concomitance	120
5.4	The archaeological quadrilateral of educational evaluation, management theory and political economy	122
6.1	The study of language, sociology and educational evaluation as fields of concomitance	137
6.2	The archaeological quadrilateral of educational evaluation, sociology and the study of language	141
7.1	The epistemic quadrilateral of educational evaluation	146

Tables

1.1 Four modalities to interrogate regimes of government 18
1.2 The identification of the objects of discourse 33
1.3 The identification of a subject as enunciative modality 36
1.4 Grasping the formation of concepts 38
1.5 Grasping the formation of concepts 40
1.6 The archaeological gaze deployed within an analytics of government 46
2.1 Educational evaluation as a governmental techne 67

Boxes

3.1 The case of school effectiveness research   83
3.2 The case of school improvement and its relations
     to economy and biology   84

Acknowledgements

The writing of this book has been for me possible thanks to a series of encounters with colleagues and friends who have profoundly changed the way I think and do research as a sociologist of education. Foremost among them is Stephen J. Ball, from whom I learned how to think differently about education and sociology of education, mobilising Foucault as a theorist of freedom and a methodologist. My heartfelt thanks go to Roberto Serpieri. Without his insightful impulses and outside our common intellectual journey this book would not have been possible. Paolo Landri continues to be for me an invaluable source of inspiration and helps me to feed off the intellectual curiosity and the passion for education that have originated this book. I am also very especially indebted to Helen M. Gunter for her comments and support at the initial stage of this writing project. I also want to acknowledge Martin Lawn, Eric Mangez, Romuald Normand and Jennifer Ozga and Pat Thomson for their helpful remarks on earlier presentations and public lectures based on parts of the book. I seize the occasion to thank many colleagues at the Department of Social Sciences of University of Naples Federico II who have offered valued comments, insights and support at different stages of the writing process. They have contributed to the book in more ways than they know. While I am indebted to all these people who have helped me to think and write productively, I take full responsibility for the text. Finally, I need to thank my family, Elena, Sveva, Bianca, Rosa, Umberto and Alessio. Without their love, patience and encouragement, this book would never have been finished. In the writing of the book, my thoughts often went to Ubaldo and our discussions on much of the topics covered in the book.

Foreword

Stephen J. Ball

Foucault said, 'Everything I do, I do in order that it may be of use' (Defert and Ewald 2001: 911–12). In this respect, he is not a theorist in the traditional sense, his work is about acting on the world, acting in the world, changing the possibilities of how the world might be and how we might be 'in' the world. Emiliano Grimaldi's book is also useful in these same senses, but also in another way – it offers, to borrow Foucault's words, a 'meticulous, erudite and exact' application of the method of archaeology. The book is a guide, a template, an exemplar of the archaeological method and very specifically how it may be used and applied, in this case to the field of educational evaluation as a general system of thought. The importance of this cannot be underestimated – much is said and written about the archaeological method, but it is rarely put into practice, thorough-going applications are very few and far between. Students eager to explore the promise of the method are typically mystified and confused by the challenges involved and the absence of commentaries or examples that are able to render Foucault's exhortations into techniques of application. This book responds to this absence to make archaeology into something sensible, doable and powerful as a means of critique: a vehicle for thinking about the ways in which current social arrangements and practices produce and constrain, at the same time, our possible modes of action and being. Stage by stage, level by level, dimension by dimension, drawing on Foucault's *The Order of Things*, the book unpicks the enunciations, regularities and inter-discursive configurations of evaluations. It shows us how archaeology can be done!

The aim of archaeology as laid out in this book is not oriented toward 'a theory of the knowing subject, but rather to a theory of discursive practice' (Foucault 1970/1994: xiv). It seeks to render visible in careful and exact fashion 'the provenance of the very apparatus within which we think' (Mills 1997: 76), that is our enmeshment in discursive practices. This endeavour is both practical in a philosophical or sociological sense and eminently political.

> ... the political, ethical, social, philosophical problem of our days is not to try to liberate the individual from the state, and from the state's

institutions, but to liberate us both from the state *and* from this type of individualisation which is linked to the state. (Foucault 1983: 216, emphasis added)

The apparatuses and practices of educational evaluation is the specific focus here and the forms and meaning of education and possibilities of subjectivity produced within these. Evaluation, as Grimaldi puts it, is 'a constitutive and distinctive trait of our educational present', an authoritative voice within the current possibilities of education, an epistemological space of professionalisation (which is part of a more general de-politicisation and technisation of education), a space of expertise and a field of visibility within which new kinds of educational subjects are made-up. Educational evaluation is also one area and one set of polyvalent techniques within a general, contemporary dispositif of government that is now referred to as 'governing by numbers'. The subject under such a regime is made calculable rather than memorable, malleable rather than committed, flexible rather than principled, productive rather than truthful – or more precisely is rendered into a particular form of the truth, a numerical truth. Very particularly within the contemporary technocratic market regime of neoliberalism, the relationships of truth and power are articulated and operationalised more and more in terms of forms of performance, effects or outputs and outcomes, all expressed in the reductive form of numbers; the 'numericisation of politics' as Legg (2005: 143) calls it. Grimaldi takes us beneath the seductive positivities of numericisation to reveal the forms of knowledge, the modes of being and the semantic claims that evaluation bring into existence within education. Within an archaeological approach, this is addressed by mapping the *'unconscious* of knowledge', its aim is 'not to uncover the truth or the origin of a statement but rather to discover the support mechanisms which keep it in place' (Mills 1997: 49).

This remarkable and compelling book renders our educational present and its prevailing positivities fragile and revocable. It makes these, and evaluation in particular, 'not as necessary as all that' (Foucault 1971: 8). It undermines the self-evidence of measurement and its horizon of silent objectification within which we are articulated, and in doing so it opens up spaces for acting and thinking differently about education and as educators our relation to ourselves and to others, to our students. To paraphrase Foucault, Grimaldi's archaeological analysis shows us that we are much freer than we feel, that and what we accept as truth, as evidence, can be criticised and destroyed (see Foucault 1988: 9). Evidence and evaluation are not necessarily bad, but they are very, very dangerous.

Introduction
Of other evaluations in education

This book is an experiment that originates from the will to question evaluation as a constitutive and distinctive trait of our educational present. Its specific remit is the analysis of the epistemological space where the contemporary regime of practice of educational evaluation finds its conditions of possibility.

My interest in the topic stems from the acknowledgement of three different but interrelated aspects of contemporary education. First, evaluation is nowadays a key semantic device in every claim on education. It acts as an obligatory passage point for whatever voice has the ambition to be heard and be recognisable as authoritative when speaking about education. Importantly, an evidence-based, outcome-oriented and standardising evaluation is presented as a necessary constitutive element of education and its government, as a neutral and eminently technical activity, whereas its politics and historical contingency are concealed and its effects in term of power are made invisible. Second, in the last decades evaluation has become an identifiable and unavoidable component of the broader governmental and professional establishment of education at the global level on the basis of the assumption that it can provide actual and potential contributions to improving learning, teaching and administration, and in general the quality of education. Third, as teachers, students, parents, academics, researchers or administrators, we are continuously made and remade into subjects and objects of evaluations through scholarship, policy and practice at different scales and for different purposes.

Of course, this is not something specific to education. Dahler-Larsen (2012: 3) has recently noted how evaluation is part of 'a larger societal trend that also includes activities such as auditing, inspection, quality assurance and accreditation – which together constitute a huge and unavoidable social experiment which is conspicuously cross sectional and transnational'. Yet, education is a field where this trend manifests itself as particularly cogent and, somehow, disruptive. As part of this unavoidable social experiment, our contemporary experience of education implies the recurrent engagement with multiple and increasingly pervasive practices of evaluation that influence how education is thought and practiced as well as the ways its qualities are conceived and appraised.

A wide array of activities is ranged under the conceptual umbrella of educational evaluation: student assessment, measurement, testing, program evaluation, school personnel evaluation, school accreditation and curriculum evaluation. More and more education systems in the world are transformed by 'ambitious school reform programmes which include a strong element of evaluation and assessment' (OECD 2013: 3). As Kellaghan *et al.* (2003) observe, evaluation 'occurs at all levels of education systems, from the individual student evaluations carried out by classroom teachers, to evaluations of schools and districts, to district-wide program evaluations, to national assessments, to cross-national comparisons of student achievement' (p. 1). These reform programmes adopt in a more or less coherent way a holistic evaluative framework that addresses five levels: system evaluation, policy evaluation, school evaluation, staff appraisal and student assessment. In doing so, they mobilise and are mobilised by bodies of evaluative knowledge that can be related to specific fields of theoretical and empirical investigation: product, personnel, policy and program evaluation (Scriven 1991). Through these bodies of evaluative knowledge, educational people, objects, activities, organisations, systems or the diverse combinations of them are governed, made and continuously transformed.

Within such a field of knowledge, evaluative theories and models with very different political underpinnings coexist and confront each other (Madaus and Stufflebeam 2002: 18). At the same time, it is widely acknowledged how, within these confrontations, neoliberalism and neomanagerialism are co-opting evaluation, establishing a *doxa* and subjugating or marginalising alternative views. Interestingly, the epistemological space where the struggles between alternative educational evaluation theories and models occur seems to have a distinctive style that is particular ways of looking at things and people, practices of division, analytical strategies and modes by which things and people are made visible.

The ambition of this book is to take seriously this last point, attempting a detailed analysis of the distinctive style of the epistemological space of educational evaluation. Such an analysis will be carried on in a general frame that looks at the interplay between the questioning of the forms and limits of evaluative knowledge through an archaeological method (Foucault 2002a, 2002b) and a critical ontology of ourselves (Foucault 1997a; Dean 2010) that problematises the ways in which educational evaluation is imbricated in the fabrication of a regime of truth and, more widely, in the making and government of ourselves as educational subjects. Using foucauldian archaeology as a method, the book outlines how theories and models currently employed to evaluate educational systems, education policy, schools as organisations, educational professionals and students learning find their epistemological conditions of possibility in a specific set of conceptual transferences from mathematics and statistics, political economy, biology and the study of language (Foucault 2002a).

The ultimate aim of the analysis is to identify a set of epistemological and ethico-political paradoxes that affect contemporary educational evaluation as an enunciative field and, more widely, as a regime of practice. In doing so, the book intends to offer a critical (but constructive) contribution to the debate on evaluation and its possible theoretical and practical development. In fact, the analysis ends discussing the epistemological challenges to be explored in the attempt to go beyond the tyrannies of contemporary evaluation and think differently about the subjects, the objects and the ethics of educational evaluation.

This introductory chapter defines the scope, the analytical frame, the remit and the limits of the book. I unpack the conceptual and ethical moves that I have outlined above, discussing more in details what is the relevance of the analysis, to what extent the questioning of educational evaluation as a feature of our educational present stands as part of a critical ontology of ourselves and, finally, how this book represents an attempt to enlarge the space of possibility for educational evaluation, contributing to a new evaluative politics and practice.

Questioning educational evaluation as a critical ontology of ourselves

The analysis of the epistemological space of educational evaluation is located in a framework that addresses evaluation as the recursive interplay between a form of knowledge, a variety of related governmental technologies and techniques and a kind of ethical work. As an archaeology of educational evaluation, this book is inspired by a research sensibility where the analytical is mutually constitutive of the ethical or, to put it in another way, where *critique* acts as connection between an archaeological gaze as *clinique* and an emancipatory research *ethics*. If in fact this is mainly a clinical work with an aim to describe evaluation as a form of truth production in the field of education, then such a description is ethically devoted to the opening of spaces of agonism (Oksala 2012) and the questioning of the limits it imposes on us (Fimiani 1997). This is an exercise of a critical ontology of ourselves as contemporary educational subjects in our relation to evaluation as a key regime of practice and its role in the production of truth about education, its objects, processes and subjects.

Critique

What does it means to say that evaluation, as knowledge, technology and ethical work, marks the distinctiveness of our educational present? In the perspective of the book, our experience as contemporary educational subjects is conceptualised as difference in space and time. Experience is unanticipable, but also constituted through the repetition of anterior evaluative events that are delimited by concrete socio-historical conditions.

Ontologically, the perspective adopted in this book is a form of reverse Platonism (Foucault 1970) that 'establishes the general ontological priority of the event over the object' and 'the specific ontological priority of thought as an event over thought as any structure or system' (Faubion 1998: xxii). Educational present is not merely a temporal notion here. On the contrary it is what we are as educational subjects, and it is possible only within a social architecture, a scene that suspends time as mere succession and shows its constitutive spatiality.

As something that happens now in a field of multiple and conflicting forces, our present is what 'embodies the limitations of what we are now, what will be left behind, and what will be transformed' (Gilson 2014: 11). The scope of the book is to address educational evaluation as a constitutive trait of our present. Educational evaluation is conceived as a set of different and repeated events that pervasively link up contemporary educational institutions and perform a distinctive capacity of being effective in the ways in which, as educational subjects, we are governed and try to govern ourselves and the others (Foucault 1991; Dean 2010; Peters *et al.* 2009).

Multiple and interrelated processes are at stake here. In the scientific and political domains, at different scales, evaluation is increasingly framed as a universal good, as knowledge and practice that cannot be rejected or opposed, because of their promises of enlightenment and improvement, social betterment and democracy, increased efficiency and – paradoxically – equity, transparency and responsibilisation. In the space of the social and economic sciences, it has progressively acquired an authoritative voice as a distinct and powerful discipline that employs scientific procedures to produce knowledge on education and, more generally, 'the social'. Through the influential and pervasive action of global public and private players (international institutions and organisations, global consultants, philanthropies, networks of expertise and so on), evaluation and the related socio-material paraphernalia are naturalised as the reasonable, plausible and necessary way to produce veritable knowledge on the qualities of education, its subjects and outcomes and to govern the field. As an instrument of economic and social knowledge, evaluation is co-opted by multiple political rationalities, prominently liberalism, neoliberalism and neoconservatism (Dean 2007), to serve different political purposes and programmes of control. In fact, evaluation contributes to and is constitutive of various political projects that work across national boundaries and range from the neoliberalisation of education through the making of educational markets (Ryan and Cousins 2009), to the reconstruction of the organisational forms of public education and the education states according to New Public Management (Gunter *et al.* 2016). It is part of the reinvention of the governmentality of education through the establishment of new governmental technologies that reflect a liberal, neoliberal or neoconservative conception of the relations between the state, the market, the profession and rational action (Power 2011).

But how to relate to evaluation as a constitutive trait of our present? The attempt of this book is to enter in a particular relation to evaluation as a present educational reality, making of it an 'actuality' (Foucault 1997a). This means to enter in a relation to evaluation as something that counts for us as contemporary educational subjects, problematising it and breaking with the current concrete socio-historical conditions that define its historically contingent and yet apparently necessary forms (Foucault 1997b). The production of truth is a key focus here, in so far as the analysis of the present as actuality assumes an ethical form where the aim is to 'freeing thought from its tendency to sort images according to truth and falsity, to allow it to measure the effects they hold for subjectivity' (Tanke 2009: 127).

In this guise, this work is animated by the endeavour to trouble the apparent inevitability of a historically contingent mode of evaluation, moving from the 'desire to make out what is concealed under [our] precise, floating, mysterious, utterly' educational present (Foucault 2001: 443). My ambition here is to enter in relation to educational evaluation as a key part of our own historicity, to understand our fabrication within power/knowledge, and to learn the possibility of modifying our mode of existence (Ball 2017: 35). The aim is to enlarge the possibilities of going beyond the limits that the current historical forms of evaluation, as knowledge and practice, impose on us as educational subjects.

Problematisation is a key concept here, because it defines the envisaged form of criticism, and also represents the conceptual link between critique and the adopted analytical gaze (Koopman 2013). As a form of criticism, problematisation is intended as that particular attitude with the aim to dismantle objects as taken for granted fixed essences and to show how they have come to be, (re)making them as something that enters 'into the play of the true and the false and constitutes it as an object for thought' (Bacchi 2012: 4). Paraphrasing Foucault, this is a work of problematisation in so far as it has the ambition to allow for a step back from a historically contingent manner of evaluating educational systems, organisations, processes, professionals and outcomes, 'for putting it forward as a thought-object and interrogating it about its meaning, its conditions, and its ends' (Foucault 1997b: 117).

In such a perspective, as an experiment of a critical ontology of ourselves, this book is an act of criticism that calls into question evaluation as a regime of practice in the contemporary government of education because of its key role in delimiting what we can be, think, say and do as educational subjects. It is a movement to detach ourselves from a historically contingent evaluative practice, and to disclose 'the possibility of no longer being, doing, or thinking what we are, do, or think' (Foucault 1997a: 315–16) as subjects and objects of evaluation in education. The aim of the book is to create a space of problematisation from which critique and transformative action can occur, problematising what has acquired the status of a situation inherent in the natural order of things and creating cracks in what is commonly regarded as a secure foundation.

Clinique

Truth, or better, the relation between truth and subjectivity is the key analytical focus of the book as a clinical work. The analysis of the epistemological space of educational evaluation is located, in fact, in a wider attempt to problematise educational evaluation as a regime of practice, that is a relatively organised and systematised way of producing judgements on education, its subjects, processes and outcomes that occur through the recursive assemblage of a distinct set of forms of knowledge and a variety of related techniques and practical ways of thinking, knowing, acting and judging. More in details, the regime of practice of educational evaluation is conceived here as unfolding through the recursive intertwining between:

- evaluation as a mode of inquiry that defines a distinct set of objects, ways of dealing with them, aims and authoritative agents of expertise;
- a set of related and highly specific categorising and dividing practices that individuate and operate on the conducts of organisations, groups and individuals, and rely upon definite evaluative mechanisms, techniques and technologies;
- evaluation as ethical work, as practices of self-formation through which we turn ourselves into subjects and objects of evaluation (Foucault 1982b).

The concept of problematisation defines also the space of analysis of the book. As a key regime of practice in the governing of education, evaluation is connected to a set of powerful modes of problematisation that defines objects, rules of action and modes of relation to oneself (Foucault 1997a: 318). Evaluation responds and contributes to (re)produce them. These modes of problematisation relates both to the epistemological and political foundations of modern education as social practice and to its government, functioning and ends in modern society. In this respect, the book as clinical endeavour is not interested in exploring the origins, the fulfilment, the internal ends or even the teleology of contemporary educational evaluation, but rather to identify the epistemological and political paradoxes that are connected to those modes of problematisation that 'act as limits on who we are and who we might yet become' (Koopman 2014: 401) when we engage with practices of evaluation in education.

In this respect, the critical interrogation of educational evaluation as actuality can be regarded as a contribution to the problematising of the meta-narratives of Enlightenment[1] and modernity (Olssen 2014: 216; Aronowitz and Giroux 1991). The assumption underlying the book is that educational evaluation is a regime of practice where we experience a singular inflection of the Kantian enigma, that is the tension between a world which is at the same time made and given, a task and an obligation, and an individual who is at the same time element of the world itself and actor/agent (Fimiani 1997).

This is a constitutive paradox of modernity and, as Foucault recognised, it is still giving a form to the possibility for thinking, being and acting in our present, in education as in other spheres of social life (Foucault 2002a).

Of course, this book is not an attempt to overcome such a paradox in a definitive or complete mode in relation to educational evaluation. It is not in my intentions, neither in my possibilities. Rather, this intends to be a modest contribution to the freeing of thought on educational evaluation from the tyranny of repetition, contributing to the critical literature that shows to what extent our structures of experience and our place in the process of knowing are creations of modernity and of the doctrinal elements of Enlightenment. In this respect, this work is situated in an intellectual and ethico-political space that unfolds starting from a double nostalgia produced by the Kantian enigma: (a) the aspiration to question the forms and limits of our knowledge, treating educational evaluation as contingent, specific, local and historical form of knowledge and (b) the desire to reflect on the ontology of ourselves, that is how we are made and made ourselves and the others as subjects and/or actors of evaluation.

The questioning of the forms and limits of our knowledge are carried on in this book starting from the choice of the relation between truth and subjectivity as the privileged focus of analysis. This cut is underpinned by a relational understanding of the nexus between truth, power and ethics. Moreover, it is premised on both the will to recapture something that is within the present (and not beyond or behind it) and an 'attentiveness to the delimiting conditions of the present' (Gilson 2014: 12). The attitude towards problematisation as mode of inquiry and the option for problematisation as the space of analysis converge here into the attempt to question the meanings, spaces and effects of historically contingent modes of evaluation, disentangling the coagulations between truth, the functioning of power and the making of the educational subjects (Ball 2016). The privileged focus on the epistemological space of educational evaluation responds to the goal to make the criteria that establish educational evaluation as a regime of practice more noticeable, undermining their taken-for-grantedness and opening up for 'examination both the complex relations that produced them and the effects of their operation' (Veyne 1997: 154). The aim of the book relates to the understanding of what makes the plurality of evaluations possible, the roots of their simultaneity and the 'soil that can nourish them all in their diversity and sometimes in spite of their contradictions' (Foucault 1997b: 118). It stands as a contribution to the understanding of the interferences between science, politics and ethics 'in the formation of [educational evaluation as] a scientific domain, a political structure, a moral practice' (ibid. 116).

In addressing the complex tangle between evaluation as a scientific domain, political technology and moral practice, one needs to find a starting point. Different analytical strategies are possible. Archaeology represents a possible choice. Its specific remit is to explore the historical conditions of possibility for the subjects and the objects of educational evaluation as enunciative field and to outline 'the site where truth names the constraints and modalities required of both subject and object to enter the positivity of reality and engage in a set of possible relations' (Deere 2014: 518). In relation to analysis of educational evaluation as regime of truth, archaeology is adopted here as an anti-method (Shiner 1982) that allows us to suspend 'what is taken as given, natural, necessary and neutral', to search for regularities in the formation of the enunciative field of educational evaluation and to challenge 'trans-historical schemas and teleologies which claim to be able to account for the truth of our [educational] present' (Dean 2010: 3–4).

Inhabiting other evaluative spaces

The critical ontology of ourselves and, within it, the questioning of the forms and limits of educational evaluation through archaeology are the poles that organise the space and scope of this book, together with an ethical disposition that is carefully normative, emancipatory and experimental. Archaeology is what allows here a double movement through an activity of cutting with an ambition to interrupt and divide our educational present as a time of repetition and contribute to a movement beyond the limits of the present. It is an activity of writing on educational evaluation as part of the educational present in a field of power relations and political struggle. The aim is to point out that there are other reasonable options.

The archaeological work stands as a preliminary and yet necessary act of freedom that reflects on the consequences of educational evaluation as a set of rules to produce truth on educational value and allows to interrogate our educational present through a double detachment: (a) from how we are governed and govern ourselves and the others through evaluation in the field of education; and (b) from the conflict between evaluative theories, models and ideas. The question relates to what are the current problematisations that have historically constructed the problem of evaluation in education and set out the conditions in which possible responses to this problem can be given, and what are their constitutive elements that need to be put under scrutiny in order to think differently about educational evaluation.

Ethics

Few more words are needed in order to clarify what I mean with emancipatory and experimental research ethics here. The analysis of this book is underpinned by a 'sober and careful' kind of normativity (Fimiani 1997: 21), where the contemporary discursive and practical forms of educational evaluation will be judged 'against an ideal of a minimum of domination' and against their relative capacity to recognise and promote difference (Foucault 1997c: 298). Again, the issue of government is pivotal here. In this respect, this book intends to represent an emancipatory tool that contributes to the 'constitution of ourselves as autonomous [educational] subjects' (Foucault 1997a: 313), where autonomy is related to the growth of capabilities disconnected from the intensification of power relations that lead to discipline, normalisation and over-regulation. This implies to exit from a condition of 'excess of authority', challenging 'effects of domination which may be linked to structures of truth or institutions entrusted with truth' (Foucault 1997c: 295). It stands as a tool to cultivate the 'art of not being governed like that and at that cost' (Foucault 2007: 45) and to 'refuse everything that might present itself in the form of a simplistic and authoritarian alternative' (Foucault 1997a: 313).

So, it is not my intention to theorise against or argue for a radical opposition to any form of educational evaluation, neither this is a plea for radical freedom, absolute spontaneity or the eliciting of any form of institutional constraining and accountability. This is not an attempt to be 'for' or 'against' educational evaluation or any specific evaluative approach, theory or model. Neither, the book is a gesture of rejection, or a contribution to the establishment of clear dividing lines between the good and bad educational evaluation or, more, the drawing of another inside/outside divide to determine what good and bad elements there may be in contemporary educational evaluation. Thinking of educational evaluation as a problem entails to admit that there isn't, probably, 'any politics that can contain the just and definitive solution' (Foucault 1997b: 114), and at the same time struggling to challenge evaluative politics in education, highlighting paradoxes and raising questions, asking politics itself to answer these questions, being aware that no complete answers are possible. Recalling Foucault's words (ibid.), it is a question, then, of thinking about the relations of educational evaluation to education politics, in the attempt to elaborate and pose political questions that may make possible the future formation of a collective, a 'we' that could also become a potential community of action.

Rather, this book is an attempt to carry on an analysis of ourselves as beings who are historically determined, to a certain extent, by educational evaluation and to search for a way out from the imposed alternative between acceptance and criticising. As an exercise of freedom that seeks to 'denaturalise' what is given, necessary and obligatory, it is an act of belonging and rupture, which critically contests, in particular, the status of the subject and the mode of individualisation proper to contemporary educational evaluation. Thus, the aim of this book is to enhance an extension of our participation in the present evaluation systems (see Foucault 1977b: 230). Criticism is here a positive act of imagination, a productive and not a destructive endeavour. It is emancipatory in so far as it aspires to increase freedom, making available resources to change our relations to truth and power through a negative use of our capacities for reasoning/thinking. Freedom is intended here as the ability to modify ourselves, to produce ourselves exploring limits to authorised forms of subjectivity and 'questioning any received standpoint' but 'in the context of the social influences at work on us' and 'drawing on the resources society makes available to us' (Bevir 1999: 76). Criticism and an emancipatory ethics meets archaeology as analytics here in so far as 'one can criticize [...], but one can only do so by playing a certain game of truth' (Foucault 1997c: 295), where game means here the 'set of rules by which truth is produced, [...] a set of procedures that lead to a certain result, which, on the basis of its principles and rules of procedure, may be considered valid or invalid' (ibid. 297).

As an attempt to play a game of truth, thus, this book is experimental and oriented towards the crossing over of the limits imposed on us by educational evaluation as scholarship and governmental practice that creates a sociohistorical distinctive set of conditions of our thinking and acting, and ultimately for the government of ourselves and the others. As such, it is a fiction, an attempt to soliciting an ethical enthusiasm and agonism (Oksala 2012) and produce an interference between our reality and our past through de-familiarisation and disaggregation, resulting in the opening up of a possible future and a transformation of the relation which we have with ourselves and the world (O'leary 2006: 102).

If the writing of this book is thus 'in itself a form of action or intervention' (Dean 2010: 6) in the milieu of contemporary education, its privileged interlocutors are those teachers, head teachers, educators, students, parents, researchers or administrators whose actuality is permeated by evaluation and who, in relation to that, experience a series of discomforts. The first and major discomfort relates to the perception of the normalising effects of an evidence-based, standardising and performance-oriented evaluative practice that presents itself to us as necessary, obvious, naturally benign and, at the same time, performs the power to silence critical voices and/or to marginalise them into positions that appear as ethically untenable (against evaluation, against improvement, against evidence; Biesta 2007; Hammersley 2013). The second discomfort is related to the difficulties to challenge a historically contingent truth on evaluation that establishes itself as a self-evident and undisputable, and to find alternative ways of doing evaluation that do not reproduce the reductionist and normalising effects of the dominant discourse and technologies (Dahler-Larsen 2012). The third discomfort is related to the rational and emotional acknowledgment of the violence exerted on us as educational subjects by an expanding evaluative machinery that forces us to 'set aside our personal beliefs and commitments' and 'to live an existence of calculation' (Ball 2003: 215).

Facing these discomforts, that I entirely share as teacher and researcher, this book stands as an experiment suspended in between a molecular theorising (the acknowledgement to be part of a plural and dispersed intellectual production) and the ambition to contribute to enact a generalising experiencing. The ambition is to produce emancipatory and liberating effects through a mobilising discursive modality that challenges the hegemonic effect of a historically contingent regime of evaluative truth and attempts to re-enact the expelled diversity.

Book overview

The book is organised in eight chapters. Chapter 1 presents the main traits archaeology as method, locating it within the framework of an analytics of government and a general sensibility towards the governmentality studies. The chapter draws on Foucault's works and the main literature in the field to present archaeology as a generative method to analyse enunciative fields and regimes of truth and, relatedly, to contribute to a critical ontology of ourselves. The chapter argues that archaeology provides us with a set of distinct analytical strategies to address the analysis of the fields of visibility and forms of rationality that organise the ways of doing things and the freedom with which human beings act within specific regimes of government. Chapter 2 stands as a preliminary step towards the archaeological analysis, addressing educational evaluation as an enunciative field and suspending its immediate forms of unity. Educational evaluation is analysed as a form of rationality, a way of seeing and perceiving, a governmental techne and a mode of identity formation. The chapter discusses this enunciative space as the field of investigation of the book and its conditions of possibility as the specific object of analysis.

Drawing on Foucault's analysis in *The Order of Things* (2002a), Chapter 3 locates educational evaluation in a tridimensional epistemological space, interpreting it as a mode of inquiry that: (a) has the project to establish itself, at different levels, a mathematical formalisation; (b) proceeds through models and/or concepts transferred from biology, political economy and the study of language and (c) explores some distinctive empirical manifestations of 'that mode of being of [modern man] which philosophy is attempting to conceive at the level of radical finitude' (ibid. 379). The chapter also highlights how the rise of educational evaluation is strictly related to the complex tangle of governmental processes that develop around the interrelationship between the problem of the government of population, the foundation of the modern state, statistics and expertise. The analysis deals with the inescapable relation that educational evaluation has with mathematics, numbers and the tension towards the application of mathematics to the empirical domain. Nevertheless, the chapter warns against the risk of thinking to numbers as devices with some intrinsic characters and emphasises the need to address the regimes of language and value or, to put it another way, the political rationalities and regimes for the production, delimitation and authorisation of truth within which numericisation occurs. The need is highlighted for an archaeological analysis of the epistemological figures of labor, life and language (and their transferences), which are interpreted as conditions of possibility for the emergence of educational evaluation as an enunciative field and a governmental practice.

Chapter 4 starts the archaeological analysis of educational evaluation as an enunciative field in search of its regularities as rules of formation and relations between statements. It focuses on those regularities that can be understood as the effect of a distinct set of processes of transference from biology through organisational theory as a concomitant enunciative field. Using the foucauldian tree of enunciative derivation and an analytics of interdiscursive configurations as heuristics, the chapter discusses the role of the figures of living system and organisation as grids of specification that constitutes the objects of the evaluative analysis and the related analytical strategies. The chapter discusses how these epistemic traits determine the kind of relationships that evaluative knowledge in education is naturally brought to seek out at the analytical level and to establish at the normative level. Adopting a similar strategy, Chapter 5 addresses the regular occurrence of further grids of specification and methods of characterisation that allow valuing, diagnosis and ordering as practices that are functional to the management of the educational evaluand. The chapter expands the archaeological analysis looking at the figure of 'labour as production' as a second regular grid of specification that constitutes the objects of the evaluative analysis and provides methods and analytical strategies for their characterisation. It understands such a regularity as the effect of a distinct set of transferences from political economy through the mediation of management theory as a concomitant enunciative field. Chapter 6 shows how it is possible to recognise in the interstices of the paradoxes produced by the transferences from biology and political economy a further set of regularities in the enunciative field, where the evaluand is formed as pertaining to the domain of meaning. In particular, the chapter discusses the regular occurrence of the figure of system of meaning as a third key grid of specification in the field of educational evaluation, interpreting it as the analogical and differentiating effect of a distinct set of transferences from the study of language through the mediation of sociology as concomitant enunciative field. It discusses how, through those transferences, the evaluand is located within a paradoxical time made of discontinuity and continuity. Chapters 4 to 6 all end outlining how the described epistemic transferences make thinkable a particular kind of *homo of evaluation* (hereafter HoE) and historicity of the objects/subjects of evaluation as learning, productive and sense-making entities. Those entities live in a space-time where forces that drive towards the fulfilling of a function, productive process or understanding struggle against, in an ongoing dialectic, the dangers of ineffectiveness, scarcity or insignificance within determined and determining conditions of existence.

Building on the analyses in the previous chapters, Chapter 7 delimits the archaeological quadrilateral of educational evaluation, that is the epistemic space within which it finds its conditions of possibility as a mode of inquiry, governmental practice and ethics. Such a quadrilateral, it is argued, articulates itself around the figure of the HoE, a particular inflection of modern man. The chapter analyses the key traits of the HoE, his character as empirical-transcendental doublet and his perennial oscillation between the promises of Enlightenment and fulfilment. The analysis emphasises how, inhabiting such an epistemic space, educational evaluation stands as: (a) a paradoxical science of truth, entrapped in a perennial oscillation between an ingenuous reduction of truth to the empirical and a prophetical promise; (b) a modern ethic that does not formulate explicitly a morality of effectiveness or improvement, in so far as the imperative is located within the evaluative thought and its movement towards the apprehension of the unthought and (c) a dialectical and teleological mode of inquiry that assumes a conception of time as fulfilment that can be known as a succession and has an inherently teleological nature (Foucault 2002a).

Moreover, the chapter reconnects the archaeological terrain to the problem of government, showing how the configuration of this epistemic space produces a distinct set of political paradoxes and makes it possible to understand the complexities of the relationships between educational evaluation and a distinct set of political rationalities, namely liberalism, neoliberalism and risk, that co-opt the HoE and give him particular kinds of inflections.

The concluding chapter presents some perspectival considerations on the possibility to think educational evaluation otherwise and to overcome the shortcuts, reductionisms, paradoxes and frustrations that the current doxa of educational evaluation produces in the scholarly, professional, policy and public debate. I argue that the archaeological analysis invites us to explore the interstices of the empirical/transcendental paradox and to engage with the transgression of its anthropological postulate. The chapter identifies two related intellectual paths of reflection: to free the HoE from the utopia of fulfilment and to historicise him (Popkewitz and Brennan 1997). In turn, this implies practicing three distinct epistemological ruptures: (a) rethinking the spatial dimension in educational evaluation, focusing on the constructing of identities through the formation of social spaces; (b) thinking of time as a multiplicity of strands moving with an uneven flow and (c) escaping from the enduring evolutionary principle that results in the centrality of the logic of comparison and the tendency to create differentiation drawing on some norms of unity (Popkewitz 1997). The book ends with the proposal to understand evaluation as a way of constructing critical histories about how our subjectivities are formed, opening up in front of a subject who reflects on his educational activity a truly free space where his search for a mode of being, acting and thinking is not overdetermined by the tyranny of what is defined as an impossible but unavoidable task.

Note

1. This is not in any way an anti-Enlightenment work and endeavour. On the contrary, my aspiration is to present this book as an attempt to practice Enlightenment as an ethical attitude that needs to be permanently reactivated, as the root for a type of interrogation that 'simultaneously problematizes man's relation to the present, man's historical mode of being, and the constitution of the self as an autonomous subject' (Foucault 1997a: 312). As Foucault has repeatedly argued, we are free in so far as we adopt the ethos of Enlightenment as permanent critique of our historical era (Bevir 1999: 77).

Chapter 1

Governmentality, evaluation and education

An archaeological gaze

In the introductory chapter, I have framed this book as an experimental and emancipatory exercise to question educational evaluation as a form of knowledge production and the limits it imposes on us, locating it as a contribution to a critical ontology of ourselves as contemporary educational subjects in our relation to government. In the chapters of the book, I will engage with educational evaluation as a key form of knowing in the governing of contemporary education and will analyse it searching for a set of rules for the production of truth about the value of education, its objects, aims and subjects. In focusing on the effects of educational evaluation as a form of truth production, my analysis will address the nexus between truth and subjectivity and its relation to the ways in which we are governed and govern ourselves as educational subjects and, within this, we are constituted and constitute ourselves as subjects of knowledge. As emphasised in the outline of the book, the aim of the analysis will be to highlight the political paradoxes produced by the contemporary hegemonic modes of educational evaluation and the epistemological ruptures to be practiced in order to imagine and inhabit other evaluative spaces. This requires to address the complex tangle between educational evaluation as a scientific domain, political technology and moral practice, reflecting on how educational evaluation is implicated in the ways in which we constitute ourselves as subjects of knowledge, as subjects acting on others and as moral agents (Foucault 1982a: 237). Before entering the main body of the book, in this chapter I present the key concepts and theoretical resources that I mobilise to problematise educational evaluation. Specifically, I attempt to explain how and why this book can be conceived as genealogical in its design and archaeological in its method (see Foucault 1997a: 315).

Educational evaluation as a governmental practice

This book is located within the tradition of the governmentality studies (Foucault 1991; Barry *et al.* 1996; Peters *et al.* 2009; Dean 2010), and its overall aim is to push further our understanding of the governmentalisation of education. Its ambition is to reflect on educational evaluation as part of the 'ensemble formed by the institutions, procedures, analyses and reflections, the calculations and tactics that allow the exercise of a [governmental] form of power' (Foucault 1991: 103), where:

- the targets are educational professionals and students;
- the forms of knowledge and the techniques of the human and social sciences play a major role in defining the entities to be governed, the means to be employed and government's ends and goals;
- the disciplinary techniques and institutions are re-inscribed within an art of government where the objects are 'the forces and capacities of living individuals, as members of an [educational population], as resources to be fostered, to be used and to be optimized' (Dean 2010: 29).

Analytically, the work moves from a definition of government as:

> any more or less calculated and rational activity, undertaken by a multiplicity of authorities and agencies, employing a variety of techniques and forms of knowledge, that seek to shape conduct by working through the desires, aspirations, interests and beliefs of various actors for definite but shifting ends and with a diverse set of relatively unpredictable consequences, effects and outcomes. (Dean 2010: 18)

Such a definition has some conceptual implications and will shape much of the analytical moves in the book. First, government is conceptualised as activity that is as the set of organised practices through which we are governed and govern ourselves and the others in a specific domain, which in turn involves the production of knowledge and truth, the exercise of power through ordering and calculation and the establishment of norms and ends. In what follows I will refer to this set of organised practices as a *regime of government*.[1] Second and consequently, regimes of government are conceived as assembling processes that involve the mobilisation of multiple and heterogeneous elements that vary from routines, technologies, ways of doing things and agencies to theories, programmes, knowledge and expertise. Thus, the analysis of regimes of government is a materialist analysis that looks at practice and assumes the co-constitution of the material and the discursive, but which is profoundly concerned with thought as a non-subjective, technical and practical domain (Rose 1989; Olssen *et al.* 2004; Olssen 1999). In fact it places particular emphasis on the 'forms of knowledge and truth that define [the] field of operation and codify what can be known' within each regime (Dean 2010: 41). Third, government can be interpreted as an intentional and yet non-subjective attempt to direct human conduct, which is conceived as 'something that can be regulated, controlled, shaped and turned to specific ends' (ibid. 18). As an attempt to direct human conduct, government is intimately linked to ethics and has ethical effects in so far as its practices and knowledge assume a definition of what constitutes a desirable, responsible and valuable conduct.

Such a conceptualisation of government as the field for investigation of a materialist and thought-concerned analysis invites to think about the connections between questions of government, authority and politics and those of identity and self. Relatedly, it looks at government as involving a complex interplay between regulation and self-regulation and thinks at governmental practices as making human life a domain of power and knowledge. It brings to the forefront how there is an invariable evaluative and normative dimension implicated in the processes of government, that is embodied in 'set of standards or norms of conduct by which actual behaviour can be judged, and which act as a kind of ideal towards which individuals and groups should strive' (Dean 2010: 17–18).

But how to approach the analysis of regimes of government as practical systems and fields of possible experiences? How to carry on a materialist analysis of practices of government as assembling processes that involve multiple and heterogeneous elements that vary from routines, technologies, ways of doing things and agencies to theories, programmes, knowledge and expertise? Following Dean (2010: 40–41; see also Rose 1999; Miller and Rose 2008), it is possible to disentangle the assemblages of government activities isolating four different foci of an *analytics of government* (Dean 2010; see also Lemke 2007), that is a perspective that engages with examination of the conditions under which regimes of government 'come into being, are maintained and are transformed' and 'particular entities emerge, exist and change' (Dean 2010: 30–31). Regimes of government as historically constituted assemblages of governmental practices can be known through a set of analytical cuts focusing on their:

- *forms of rationality*, that is of 'distinctive ways of thinking and questioning' that mobilise specific 'vocabularies and procedures for the production of truth' (Dean 2010: 33) in a regime of government. The analytical focus here is constituted by those thoughts, forms of knowledge, expertise, strategies, programmes and means of calculation that are employed in and inform the practices of government. The examination of forms of rationality develops through the analysis of scientific, policy, narrative or juridical texts, regulations, graphic formalisations, images and any other material form assumed by thought in space and time. The key question in this examination relates to how these material forms of thought are involved in rendering governable a specific domain of practices through the production of 'specific forms of truth' (ibid. 42). Regimes of truth, in relation to government, imply the intentional but non-subjective formation of distinct ways of 'viewing institutions, practices and personnel, of organizing them in relation to a specific ideal of government' (ibid. 43).

- *fields of visibility*, that is ways of seeing and perceiving that are characteristic of a regime of government and are necessary to its operation. The focus here is on those governmental practices through which light is shed on certain objects, meanings and understandings whereas 'darkness obscures and hides others' (ibid. 41). The creation of fields of visibility unfolds, for instance, through the mobilisation of models, tables, figures, charts, maps and graphs as ways for visualising fields to be governed. These tools for visualisation establish spaces where what becomes visible are entities (substances and subjects) to be governed, relations of authority, connections between locales and agents, problems to be solved, objectives to be pursued and solutions to be adopted. What is at stake here is the analysis of the 'visual and spatial dimension of government' (ibid. 41).
- the distinctive *forms of ruling* of a regime of government, that is its peculiar modes of 'acting, intervening and directing' that combine distinct practical rationalities, expertise and know-how and rely on 'definite mechanisms, techniques and technologies' (ibid. 33). The concern here is with those modes of operation of the means, mechanisms, technologies, procedures and vocabularies that define and limit the possibility of acting, thinking and being. The analysis aims at shedding light on how these modes of operation constitute authority and guarantee that rule is accomplished (ibid. 42). In this respect, it is important to distinguish between 'techniques of government' and 'technologies of government'. Techniques of government are, in fact, those modes of intervention (e.g. systems of accounting, methods of the organisation of work, forms of surveillance, methods of timing and spacing of activities in particular locales, etc.) that are and can be assembled through particular governmental programmes in diverse 'technologies of government' (e.g. types of schooling, forms of administration and 'corporate management', systems of intervention into various organisations, and bodies of expertise) (Dean 1994: 187–88).
- *identity formation*, that is those 'characteristic ways of forming subjects, selves, persons, actors or agents' within a regime of government (Dean 2010: 42). The practices under investigation here are those that form the individual and collective identities assumed of those who exercise authority and are to be governed (in terms of forms of person, self and identity, related statuses, capacities, attributes and orientations, expected forms of conduct and set of duties and rights) through which government operates. In the examination of identity formation, a particular attention is directed to classificatory and grouping practices that 'elicit, promote, facilitate, foster and attribute various capacities, qualities and statuses to particular agents' and the ways in which capacities and attitudes can be and have to be fostered, duties enforced and rights ensured (ibid. 43–44).

Table 1.1 presents the four set of governmental practices that can be addressed as potential foci of a materialist analysis of regimes of government.

Table 1.1 Four modalities to interrogate regimes of government

The analytics of government	Focus	What is	What to look at
A materialist analysis of practices of government as assembling processes that involve multiple and heterogeneous elements that vary from routines, technologies, ways of doing things and agencies to theories, programmes, knowledge and expertise	Forms of rationality	The distinctive ways of thinking and questioning that mobilise specific 'vocabularies and procedures for the production of truth' in a regime of government	Thoughts, forms of knowledge, expertise, strategies, programmes and means of calculation that are employed in and inform the practices of government
	Fields of visibility	Ways of seeing and perceiving that are characteristic of a regime of government and are necessary to its operation	Models, tables, figures, charts, maps and graphs that are mobilised as ways for visualising fields to be governed
	Techne	Peculiar modes of acting, intervening and directing that combine distinct practical rationalities, expertise and know-how and rely on definite techniques and technologies in a regime of government	Techniques of government', conceptualised as modes of intervention (e.g. systems of accounting, methods of the organisation of work, forms of surveillance, methods of timing and spacing of activities) that are and can be assembled through particular governmental programmes in diverse technologies of government (e.g. types of schooling, systems of intervention into organisations).
	Identity formation	Characteristic ways of forming subjects, selves, persons, actors or agents' within a regime of government	The forms of person, self and identity presupposed by practices of government, the 'statuses, capacities, attributes and orientations' assumed of those who exercise authority and are to be governed, the expected forms of conduct and the set of duties and rights associated with those identities.

Source: Adapted from Dean 2010; Grimaldi and Barzanò 2014.

What emerges is a set of modalities to interrogate a regime of government, directing the analysis on how such a regime works in practice in the very production of truth, in the visualisation of a world made of entities and substances, in the production of an order and the creation of ethical subjects. It is an invitation to both rejecting any a priori distribution of knowledge, power and ethics, and assuming a dynamic perspective. This involves analysing government in terms of regularities and changes in its mundane functioning because of shifts and contingencies in the very processes of assembling of its constitutive heterogeneous entities.

There is of course a mutually constitutive relation between the subsets of governmental practices in each regime of government. Forms of rationality and fields of visibility represent the forms of knowing and visualising that inspire the activity of governing, make distinctive techniques and technologies possible and, at the same time, originate from them. They also establish and presuppose knowing and knowable subjects. Symmetrically, techniques and technologies of government operate through and mobilise rationalities, forms of knowledge and knowing, expertise, know-how, modes of representation and distinctive subjectivities in their design and operation. There is a mutually constitutive relation between the dimensions of government here, where techniques as modes of intervention and technologies as forms of ruling are essentially systems of relations connecting regimes of visibility and enunciability and things into actual practices of government. As such they have forms of rationality and field of visibility inscribed within them (think for instance of means of government such as statistical tables, graphs and reports that can be both analysed as intellectual technologies of government that render specific aspects of governed reality amenable to governing, but also knowable). Finally, practices of identity formation involve the enactment of forms of knowing/visualising and modes of ruling the conduct and, vice versa, this enactment is made possible through the establishment of knowing, seeing and acting subjects. This means that the option for one of these foci implies an ordering of concerns in the disentangling of the governmental assemblages, whereas the choice for the form of rationality, the fields of visibility, the forms of ruling or the processes of identity formation as entry-points implies inevitably the necessity to deal with all of them, their intertwining and their dynamics of mutual constitution.

Yet, opting for one of the four foci listed in Table 1.1 as entry-point means to locate at the centre of an exercise in the historical ontology of ourselves four different but related open set of questions and the 'labor of diverse inquiries' (Foucault 1997a: 319). These inquiries are complementary and necessarily intertwined in constituting critical ontology of ourselves as a critique of what we are and, relatedly, as both a historical analysis of the limits imposed on us and as an experiment with the possibility of going beyond them. To qualify those diverse inquiries,[2] one could say that it is possible to carry on a historical ontology of ourselves in relation to truth and this implies to focus primarily on the formation of a domain of recognitions (*savoir*) that constitute a specific knowledge of a reality and on questions related to the ways in which we are constituted and constitute ourselves as subjects and objects of our own knowledge. In the case of this book, this would mean to ask how material forms of evaluative thought are involved in rendering governable the domain of education through the production of specific forms of educational truth (ways of viewing institutions, practices and personnel, of organising them in relation to a specific ideal of government). Moreover, it would imply to ask how material forms of evaluative visualisation establish spaces where what becomes visible are entities to be governed, relations of authority, connections, problems, objectives and solutions. A second possibility is to engage with a historical ontology of ourselves in relation to a field of power and the 'organization of a normative system built on a whole technical, administrative, juridical [...] apparatus' (Foucault 1984: 336) with a distinct purpose and, relatedly, to give centrality to questions concerned with the ways in which we are constituted and constitute ourselves 'as subjects who exercise or submit to power relations' (Foucault 1997a: 317–18). In the case of the book, this would mean to reflect on how modes of operation constitute authority and guarantee that rule is accomplished and, relatedly, constitute subjects who exercise or submit to power relations. Third, it is possible to attempt a historical ontology of ourselves in relation to ethics, and this, in the case of the book, would involve to question evaluation as a mode through which we are constituted and constitute ourselves 'as moral subjects of our own actions' in relation to oneself and to others (ibid).

Government, evaluation and truth

In the space of interrogation opened by the perspective of an *analytics of government* (Dean 2010; Lemke 2007), this book approaches educational evaluation as a pivotal form of rationality in the contemporary government of education, as a way of thinking, reasoning, calculating, questioning and producing truth about educational reality that mobilises a specific set of bodies of knowledge, vocabularies, expertise and means of calculation, and a related set of means to make visible or hide the entities and substances populating such an educational reality. More specifically, in addressing educational evaluation as a form of truth production on the value of education and its subjects, I will focus on its relation to formal bodies of knowledge and expertise derived from human sciences, and I will attempt to problematise this as practical and collective modes of reasoning which become increasingly taken for granted and are not generally questioned by those who are involved in a historically contingent regime of practices.

There is, of course, an intimate relation between government, evaluation and truth. Foucault's entire oeuvre has shown us how 'the direction of human conduct is always compelled by a discourse or ordering of the true and the false' and political power becomes 'unintelligible without the deployment of truth as a matrix through which subjects govern themselves and others' (Deere 2014: 522). Modern governmentality finds a central pillar in the process of veridiction, where the production of truth, more than jurisdiction, becomes a fundamental means of verification, rationalisation and individualisation. With 'production of truth' what is meant here is the setting up of the rules of the game in which the production of the true and the false is regulated (Bacchi 2012: 4). Clearly, educational evaluation plays a key role in this process of veridiction, being a distinctive way to produce 'totalizing grids of all possible subjects to be known and controlled' and to set up the conditions for the educational subjects 'to be observable, controllable, and visible' (Deere 2014: 522). As a way for producing truths about who we are, what aspects of our existence we should work on, how we should work on these aspects, with what means and ends, educational evaluation performs nowadays a prominent role in the contemporary governmentality of education and has shown a distinctive capacity to act as a pivotal form of truth production within advanced liberal societies, entering a relation of mutual co-option with liberal, neoliberal and risk political rationalities (Ball 2012). If we assume the attempt to work through the freedom or capacities of acting and thinking of the governed as the distinctive feature of the advanced liberal modes of government, then it becomes clear how evaluation stands, in education as in other domains, as an apparently technical and scientific way to define the nature and utility of such freedom and capacities and, relatedly, to shape and mobilise them to securing the aims of government. Educational evaluation as a form of truth production within advanced liberal societies works on the 'choices, desires, aspirations, needs, wants and lifestyles of [educational] individuals and groups' (Dean 2010: 20) and, as such, contributes in giving a specific structure to the field of possible action and thinking for educational subjects when it comes to the governing of themselves and the others (ibid. 23–24). Moreover, educational evaluation, as a plurality of rational and calculated activities, becomes a key pillar in the government of education, in so far as, within that plurality, it assumes the possibility to regulate and control rationally or deliberately the behaviour of a variety of educational subjects and establishes a plural but ordered space of knowledge, techniques and authoritative subjects who are responsible for the occurring of this regulation and control.

In this respect, I want to emphasise here how the present analysis of educational evaluation as a form of truth production on educational reality is ultimately interested in understanding 'the correlative formation of domains and objects and the verifiable, falsifiable discourses that bear on them' and the effects in the real to which they are linked (Foucault 1981: 8–9). Within this, the aim is to reflect 'on the formation of what it is to be a human being, a citizen, and a governed and governing subject, which reveals his deepest ethical concerns (Dean 1994: 186). Thus, recalling Deere (2014: 517), one of the aims of the book is to address the analysis of educational evaluation in contemporary educational governmentality looking at the relations between subjectivity and truth, that is looking at how 'discourse, institutions, politics, and subjects are established within [educational] regimes of truth' that make, through evaluation, knowable objects and subjects to emerge in reality. As Deere puts it (ibid), 'to emerge as a knowable object in reality is also always to enter into a regime of truth' and 'a regime (or game) should be understood as a set of rules and constraints divided between true and false discourses and practices'. This is why, within the wider problematic of educational government, my analysis will opt for an approach to educational evaluation as a set of rules for the production of truth about the worth and value of education, its objects and subjects. In this perspective, truth is conceived as part of history, as an event that emerges within historically specific circumstances and has productive effects in terms of government (i.e. regulation of human conduct). As such, methodologically, truth-event requires an examination of its conditions of emergence, its rules of construction and its geography of instantiation.

Genealogy and archaeology: Two complementary gazes on regimes of government

Consistently with the perspective of an *analytics of government* and the centrality of the concern for truth, the analysis will address a selected array of material forms assumed by the evaluative thought in space and time in the government of contemporary education. The documentary basis of the work will be made of scientific, policy, advisory or juridical texts, regulations, graphic formalisations and images where educational evaluation assumes the form of a key governmental rationality in contemporary education on a global scale. Moreover, models, tables, figures, charts, maps and graphs enacted in those texts and material forms will be analysed as means of visualisation. These material forms of evaluative thought will be selected and approached as having a pivotal role in the codification of teachers, educators and students as distinctive forms of educational person, self and identity who are selectively asked to exercise authority and/or are to be governed, with all the related arrays of statuses, capacities, attributes and orientations, expected forms of conduct and set of duties and rights. This will require looking at the tangle between educational evaluation as a scientific domain, a political technology and a moral practice.

But how to analyse material forms of evaluative thought? This work, as a historical ontology of ourselves in relation to truth, will project on the realm of educational evaluation an archaeological gaze and the related analytical tools.

The position underpinnings this book is that the diverse inquiries through which it is possible to carry on a historical ontology of ourselves in relation to truth, power and ethics find their theoretical coherence in the identification of the realm of practices as a homogeneous domain of reference and their methodological coherence in the combined or alternating projection on this realm of an archaeological and a genealogical gaze. The deployment of these two gazes can be understood as two complementary ways to carry on critical histories of the present that 'problematize dimensions and regions of social existence and personal experience' which are 'taken-for-granted, assumed to be given, or natural within contemporary social existence' (Dean 1994: 35). Archaeology in particular becomes a means of analysis, that is necessary in any genealogically designed attempt to problematise our present. As Dean (1994: 33–34) powerfully argues:

> Genealogy 'allows us to establish a historical knowledge of struggles and to make use of this knowledge today'. But genealogy can only do this on the basis of archaeology. This historical knowledge of struggles, and the entertaining of the local, discontinuous, illegitimate forms of knowledge disqualified in the course of such struggles, can only be analysed because archaeology provides the point of attack on discourse we defined above. 'If we were to characterise it in two terms,' Foucault clarifies, '"archaeology" would be the appropriate methodology of this analysis of local discursivities, and "genealogy" would be the tactics whereby, on the basis of the descriptions of these local discursivities, the subjected knowledges which were thus released would be brought into play'. The roles of genealogy and archaeology appear complementary, the latter performing analyses that are a necessary condition of the former. If, from the perspective of the production of a knowledge of discursive formations, archaeology remains the indispensable methodology, from the practical, polemical and strategic perspective of the use of historical analysis, genealogy [...] connects the empirical analyses revealed to concerns activated in light of particular contemporary struggles.

If, generally speaking, an archaeological gaze focuses on practices as the forms of rationality that organise our ways of doing things, a genealogical one approaches practices as 'strategic games of liberty' (Foucault 1997a: 317–19). If archaeology stands as a movement of detachment, genealogy is a method of involvement that looks at the positivity of ensembles of discursive and non-discursive practices. As Dean (1994: 32–33) puts it, archaeology aims at identifying the rules of formation of discourses, whereas 'genealogical description addresses both the rarity of statements and the power of affirmation' in the attempt to 'uncover a positive and productive form of power underlying every movement of institutional or discursive delimitation of statements'. Archaeology can be understood as a form of history that suspends and brackets the norms, criteria of validity and operations of a particular field of knowledge and explores the imbrication between scientific, political and ethical discourses. As such it represents a method of detachment that attempts to identify the rules that govern what counts as truth within a particular discursive order or the *conditions of emergence, existence, and transformation* of established ensembles of knowledge (Dreyfus and Rabinow 1982). Genealogy has the ambition to 'explain the existence and transformation of elements of theoretical knowledge (*savoir*) by situating them within power structures and by tracing their descent and emergence in the context of history' (Olssen 1999: 12).

What is continuous in the deployment of these two gazes 'is the concern for the historicity of truth[3] and [the] interest in the "games of truth" involved in any activity through which being is historically constituted as something that can and must be thought and governed' (see Foucault 1985: 6–7; quoted in Dean 1994: 34).

Because of their common interest in games of truth, both genealogical and archaeological analyses 'are concerned with the present configuration and organisation of knowledge' and 'give explicit acknowledgement of the fact of their own immersion within an existing, mobile field of knowledge', in so far as 'their objective is not to produce the truth but to grasp the conditions which hold at any one moment for 'saying the true'' (Dean 1994: 23–24). Moreover, these two gazes are constituted by some common methodological strategies that have to do with the analysis of logical relations. In fact, they are inspired by a form of anti-atomism, and the idea that the analysis has to focus on relations among elements, where these relations form a transformable structure (Olssen 1999: 16–17; see also Webb 2003). As attempts to analyse forms of determination, genealogy and archaeology stand as methods of *synchronic analysis* that seek to identify logical (rather than causal) relations in the texture or configurations of social life (see Davidson 1997), acting as 'necessary components of the one evolving framework' (Dean 1994: 34; see also Olssen *et al.* 2004: 47).

It is in such a perspective that this book can be considered genealogical in its design and archaeological in its method (Foucault 1997a: 315). Through a movement of detachment, the analysis explores the imbrication between scientific, political and ethical statements, attempting to identify the rules that govern what counts as truth within the discursive order of educational evaluation. Through an archaeological gaze, the book aspires to problematise the historicity of educational evaluation as a form of truth production, asserting its radical contingency. Such problematisation is intended here as a point of attack on educational evaluation, as a necessary and unavoidable preparatory work for any attempt to trace its descent and emergence within history, charting its manifold interconnections with social structure, power and its microphysics dynamics (Dreyfus and Rabinow 1982) and, most of all, connecting such an empirical analyses to concerns activated in light of contemporary struggles in the field of education. In the rest of the chapter I will present the distinctive traits of such a gaze, its machinery, vantage points and limitations.

The archaeological method within an analytics of government

In what consists the distinctiveness of archaeology as an analytics[4] when it comes to the method? As Dean argues (1994: 17) 'archaeology marks the advent of a materialist approach to the analysis of knowledge and belief if by that is meant an approach that respects the being of discourse, its materiality, its location in time and place'. In the context of this book, as a method to carry on a historical ontology of ourselves in relation to those truths through which we constitute ourselves as subjects of evaluation in education, archaeology looks at the positivity of educational evaluation, attempting a systematic description of the organisation of evaluative statements into discursive formations and their constitutive rules. An archaeological gaze analyses a field of discursive regularities, looking for historical conditions of possibility of educational evaluation as form of truth production. In the following paragraphs I will try to translate this apparently arcane sentence into concrete analytical moves.

As a form of inquiry, archaeology is historical and spatial (Deleuze 1992). In fact, it is concerned with discursive events, actual occurrences and their effects (Gutting 1989: 228), always bearing upon and departing from a body of determined practices (Foucault 1997a: 318). At the same time, archaeology aims at describing an open logical space in which certain discursive practices occur (Dreyfus and Rabinow 1982: 51). In the archaeological language, practice is a key term and discursive practices have to be intended as 'the local socio-historical material conditions that enable and constrain disciplinary knowledge practices such as speaking, writing, thinking, calculating, measuring, filtering, and concentrating' (Barad 2003: 819). As such, these conditions produce the 'subjects' and 'objects' of knowledge practices and have to be intended as 'immanent and historical rather than transcendental or phenomenological' (ibid), where knowledge becomes something immanent to what people do rather than a transcendent phenomenon to be discovered (Bacchi 2012: 3).

Given such a conceptualisation of discursive practices, the archaeological task is to pursue a pure description of discursive events (Webb 2003: 55), analysing within what space of order a specific knowledge is constituted (Foucault 2002b). In this perspective, this book mobilises archaeology as a mean to carry on a critique of the self-evidence of educational evaluation from a distinct vantage point, situating the problem of truth of evaluation at the historical level and excavating its historical conditions of possibility (Deere 2014: 518), intended as 'actual historically situated social conditions' (Barad 2003: 819). Thus, to reinforce what is already noted, archaeology represents a non-interpretive and non-anthropological[5] attempt to provide a description of regularities, differences and transformations, 'eschewing the search for authors and concentrating instead on statements (and visibilities)' (Wickham and Kendall 1999: 26).

The description of discursive regularities implies to approach the open logical space in which certain discursive practices occur looking at relations between statements and searching for unities within the space within which statements circulate (Foucault 2002b: 29–30). The statements and the relations among them are the foci of the archaeological description. In the *Archaeology of Knowledge* Foucault defines the statements as discursive events which are at once tied to a historical context and capable of repetition (Olssen 1999: 9). Not all discursive practices can be regarded as statements and constitute the objects of an archaeological analysis. Statements are discursive events of certain kinds, where it is possible to detect an enunciative function that relates a group of signs to a field of objects, a number of possible subjective positions, a domain of coordination and coexistence and a space in which they are used and repeated.

If archaeology has fundamentally to do with the description of regularities in the relations between statements, intended as enunciative functions, that have to be searched for in practices, the space of the archaeological analysis is what Foucault calls the archive, that is the general system(s) of the formation and transformation of statements. This means that archaeology moves from the recognition of 'a corpus of statements whose organisation is regular and systematic' and develops through the identification of the rules that make this corpus being regular and systematic (Wickham and Kendall 1999: 42). Of course, what is important to bear in mind is that the kind of rules that archaeology looks for are 'nothing but the ways the statements are actually related' (Dreyfus and Rabinow 1982: 55).

As a relational analysis, a key methodological principle in the archaeological analysis is the shift from the linear to the tabular, 'in the attempt to draw up the relations between elements within series, their limits and divisions' (see Webb 2003: 44) and link over different scales of heterogeneous kinds of events and the forms of relations that exist between them. As Wickham and Kendall argue (1999: 42):

> The systematic character of a discourse includes its systematic articulation with other discourses. In practice, discourses delimit what can be said, while providing the spaces - the concepts, metaphors, models, analogies, for making new statements within any specific discourse. [...] every discourse [can be understood] as the result of a practice of production which is at once material, discursive and complex, always inscribed in relation to other practices of production of discourse. Every discourse is part of a discursive complex; it is locked in an intricate web of practices, bearing in mind that every practice is by definition both discursive and material. (Henriques *et al.* 1984: 105–6)

The tables that archaeology draws up are spaces of dispersion, where 'dispersion designates a multiplicity of times or spaces [...] which may be modified structurally through their contact [and] is therefore operative first of all at the level of rules, rather than things, events or elements' (Webb 2003: 45).

From this initial exposition of the archaeological method, it should be clear that archaeology is distinguished by a distinctive set of methodological moves and strategies that concern the *what* (regularities as rules and relations among statements), *where* (archive as the space of analysis) and *how* (archaeological description) of the analysis. In the next sections, I will approach each of them more in details.

Discursive regularities

As a spatial kind of analysis, that is interested in detecting regularities within spaces of dispersion, archaeology moves from the suspension of familiar and immediate forms of unity and studies the network of discursive practices, treating it as an ensemble of interconnected elements (Dreyfus and Rabinow 1982: 58). Being non-interpretative, archaeology proceeds through the description of the links between the elements of discursive formations, showing how enunciative events are distributed in their deployed space. In doing so, it stands as a holistic analysis, assuming that 'the whole determines what can count even as a possible element' and 'there are no parts except within the field which identifies and individuates them' (ibid. 55). Accordingly, what the archaeology seeks to describe are regularities in the distribution of and relations between objects, types of statement, concepts or thematic choices (Foucault 2002b: 38). It is interested in a specific kind of discursive practice, the statement, and looks at relations between statements, searching for unities within the space within which statements circulate.

Thus, the archaeological gaze does not approach to discursive practice attempting to analyse propositional structures, sentences or speech acts. Recalling Foucault's words, statements are enunciative functions; they 'do not exist in the same sense in which a language (*langue*) exists' nor 'in the same way as the object presented to perception' (ibid. 97). Rather, the statement is 'the modality of existence proper to [a] group of signs: [...] a modality that allows it to be in relation with a domain of objects, to prescribe a definite position to any possible subject, to be situated among other verbal performances, and to be endowed with a repeatable materiality' (ibid. 120).[6] Thus, as enunciative functions, statements have a distinct relation with:

- a *referential*, that is a principle of differentiation that 'defines the possibilities of appearance and delimitation of that which gives meaning' to the group of signs and/or a value of truth to the proposition (ibid. 103);
- a *subject*, that is a distinctive position that can be assumed in certain conditions by various individuals;

- an *associated field*, that is a domain of coexistence for other statements;
- a *materiality*, that is both the substance or support of the articulation, and also a set of rules of transcription and possibilities of use and reuse (ibid. 115; Olssen 1999: 9).

But the statement is not a unity that operates independently and cannot be analysed as such. On the contrary, it is part of a complex web of discursive practices, or better of an enunciative field. In fact, to describe a statement in the exact specificity of its occurrence means to determine:

- *its referential*. Being the statement as enunciative function 'a function of existence that properly belongs to signs' that 'cuts across a domain of structures and possible unities', whose referential are the laws of possibility and rules of existence for the objects, subjects and concepts 'that are named, designated, or described within it, and for the relations that are affirmed or denied in it' (Foucault 2002b: 103). Analysing the referential of a statement is not a semantic investigation or verification, but it is a kind of description that looks at the statement in its actual practice, its conditions, the rules that govern it and the field in which it operates, addressing the relations between the statement and a field of related statements, which is intended as a space of differentiation;
- *its subject*. The statement as enunciative function produces a specific relation with a subject, which is another characteristic that enables one to describe it. Such a position does not correspond to the individual that speaks the statement or puts it into the form of writing, neither does the description of such a position have to do with the analysis of the relation between an author and what is said. On the contrary, determining the position of the enunciating subject of a statement means to describe the 'particular vacant place', the position can and must be occupied by any individual if she/he is to be the subject of it (ibid. 107) or, to put it another way, the function that is made actual in the relation that unites the enunciating subject and what is being stated. Again, in analytical terms determining the subjects of the statement is a relational endeavour, where the requisites and possibilities that, taken together, determine such a position are defined in terms of: (a) it's being fixed in a domain constituted by a finite group of statements; (b) a series of enunciative events that have occurred and represent the condition and demonstrative time in which such a position is established and (c) a set of effective operations that 'belong to the enunciating subject, which are at his disposal, and of which he may avail himself when necessary' (ibid. 106);
- *the domain of coexistence with other statements*. As it should be clear, given its nature of enunciative function, a statement 'cannot operate without the existence of an associated domain' (ibid. 108). This is a collateral space populated by other statements which act as borders for each statement,

and it is made up by: (a) 'the series of other formulations within which the statement appears and forms one element' in the immanence of its historical appearance; (b) all the statements to which the statement refers, 'either by repeating them, modifying them, or adapting them, or by opposing them, or by commenting on them'; (c) all the statements 'whose subsequent possibility is determined by the statement, and which may follow the statement as its consequence, its natural successor, or its conversational retort'; (d) all the statements 'whose status the statement in question shares, among which it takes its place without regard to linear order, with which it will fade away, or with which, on the contrary, it will be valued, preserved, sacralised, and offered, as a possible object, to a future discourse' (ibid. 110–11);

- *the materiality*. As an enunciative function, a statement must have a material form; it has to exist as a historical trace. It has to have 'a substance, a support, a place, and a date' (ibid. 113). In the archaeological perspective, the epistemic is practice to be encountered; it is time-bound and factual. This materiality is not a medium or an addition, but rather is a constitutive part of its making-up. As Foucault argues (ibid), the spatiotemporal coordinates and the material status of the statement 'are part of its intrinsic characteristics', and as such any analysis of a statement in its enunciative field cannot eschew from addressing them. When, where, how and in what form a statement has emerged as part of an enunciative field on the surface of history are all questions that an archaeological analysis cannot avoid. But here some clarifications are needed in order to make clear what is the materiality that is proper to the statement. This is crucial to understand what are the special types of repetition/regularity that it is possible to describe in the historical series of statements and how and to what extent it is possible to 'speak of the same statement when there are several distinct enunciations of it' and 'of several statements when one can recognize identical forms, structures, rules of construction, and intentions' (ibid. 114) at the level of enunciations. Foucault clarifies that the materiality of the statement is defined by its status as a thing or object (Foucault 2002b: 115) and that it pertains to the order of the institution, rather than the mere spatiotemporal localisation. In fact, the possibility to recognise identity and repetition between statements relates to the identification of a *field of stabilisation* and a *field of use*, that is a set of rules that 'defines possibilities of reinscription and transcription' of a statement (ibid. 116) and a set of 'conditions and limits [...] imposed by all the other statements' in its collateral space, 'by the domain in which it can be used or applied, by the role and functions that it can perform' (ibid). Foucault identifies the elements constituting a field of stabilisation, namely schemata of use, rules of application, constellations in which statements can play a part, statements' strategic potentialities, and a field of use, namely 'constancy of the statement, preservation of its identity through the unique events of the enunciations, its duplications through the identity of the forms' (ibid. 117). These are the elements that make 'it possible, despite all the differences of enunciation, to repeat' statements, and these are the elements that an archaeological analysis has to look at in order to identify repetition, regularities and difference in the emergence of statements on the surface of history.[7]

As it results perhaps more clearly at this point, statements as enunciative functions do not exist in isolation. Rather, as their conceptual definition implies, they appear with the relations that define and sustain their existence and 'it is the story of the formation and transformation of these relations that archaeological history tells' (Webb 2003: 54). In Foucault's terms, a statement always belongs to a series or a whole and appears in a network of statements, being part of a specific enunciative field (Dreyfus and Rabinow 1982: 54). So it can be described as playing a role among other statements, deriving support from them and distinguishing itself from them. The elementary foci of the archaeological gaze, the statements 'are not only individuated by the whole system of statements, but [...] they can be identified as elements only in the specific system in which they make sense' (ibid).

It is in this vein that archaeology has to do with the analysis of regularities in the dispersion of statements and relations among statements, where these regularities are understood as 'rules' or, more precisely, as 'laws of possibility' and 'rules of existence' (Dean 1994: 16; Major-Poetzl 1983: 3–5). It is these *regularities as relations and rules* that compose what Foucault calls a *discursive formation*, an enunciative field functioning as a rule-governed system of 'elements ordered by rules of transformation', where meaningful units 'follow one another, order one another, coexist with one another, and play roles in relation to one another [...] in a space in which they breed and multiply' (Foucault 2002b: 112).

The archive of the archaeological analysis

Where does the search for regularities as relations and rules occur? As a method that can be located within an analytics of government, archaeology has a specific documentary base made of groups of signs. We have discussed this in some details above in relation to regimes of practices/government and material forms of thought. As Foucault clarifies, archaeology is an analysis of 'a knowledge whose visible body is not theoretical or scientific discourse, nor literature either [in se] but a regulated, everyday practice' (Foucault 1997d: 6). Here everyday practice can be intended as 'the locus of particular events, regularities, relationships, modifications and systematic transformations', a field of statements approached 'as a practical domain that is autonomous (although dependent), and which can be described at its own level (although it must be articulated on something other than itself)' (Foucault 2002b: 137).

As Dreyfus and Rabinow note (1982: 59), an archaeological analysis begins like a pure empiricist endeavour, 'simply selecting as his raw data an ensemble of what were taken to be' statements in a domain, without taking at face value any originally defined set of material forms of thought and 'the concomitant classification into disciplines that it presupposes'. On the contrary, what were taken to be statements supply the raw data for an independent and distinctive systematisation.

In the *Archaeology of Knowledge* (2002b), Foucault clarifies that the analysis of discursive formations as systems of dispersion and redistribution of statements does not consist in an exhaustive description of what was said. The domain of statements that the archaeological gaze has the ambition to grasp is not an undifferentiated plain. Rather, it is a complex volume articulated according to different groups of rules (and thus different types of positivity) and divided up by distinct discursive formations into heterogeneous subspaces where specific rules operate.

This is what Foucault calls the archive, the space of the archaeological analysis of a regime of practice and its material forms of thought. Archaeology describes discursive practices as 'specified in the element of the archive' (ibid. 148):

> we have in the density of discursive practices, systems that establish statements as events (with their own conditions and domain of appearance) and things (with their own possibility and field of use). They are all these systems of statements (whether events or things) that I propose to call archive. (ibid. 144)

Some methodological clarifications are needed here in order to make this concept to operate as an analytical tool for the archaeological gaze. As Foucault has reasonably noted, an archive cannot be described exhaustively (Dreyfus and Rabinow 1982: 56). Rather, the archive as a sensitising tool is intended to identify the space of the accumulated existence of discourse, a space that is different from our present existence (Olssen 1999: 10). In approaching this space, the archaeological gaze looks for the residual character of statements, that is the ways in which they are 'preserved by virtue of a number of supports and material techniques' (Foucault 2002b: 139), in accordance with certain types of institutions and statutory modalities. It is these supports and material techniques that put them into operation. The practices that derive from them and the social relations that they form represent the privileged documentary base of the archaeological gaze when engaging in the description of discursive formations as specified in the element of the archive (or what could be termed here also as the epistemic – see Roth 1981).[8] An archaeological analysis, then, produces a fragmented figure, describes a dispersion, specific forms of an accumulation and, in doing so, it establishes a positivity, whose unity throughout time goes well beyond individual oeuvres, books, texts and other historically located groups of signs. According to Foucault (2002b: 143) 'this form of positivity and the conditions of operation of the enunciative function [that he calls the *historical a priori*] define a field in which formal identities, thematic continuities, translations of concepts, and polemical interchanges may be deployed' (ibid. 143).

Thus, the ambition of archaeology is to identify the positivity of discursive formations through a double and paradoxical movement: (a) towards the interior, attempting to turn back 'towards the rarity of statement' and to establish a law of rarity, the principle according to which 'only the "signifying" groups that were enunciated could appear' (ibid. 134); (b) towards the exterior, locating the positivity of those discursive formations within the element of the archive, or the epistemic as I propose here to conceptualise such a space. This means to locate discursive formations within a wider space articulated according to different groups of rules and divided up by distinct discursive formations into heterogeneous sub-spaces where specific rules operate.

But how to proceed in the identification of such a positivity? To make the positivity of a discursive formation visible means 'to describe statements, to describe the enunciative function of which they are the bearers, to analyse the conditions in which this function operates, to cover the different domains that this function presupposes and the way in which those domains are articulated' (ibid. 130). The *formation of objects*, *enunciative modalities*, *concepts* and *strategies* are the four domains in which the enunciative function operates as a group of rules.

The archaeological description of discursive formations

If discursive formations are groups of statements that are linked at the level of their enunciative function, in the archaeological perspective, it is possible to identify the general set of rules that govern the system of their referentials, the system that defines and prescribes the possible subjective positions, all their associated domains and the system that links all these fields of coexistence together, and finally the status of these statements, the way in which they are institutionalised, received, used, reused, combined together, the mode according to which they become objects of appropriation, instruments for desire or interest, elements for a strategy (Foucault 2002b: 129).

The Archaeology of Knowledge (ibid. 44–78) provides some detailed methodological proposals to examine those rules of formation, in order to understand how within a discursive formation a specific object is recognised and treated; what institutions are assigned to hold and care for it at times; what authorities decided about it, and according to what criteria; what methods are employed to make distinct type of operations on/with/through them; in what network of institutions and practices this specific object is both enmeshed and defined.

The formation of objects

Discursive formations produce the objects about which they speak (Dreyfus and Rabinow 1982: 61), through a complex set of operations on these objects such as naming, dividing up, describing, explaining, tracing origins and developments, indicating correlations, judging, articulating speeches to be taken in their name. To grasp the production of such kind of objects, the archaeological analysis attempts to identify the rules of formation from which the appearance of the objects of discourse and the possibilities of juxtaposition and/or succession between different objects depend. What the archaeological gaze looks for is the general system of rules through which such a production occurs, the systematic ways in which discursive practices form the objects of which they speak. This means to confront with the analysis of the practical background which makes objectivity possible (ibid. 62). Such an analysis implies to ask what has ruled the existence of a delimited set of objects as objects of discourse employing a set of research strategies (see Table 1.2):

1. to map *surfaces of emergence*, that is those institutional/disciplinary fields or spheres of social life within which discursive practices define what it is talking about, give it the status of an object – and therefore make it manifest, nameable and describable. Surfaces of emergence are the social loci where specific objects are characterised in a specific way, differentiated from other objects and established as objects of concern for a specific discursive formation (Gutting 1989: 234). In Foucault's works examples of surfaces of emergence are, for instance in the case of madness, the family, the immediate social group, the work situation, the religious community, art, sexuality, penalty, intended as fields of initial differentiation where a discourse finds a way of limiting its domain (Foucault 2002b: 46).
2. to describe *authorities of delimitation*, that is institutions, groups of individuals, bodies of knowledge and practice that have the power to delimit, designate or name objects. These are those authorities that are given the

Table 1.2 The identification of the objects of discourse

The objects of discourse		
	Surfaces of emergence	Institutional or disciplinary field or spheres of social life within which discursive practices define what it is talking about, give it the status of an object – and therefore make it manifest, nameable and describable
	Authorities of delimitation	Institutions, groups of individuals, bodies of knowledge and practice that have the power to delimit, designate or name objects
	Grids of specification	Those systems according to which the different objects are divided, contrasted, related, regrouped, classified and derived from one another as objects of discourse

power to decide what objects can be the concern of a specific discursive formation. Foucault offers many examples of what can be understood as an authority of delimitation. The most striking is probably the case of medicine in relation to the object 'madness', where medicine is intended as 'an institution possessing its own rules, as a group of individuals constituting the medical profession, as a body of knowledge and practice, as an authority recognized by public opinion, the law, and government' (Foucault 2002b: 46). But also law and penal law, the religious authority, literary and art criticism can be understood as authorities of delimitation, which delimit, designate, name and differentiate.

3 to analyse *grids of specification*, that is those systems according to which the different objects are divided, contrasted, related, regrouped, classified and derived from one another as objects of discourse. These are the systems 'whereby discursive formations classify and relate different kind of objects' (Gutting 1989: 235). Examples of grids of specification can be considered 'the soul, as a group of hierarchized, related, and more or less interpenetrable faculties', 'the body, as a three-dimensional volume of organs linked together by networks of dependence and communication' or 'the life and history of individuals, as a linear succession of phases, a tangle of traces, a group of potential reactivations, cyclical repetitions; the interplays of neuropsychological correlations as systems of reciprocal projections, and as a field of circular causality' (Foucault 2002b: 47).

Then, mapping the formation of the objects generated by discursive practices requires exploring the set of relations between authorities of emergence, delimitation and specification, intended as conditions of existence for those objects, in search for regularities. In *The Archaeology of Knowledge* (2002b: 48–49), Foucault relates to his previous archaeological work on the psychiatric discourse to provide examples of what kind of relations he is talking about and how they can be considered as giving rise to a series of objects:

- the relation between planes of specification like penal categories and degrees of diminished responsibility, and planes of psychological characterisation (faculties, aptitudes, degrees of development or involution, different ways of reacting to the environment, character types, whether acquired, innate or hereditary);
- the relation between the authority of medical decision and the authority of judicial decision (a really complex relation since medical decision recognises absolutely the authority of the judiciary to define crime, to determine the circumstances in which it is committed, and the punishment that it deserves; but reserves the right to analyse its origin and to determine the degree of responsibility involved);
- the relation between the filter formed by judicial interrogation, police information, investigation and the whole machinery of judicial

information, and the filter formed by the medical questionnaire, clinical examinations, the search for antecedents and biographical accounts;
- the relation between the family, sexual and penal norms of the behaviour of individuals, and the table of pathological symptoms and diseases of which they are the signs;
- the relation between therapeutic confinement in hospital (with its own thresholds, its criteria of cure, its way of distinguishing the normal from the pathological) and punitive confinement in prison (with its system of punishment and pedagogy, its criteria of good conduct, improvement, and freedom).

Objects of discourse are constructed and have real effects, but only exist in relation to other things (Webb 2003: 65). The archaeological analysis of the formation of the objects of discourse is not a history of the referent, neither is it an analysis of the relations between words and things (in terms of representation). Archaeology, on the contrary, attempts to de-presentify things, relating them to the body of rules that constitute their conditions of possibility and historical appearance.

To locate properly such an analysis in the perspective of the analytics of government, it is essential to note here how those relations are not internal to discourse, neither autonomous, but have to be interpreted as 'established between institutions, economic and social processes, behavioural patterns, systems of norms, techniques, types of classification, modes of characterization' (Foucault 2002b: 49). In this respect, it is crucial to highlight how the archaeological gaze looks at discursive relations, being aware that such a focus does not represent an autonomous level. On the contrary, what is at stake is an act of cutting that isolates a system of relations that are enmeshed within a complex articulation which, in turn, could be described as follows (see Foucault 2002b: 50): (a) a system of *real* or *primary relations*, that is those relations that may be described between institutions, techniques, social forms, independently of all discourse or all object of discourse; (b) a system of *reflexive* or *secondary relations* that are formulated in discourse itself and 'are what can be said about the primary relations from within existing discourses' (Webb 2003: 68). Secondary relations can be found in the way practicing subjects reflectively define their own behaviour (Dreyfus and Rabinow 1982: 63) and (c) *a system of relations* that might properly be called *discursive*, and which can be interpreted as a group of rules proper to discursive practices that define the ordering of objects and constitute the regularities that govern their dispersion.

The formation of enunciative modalities

Discursive formation produces also what Foucault calls enunciative modalities (Foucault 2002b: 55–61; see also Webb 2003: 69–72). In *What Is an Author* (1998: 221), Foucault offers a straightforward illustration of the kind of questions that archaeology poses about the conditions of possibility of enunciative modalities in the order of discourse and how this relates to the general problem of the subject:

> [...] these questions will be raised: How, under what conditions, and in what forms can something like a subject appear in the order of discourse? What place can it occupy in each type of discourse, what functions can it assume, and by obeying what rules? In short, it is a matter of depriving the subject (or its substitute) of its role as originator, and of analyzing the subject as a variable and complex function of discourse.

When it comes to the analytical strategies to explore such productive processes, *The Archaeology of Knowledge* (Foucault 2002b) offers some indications to map a field of regularity for various positions of subjectivity:

1 the first one is the *identification of those subjects who have the authority*, sanctioned by law or tradition, juridically defined or spontaneously accepted, to use a specific language. Such individuals derive their status and prestige from the exclusive use of this language and, at the same time, guarantee to that language its presumption of truth. The guiding questions are, in this case, who is speaking, who is accorded the right to use a language, who is qualified to do so, who derives from it a special quality, prestige and the assurance that what he says is true, what is the status of the individuals who have the right to proffer a discourse. Table 1.3 provides a

Table 1.3 The identification of a subject as enunciative modality

The enunciative modality	Status	Criteria of competence and knowledge Institutions, systems, pedagogic norms; legal conditions that give the right, with certain limitations, to practise and to extend knowledge
	A system of differentiation and relations	Division of attributions, hierarchical subordination, functional complementarity, the request for and the provision and exchange of information with other individuals or other groups that also possess their own status (e.g. the state and its representatives, the judiciary, different professional bodies, social groups and so on)
	Functioning	A number of characteristics that define its functioning in relation to society as a whole (e.g. the role in relation to a specific commitment and activation; the compulsory nature of its activation, the right to intervene and make decisions accorded to him; what is required of him; the payment he receives and the form of contract that he negotiates and so on)

detailed articulation of what it means to identify a subject as enunciative modality through the archaeological gaze.

Here the crucial foci of analysis become, then, the subjects' regulative and traditional statute, the criteria of competence, pedagogical norms and legal conditions connected to that statute, together with the systems of relations and differentiation between the subjects involved in the processes in focus.

2 the second one consists in the description of the *institutional sites* from which a subject is entitled to talk with authority of specific objects, telling the truth, and 'from which [a] discourse derives its legitimate source and point of application (its specific objects and instruments of verification)' (Foucault 2002b: 56). This implies to grasp the institutional sites that act as places of constant, coded, systematic observation of a distinct set of objects run by a differentiated and hierarchize staff, the fields within which observation of reality is carried on, the places for the production of truth and a documentary field.

3 the third one relates to the description of the *situation* that a subject can occupy in relation to specific domains or groups of objects of discourse. The archaeological gaze asks if the subject under focus is in a position of questioning, listening, seeing, observing, perceiving, receiving, producing, teaching and so on. Such an analysis attempts to identify if a subject is in a therapeutic or pedagogic role, if the subject acts as an intermediary in the diffusion of a distinct knowledge and if the subject has a role as a responsible representative of something in the social space. These positionings are of course intertwined with the functioning of 'a certain grid of explicit or implicit interrogations', specific 'tables of characteristic features' or the use of 'instrumental intermediaries' and, more generally, relate to 'the positions that the subject can occupy in the information networks' (ibid. 58).

Given the relational nature of archaeology, these analytical moves need to be closely coordinated with those concerning the formation of objects, grasping the relations between certain enunciative modalities and certain groups of objects produced within a discursive formation. To make again a point which has returned often in the chapter, also in the case of the complex relations involving enunciative modalities, Foucault reminds us that these relations between different elements are historical conditions of existence, where it is 'practice, that establishes between them all a system of relations, that is not "really" given or constituted a priori'. In this respect, 'if there is a unity, if the modalities of enunciation that it uses, or to which it gives place, are not simply juxtaposed by a series of historical contingencies' it is because practice makes constant use of this group of relations (Foucault 2002b: 59). The archaeological analysis has not the ambition to refer back whatever synthesis of a unitary function of a subject. Rather, it is devoted to highlight how the various enunciative modalities manifest the dispersion of the subject.

The formation of concepts

A third crucial archaeological task is describing the organisation of the field of statements where concepts emerge and circulate (ibid. 62). The analytical strategy proposed by Foucault to approach such an organisation is to trace a conceptual network on the basis of the intrinsic regularities of discursive practice, to reconstruct the grid of conceptual compatibilities and incompatibilities and, finally, to relate the emerging conceptual network to distinctive rules of formation. In doing this (see Table 1.4), the archaeological gaze looks at:

1 *forms of succession*, or set of rules for arranging the recurrent elements that may have value as concepts in series (Gutting 1989: 236). Foucault (2002b: 63) identifies some key forms of succession to look at in the analysis of different modalities of concepts' dispersion: (1) *orderings of enunciative series*, the way concepts are ordered (their spatial distribution) in the production of inferences, successive implications, demonstrative reasoning, descriptions, schemata of generalisation, progressive specification of these descriptions and generalisations; (2) *types of dependence* of the statements, where dependences can assume the form of the relations between, for example, hypothesis and verification, assertion and critique, or general law and particular application and (3) *rhetorical schemata* that link together groups of statements, combining, for example,

Table 1.4 Grasping the formation of concepts

The formation of concepts	Forms of succession	Rules for arranging the recurrent elements that may have value as concepts in series. Key forms of succession to look at are:
		1. orderings of enunciative series 2. types of dependence 3. rhetorical schemata that link together groups of statements
	Forms of coexistence	Regularities in relations between recursive and widely used concepts in discourse. Different forms of coexistence are:
		1. a field of presence 2. a field of concomitance 3. a field of memory
	Procedures of intervention	Procedures allowed to be legitimately applied to statements. Among them it is worth to recall here:
		1. techniques of rewriting 2. methods of transcription and approximation 3. modes of translating, delimitation and transferring 4. methods of systematising and redistributing

descriptions, observations, deductions, definitions, characterisations, classifications in the architecture of a text.

2 *forms of coexistence*, that is the regularities in relations between recursive and widely used concepts in discourse which establish attitudes of acceptance or rejection (Gutting 1989: 236). The distinction between different forms of coexistence is of particular interest. Foucault (2002b: 64) distinguished between: (1) a *field of presence* that comprises those already existing statements that, on the one hand, are accepted by a discourse as truth, effective description, reasonable argument or necessary assumption and, on the other hand, are criticised, discussed, judged, refused or excluded. The (explicit or implicit) relations established in this field can be the following: experimental or deductive validation, repetition, acceptance based on authority or tradition, comment, research of hidden meanings, analysis of errors; (2) a *field of concomitance* is the ensemble of statements that concern different objects and belong to different discourses, but exert a function in relation to the statements in focus, acting as points of analogy, general principles, accepted premises, transferable models and imperatives; (3) a *field of memory* constituted by those statements no longer accepted, no longer defined as a body of truth but seen as precursors, because 'relations of filiation, genesis, transformation, continuity, and historical discontinuity can be established' (ibid. 65) with the contemporary domain of validity.[9]

3 *procedures of intervention* that are allowed to be legitimately applied to statements, among which it is worth to recall here: techniques of rewriting them within different forms (e.g. from linear to tabular), methods of transcribing them according to a different language (more or less formalised), modes of translating quantitative statements into qualitative formulations and vice versa, methods to approximate statements and refine their exactitude, modes of delimitation of the domain of validity of statements by extension or restriction, modes of transferring of statements from a domain to another, methods of systematising already existing propositions, methods of redistributing in a new systematic whole statements that are already but differently linked together.

Thus, analysing the formation of concepts should aim to delimit the group of concepts, disparate as they may be in terms of origin and far-reaching chronological import, that are specific to a discursive formation and determine according to what patterns the statements are linked to each other within such a discursive formation through the establishment of forms of deduction, derivation, coherence, incompatibility, substitution, exclusion or reciprocal transformation between the concepts themselves (Foucault 2002b: 68). The archaeological gaze here approaches such a dispersion in search for patterns in regularity in the distinctive forms of relatedness between concepts, where it is 'such a group of relations that constitutes a system of conceptual formation' (Webb 2003: 74).

The formation of strategies

Discursive formations can be also approached looking for the formation of strategies (Foucault 2002b: 71), that is distinctive forms of organising concepts, regroupings objects and establishing types of enunciation which, 'according to their degree of coherence, rigour, and stability', result into themes or theories. Strategies are systematically different ways of treating objects, displace enunciative modalities and manipulate concepts. They are regulated and describable ways of practising discursive possibilities. Again, the archaeological gaze looks for regularities and a common system of their formation (ibid. 72).[10] This means to look for the points of choice, the possibilities to reanimating themes, the possibilities to play different truth games that a discursive formation makes available (Dreyfus and Rabinow 1982: 71–72). Here, the archaeological gaze identifies some privileged points of analysis to grasp the formation of strategies, which basically pertains to a focus on lateral or diagonal relations between elements of discursive formations (Webb 2003: 77) (see Table 1.5):

1   to map the theoretical choice occurred on the surface of history identifying possible *points of diffraction* within a discursive formation. In mapping these choices it is possible to follow an analytical series: (1) to look for *points of incompatibility*, which refer to the appearance within the same

Table 1.5 Grasping the formation of concepts

The formation of strategies	Points of diffraction	Mapping theoretical choices following an analytical series:
		1. to look for points of incompatibility
2. to grasp how incompatible statements become points of equivalence
3. to analyse how those alternative and yet incompatible elements become link points of systematisation
	Authorities	Understanding what are the specific authorities that guided those theoretical choices focusing on the economy of the discursive constellation to which the discursive formation in question belongs, that is the kind of relation connecting it to those discursive formations that are contemporary with it or related to it
	Function in a field of non-discursive practices	Relating the determination of the theoretical choices that were actually made to:
		1. the function carried out by the discourse under study in a field of non-discursive practices
2. the rules and processes of appropriation of it

discursive formation of statements that exist on the same level and are equally permitted by the rules of formation but are contradictory or inconsequent and cannot coexist in the same series (Gutting 1989: 237); (2) to grasp how these incompatible statements, as points from which different theoretical turns can be taken, become *points of equivalence*, through a process that translates two incompatible elements into an alternative of elements that are formed on the basis of the same rule and (3) to analyse how those alternative and yet incompatible elements become *link points of systematisation* that represent starting point to derive coherent series of statements that come to form discursive subgroups.

2 to understand what are the specific *authorities* that guided those theoretical choices that have been realised out of all the possible alternatives allowed by the rules of formation in a discursive field. In this case the archaeological gaze identifies as privileged focus, the *economy of the discursive constellation* (Gutting 1989: 237) to which the discursive formation in question belongs, that is the kind of relation connecting it to those discursive formations that are contemporary with it or related to it. Examples of relations can be to play the role of 'a formal system of which other discourses are applications with various semantic fields', to be 'a concrete model that must be applied to other discourses at a higher level of abstraction', to be 'in a relation of analogy, opposition, or complementarity with certain other discourses' or finally to be in a 'relation of mutual delimitation' (Foucault 2002b: 74). As Foucault puts it, 'this whole group of relations forms a principle of determination that permits or excludes, within a given discourse, a certain number of statements', that is 'conceptual systematizations, enunciative series, groups and organizations of objects that might have been possible [...], but which are excluded by a discursive constellation at a higher level and in a broader space' (ibid. 74–75). In this respect they result in the elimination of points of diffraction, acting as principles of the possibility of choices (Gutting 1989: 238).

3 to relate the determination of the theoretical choices that were actually made to a further authority, that is the *function* carried out by the discourse under study in a field of non-discursive practices, for example pedagogic practice, political and economic decisions, social and political struggles and the *rules and processes of appropriation* of it, which delimit the right to speak, the ability to understand, the licit and immediate access to the corpus of already formulated statements and the capacity to invest this discourse in decisions, institutions or practices (Foucault 2002b: 75).

The analysis of the formation of strategies is the point where the historicity of discursive formation emerges more clearly, where the relation of discursive formations to desire, to the processes of their appropriation or their role among non-discursive practices appears as intrinsic to its characterisation and the laws of its formation (Foucault 2002b: 76). They are not external noises but constitutive part of their formation.

Trees of derivation, interdiscursive configurations and forms of articulation

In *The Archaeology of Knowledge* (2002b), Foucault provides some further methodological indications on how to grasp the relatedness and mutual implication between objects, enunciative modalities, concepts and strategies formation. He lists six moves to approach the analysis of a discursive formation as a field of regularities.

First, Foucault suggests identifying and starting from *governing statements* to constitute *trees of derivation* of a discursive formation. Governing statements 'concern the definition of observable structures and the field of possible objects, [...] prescribe the forms of description and the perceptual codes [that can be used], reveal the most general possibilities of characterization, and thus open up a whole domain of concepts to be constructed, and, lastly, [constitute] a strategic choice, leave room for the greatest number of subsequent options' (Foucault 2002b: 164). Governing statements are those that put rules of formation of objects, enunciative modalities, concepts and strategies into operation in their most general and widely applicable form. They can be considered the starting point of the archaeological description in so far as they allow the archaeologist to begin the description of a tree of enunciative derivation where to locate other statements that put into operation the same regularity, but in a form, that is less general, delimited and localised in its extension and application. At the end of the branches of the tree or at various places in the whole, the archaeological analysis will be able to make visible how within the same field of regularities it will be possible to find discoveries, conceptual transformations, the emergence of new notions, technical improvements and, more generally, doxological oppositions, alternatives, divergences, ruptures and contradictions.

A second suggested move is to describe the *different spaces of dissension* of a discursive formation, taking contradictions as objects to be described. This means to identify: (a) the locus in which they take place in a certain description of its objects, in a set of operations on these objects and/or in the authorities that are allowed to deal with them; (b) the place where two branches of the tree of derivation join and (c) a certain domain of objects, enunciative modalities, concepts or theoretical choices from which it is possible to derive the divergence in focus (ibid. 170). The archaeological description is interested, in particular, in addressing what Foucault calls *intrinsic contradictions*, that is those contradictions 'that are deployed in the discursive formation itself, and which, originating at one point in the system of formations, reveal subsystems' or different 'ways of forming statements, [...] characterized by certain objects, certain positions of subjectivity, certain concepts, and certain strategic choices' (ibid. 171). Here intrinsic contradictions can be described in terms of *inadequation* of the objects, *divergence* of enunciative modalities, *incompatibility* of concepts or *exclusion* of theoretical options. Intrinsic contradictions as oppositions can be analysed archaeologically as bringing about an *additional development*, a *reorganisation* or a *critique* of the enunciative field.

A third move is to outline historical *interdiscursive configurations* through comparative analysis, that is describable relations between a determined set of discursive formations focusing on the law of their communications. Such an outlining develops through three moves: to compare and oppose discursive formations to one another in the simultaneity of their emergence; to 'distinguish them from those that do not belong to the same time-scale; to relate them, on the basis of their specificity, to the non-discursive practices that surround them and serve as a general element for them' (ibid. 174). This is what allows the archaeological gaze to connect the archaeological description of discursive formations (as them and in correlation to them) to that of 'an institutional field, a set of events, practices, and political decisions, a sequence of economic processes', carrying on what Foucault calls a *lateral rapprochement*. This is a crucial point to understand the specificity of the archaeological gaze. Archaeology compares the concomitant states of distinct discursive formations during a particular period, where 'the horizon of archaeology [...] is not a science, a rationality, a mentality, a culture [but] a tangle of interpositivities' (ibid. 177) whose limits and points of intersection become a key point of analysis, and the scope is not to outline a totalising unity but to produce a diversifying effect, dividing up their diversity and specificity into different figures. Through lateral rapprochement, what archaeology wishes to uncover is primarily – in the specificity and distance maintained in various discursive formations – the *play of analogies and differences* as they appear at the level of rules of formation. This means to confront with five tasks: (a) showing *archaeological isomorphisms*; that is if and how different discursive formations may be formed on the basis of similar rules; (b) defining the *archaeological model* of each formation, showing to what extent these rules do or do not apply in the same way, are or are not linked in the same order, are or are not arranged in accordance with the same model in different types of discourse; (c) pointing to *archaeological isotopia*, shedding light on how different concepts occupy a similar position in the ramification of their respective discursive formations; (d) indicating the *archaeological shifts*, showing how a single notion may cover archaeologically distinct elements and (e) establishing *archaeological correlations*, that is to show how relations of subordination or complementarity may be identified between discursive formations.[11]

As a fourth move, Foucault suggests to define *forms of articulation*, that is describing how the rules of formation that govern distinct discursive formations can be linked to non-discursive domains (institutions, political events, economic practices and processes). The archaeological gaze looks at this link through a specific lens. It is in fact interested in shedding light on how and in what form political, economic and social practices take part in the conditions of emergence and functioning of a discursive formation. The analysis of the forms of articulation develops looking at the four archaeological processes of formation, describing how political, economic and social practices take part in the division and delimitation of the objects of a discursive formation, in the according of a peculiar status to its distinct subjects, or the attribution to it of a function and modes of operation. As Foucault (2002b: 182) puts it, it is a question to show how discourse 'as a practice concerned with a particular field of objects, finding itself in the hands of a certain number of statutorily designated individuals, and having certain functions to exercise in society, is articulated on practices that are external to it, and which are not themselves of a discursive order'.

The fifth move consists of looking at *change and transformation* in discursive formations, reflecting on the temporality of discursive formations in some distinct ways through a set of moves: (a) *suspending given temporal successions*, 'to reveal the relations that characterize the temporality of discursive formations and articulate them in series' (ibid. 184). Specifically, this means to describe the emergence of new statements in correlation with 'external' events, showing the conditions that make such a correlation to exist, that is its limits, its form, its code and its law of possibility (ibid. 185); (b) *mapping the temporal vectors of derivation*, combining a synchronic and diachronic glance to discursive formations. In other words, the archaeological ramification of the rules of formation is not a uniformly simultaneous network: there exist relations, branches and derivation that are temporally neutral; there exist others that imply a particular temporal direction. Moreover, all the rules of formation assigned by archaeology to a positivity do not have the same generality: some are more specific and derive from others. This subordination may be merely hierarchical but it may also involve a temporal vector (ibid. 186); (c) *proceeding through differentiation*, that is taking as its privileged object of description differences in the attempt to identify exactly what they consist of. Differentiation is based on the distinction between different levels of discursive events within the very density of a discursive formation: statements themselves in their unique emergence; the appearance or transformation of objects, types of enunciation, concepts, strategic choices; the derivation of new rules of formation on the basis of rules that are already in operation in the element of a single positivity; the substitution of one discursive formation for another (ibid. 190). At each of these levels, the archaeological description of change grasps the details of how a system of formation, the relations between its elements, or the relations between rules of formation have been transformed. Archaeology focuses on the dynamics of continuity and transformation in the field of discursive practice, describing if and how general transformation of relations occur, and within this some elements 'remain throughout several distinct positivities, their form and content remaining the same, but their formations being heterogeneous', some 'are constituted, modified, organized in one discursive formation, and which, stabilized at last, figure in another', some others 'appear later, as an ultimate derivation [but] occupy an important place in a later formation' or 'reappear after a period of desuetude, oblivion, or even invalidation' (ibid. 191–92).

Conclusion

I am now in the position to make a final move to show in detail to what extent the deployment of the archaeological gaze contributes to an *analytic of government* and, relatedly, to a critical ontology of ourselves as contemporary educational subjects in our relation to government, evaluation and truth. As shown in Table 1.6, the archaeological method provides an analytics to address a materialist analysis of practices of government as assembling processes, projecting a distinctive gaze on each of the set of practices which constitute a regime of government. It looks at forms of rationality, fields of visibility, techne and identity formation focusing on discursive practices, that is the local socio-historical material conditions that enable and constrain knowledge practices and produce their objects and subjects, in search for regularities in the relations between the statements or enunciative functions that they establish. The aim is to identify the positivity of discursive formations as rule-governed systems. What the archaeological endeavour allows us to do is to understand how truth is produced in a regime of government through the operation of a set of rules that pertain to:

- the formation and dispersion of objects and, as such, constitute the conditions of existence of a *field of visibility*, that is of ways of seeing and perceiving that are characteristic of a regime of government and are necessary to its operation. These rules can be mapped looking at the relations between surfaces of emergence of objects, their authorities of delimitation and grids of specification;
- the formation and dispersion of concepts, which constitute the conditions of existence of a *form of rationality*, that is ways of thinking and questioning that mobilise specific vocabularies and procedures for the production of truth in a regime of government. These rules can be grasped looking at the relations between forms of succession, forms of coexistence and procedures of intervention;
- the formation and dispersion of enunciative modalities, constituting the conditions of existence of distinct modes of *identity formation*, that is ways of forming subjects, selves, persons, actors or agents within a regime of government. These rules can be analysed looking at the relations between the status, differentiation, relations and functioning of enunciative modalities, their institutional sites and situations;

Table 1.6 The archaeological gaze deployed within an analytics of government

The archaeological gaze

A historical and spatial analysis of discursive practices as 'the local socio-historical material conditions that enable and constrain knowledge practices such as speaking, writing, thinking, calculating, measuring, filtering, and concentrating' and produce the "subjects" and "objects" of knowledge practices'
In search for regularities in the relations between statements (discursive formations as rule-governed systems)
In order to understand how within a discursive formation, immanent in a regime of government, a specific object is recognised and treated; what institutions are assigned to hold and care for it at times; what authorities decided about it, and according to what criteria; what methods are employed to make distinct type of operations on/with/through them; in what network of institutions and practices this specific object is both enmeshed and defined.

The analytics of government	Focus	What is	What to look at	Archaeological focus	Privileged points of analysis
A materialist analysis of practices of government as assembling processes that involve multiple and heterogeneous elements, that vary from routines, technologies, ways of doing things and agencies to theories, programmes, knowledge and expertise	Forms of rationality	The distinctive ways of thinking and questioning that mobilise specific vocabularies and procedures for the production of truth in a regime of government	Thoughts, forms of knowledge, expertise, strategies, programmes and means of calculation that are employed in and inform the practices of government	The formation of concepts	Forms of succession Forms of coexistence Procedures of intervention
	Fields of visibility	Ways of seeing and perceiving that are characteristic of a regime of government and are necessary to its operation	Models, tables, figures, charts, maps and graphs that are mobilised as ways for visualising fields to be governed	The formation of objects	Surfaces of emergence Authorities of delimitation Grids of specification

Techne	Peculiar modes of acting, intervening and directing that combine distinct practical rationalities, expertise and know-how and rely on definite techniques and technologies in a regime of government	Techniques of government', conceptualised as modes of intervention (e.g. systems of accounting, methods of the organisation of work, forms of surveillance, methods of timing and spacing of activities) that are and can be assembled through particular governmental programmes in diverse technologies of government (e.g. types of schooling, systems of intervention into organisations).	The formation of strategies	Points of diffraction Authorities Function in a field of non-discursive practices
Identity formation	Characteristic ways of forming subjects, selves, persons, actors or agents within a regime of government	The forms of person, self and identity presupposed by practices of government, the 'statuses, capacities, attributes and orientations' assumed of those who exercise authority and are to be governed, the expected forms of conduct and the set of duties and rights associated with those identities.	The formation of enunciative modalities	Enunciative modality Institutional sites Situations

- the formation of strategies, that is theories (or theoretical choices) that outline peculiar modes of acting, intervening and directing that combine distinct practical rationalities, expertise and know-how and rely on definite techniques and technologies (*techne*) in a regime of government. These rules can be approached looking at the relations between points of diffraction, authorities and the functions in a field of non-discursive practices.

Used in this way to analyse regimes of government, archaeology stands as a double distancing, from truth and from ourselves. It has the ambition to allow the folding on the limits of validity of the world that we inhabit, opening spaces for the possibility of dissent and for thinking otherwise (Rabinow 1997: xxxv). It is in this vein that this book entails a form of historical and not transcendental criticism that could be defined, with Foucault, as a limit attitude.

In fact, it will attempt to analyse educational evaluation as the contemporary practice of evaluating those who educate and are educated, interpreting it as a domain of historical discursive events that set the possibilities for us to think, say and do education. Archaeology here constitutes a method for examining the historicity of truth by describing rules that undergird ways of looking at evaluation, its objects (the *evaluand*), concept (*evaluation*), enunciative modality (the *authorities* of evaluation) and strategies (various uses of evaluation and work in the *treatment of the evaluand*). These rules are intended as regularities that determine the systems of possibility as to what is considered as true and false. They determine what counts as grounds for assent or dissent, as well as what arguments and data are relevant and legitimate (Olssen 1999: 10), what statements are excluded or marginalised as well as what problems and solutions can be thought and how can be hierarchised and enacted by policymakers, professionals, educators, technicians, students and so on. But there is not any form of determinism here. As a form of bracketing, archaeology has the ambition to lay down the basis for exploring the relation of games of truth to power relations and to the self (see Gutting 2014: 18), standing as a move towards the opening of a space of analysis where the discursive and the non-discursive relations can be addressed (see Gutting 1989: 225). As a form of detachment, archaeology separates out 'from the contingency that has made us what we are, the possibility of no longer being, doing, or thinking what we are, do, or think' (Foucault 1997a: 315–16) as subjects of educational evaluation. In this respect, as a work of freedom which is in a condition of perennial becoming,[12] such a criticism, is also experimental, it is oriented towards 'contemporary reality', in the attempt to test the limits that can be crossed-over and to explore 'the points where change is possible and desirable' (Foucault 1997a: 316).[13]

Before to enter the archaeological analysis of educational evaluation as a key form of truth production in the contemporary government of education, I need however to provide here two further specifications. First, in presenting archaeology as a gaze to approach an analytics of government I have often emphasised the need to look at the relatedness and mutual implication between objects, enunciative modalities, concepts and strategies formation. If a regime of government cannot be known isolating subgroups of practices, at the same time any archaeological analysis needs to identify an entry-point. In this work, choosing from the multiple entry-points made available by the archaeological gaze, I will opt for the formation of objects and concepts in the field of educational evaluation, mainly focusing on the entities formed through educational evaluation, the means by which truth about their value is produced, and the criteria of rationality that they establish (see Olssen 1999; Machado 1992). This choice originates from the acknowledgement of the historical specificity of educational evaluation as a discursive domain emerged within the epistemological space of possibility of the human and social sciences. As such, it has historically developed through processes of conceptual transposition from other discursive domains. If this premise is accepted, then the point of analysis that demands a closer attention and could allow a better 'grip' on the processes of formation of the evaluation enunciative modalities and strategies is to approach first the regularities in the distinctive ways of objectifying, thinking and questioning that mobilise specific vocabularies and procedures for the production of truth. In archaeological terms, this means to focus on evaluation as a field of discursive practices attempting the reconstruction of the spatial organisation of a field of visibility and the dispersion of its concepts and their rules of formation. It is starting from the identification of the rules that govern the formation of objects and concepts in terms of grids of specification, forms of succession, forms of coexistence and procedures of intervention that the analysis inevitably will move, time by time, to the formation of enunciative modalities and strategies looking at their relatedness.

Second, the analysis will try to chart the movement of educational evaluation as a discursive formation 'across the various thresholds of epistemologisation and scientificity' (Dean 1994: 31). Educational evaluation will not be addressed as a particular discipline, corpus, or branch of knowledge (*connaissance*), but rather as a discursive formation that gives rise to practical, political, legal, literary, aesthetic, philosophical, common sense or ethical knowledge, in search for the regularities which govern the emergence of evaluation objects, concepts, theories, and forms of subjectivity within knowledge (*savoir*). Thus, the point of attack of the analysis will be the regularity of statements within educational evaluation as a discursive formation, their system of formation which delimits the statements that can be made, the relations they have with one another, their modes of transformation (ibid. 32). The unity of what I will attempt to analyse through the archaeological lenses lies in the rules immanent to educational evaluation as a practice of government (Gutting 1989: 232) and, as such, it will be not congruent with any discipline, will not appear to have the same surface or the same articulations (Webb 2003: 68). It is such a disperse and heterogeneous space that will constitute the archive of the present analysis.

Notes

1. Dean (2010: 268) defines regimes of practices as the 'relatively organized and systematized ways of doing things such as curing, caring, punishing, assisting, educating' and regimes of government as 'the subset of regimes of practices concerned with ways of directing the conduct of the self and others'. The latter constitute the object of an analytics of government.
2. In the essay *On the Genealogy of Ethics: An Overview of Work in Progress* published in the *Foucault Reader* edited by P. Rabinow (Foucault 1984: 352), Foucault defines these enquiries as three possible domains of genealogy, which were all 'present, albeit in a somewhat confused fashion, in Madness and Civilization', whereas he clarifies that 'the truth axis was studied in *The Birth of the Clinic* and *The Order of Things*, the power axis was studied in *Discipline and Punish*, and the ethical axis in *The History of Sexuality*'.
3. In *The Subject and Power* Foucault describes the general theme of his research as the ways in which 'human beings are constituted as subjects' (1982: 208–9). In relation to the discontinuities and disjunctions in Foucault's definition of the general themes of his research, Dean argues that 'there is more continuity in his reworking of historical approach than in his formulation of his general themes and objects' and that 'one can discern varying degrees of concern for and balances between issues of power and government, truth and rationality, and subjectivity and ethical practice' (Dean 1994: 35).
4. The word analytics is intentionally employed here to highlight that archaeology is 'a method of decomposition into context-dependent categories of statements and their context-dependent transformations rather than atomic elements and abstractable rules of formation' (Dreyfus and Rabinow 1982: 56). On the basis of these considerations, Dreyfus and Rabinow conclude that archaeology 'could better, following Kant, be called an analytic, since it seeks to discover the a priori conditions that make possible' any historically and socially situated analysis.
5. Most of the key terms and concepts of the archaeological method (e.g. discontinuity, threshold, limit, series or transformation) are derived from mathematics and make evident the strong relation existing between Foucault's archaeology and the works of Bachelard, Cavaillès and Serres (Webb 2003: 54; Major-Poetzl 1983). Archaeology, in this respect, stands as an attempt to 'draw on resources from science and mathematics to undo habits of thought entrenched in philosophy, and above all in forms of thought allied to the human sciences through their shared commitment to the idea of the human' (Webb 2003: 48). However, if located in Foucault's entire intellectual trajectory, it is clear how such an undoing is not devoted to a radical decentering of the human subject, neither to a radical critique to human sciences and the idea of the human. On the contrary, Foucault's analyses have the ambition to account for the constitution of the subject within a historical framework (Foucault 1980: 117), not rejecting 'all humanism' but resituating 'humanism by historicizing the conceptions of actors and reason through which practice and purpose are constructed' (Popkewitz and Brennan 1997: 297–98). As Webb has argued (2003: 54), Foucault's ambition, after all, is to open up the 'synthesis of experience to reveal its operation as a historical process'.
6. In order to fully understand what is the domain of analysis of the archaeology and eschew from some confusions and reductionisms that it is possible to recognize in some attempt to employ Foucauldian archaeology, it seems useful to bear in mind how, through this definition, Foucault distinguishes the statement from *linguistic performance*, that is any group of signs produced on the basis of a natural (or artificial) language (langue), *formulation*, that is the individual or collective act (an event) that reveals, on any material and according to a particular form, that

group of signs, *sentence or proposition*, that are the units that grammar or logic may recognize in a group of signs. The statement is the modality of existence proper to that groups of signs.
7. Interestingly enough for a sociologist, in the *Archaeology of Knowledge* (2002b), Foucault demonstrates a clear sense of the kind of bracketing that an archaeological gaze operates in choosing the enunciative field and function as objects of the analysis and how this de-emphasize the role that humans have in making their history (Gutting 2014: 16). In his discussion of the repeatable materiality of the enunciative function, Foucault (2002b: 118) defines the statements as paradoxical 'objects that men produce, manipulate, use, transform, exchange, combine, decompose and recompose, and possibly destroy. Instead of being something said once and for all [...] the statement, as it emerges in its materiality, appears with a status, enters various networks and various fields of use, is subjected to transferences or modifications, is integrated into operations and strategies in which its identity is maintained or effaced. Thus the statement circulates, is used, disappears, allows or prevents the realization of a desire, serves or resists various interests, participates in challenge and struggle, and becomes a theme of appropriation or rivalry'.
8. This is a controversial point and it is possible to criticize the kind of conceptual equivalence that I am suggesting here. As Lynch (2014: 20) observes, Foucault uses the term 'archive' most commonly in the years 1967–1969, offering several variations on the notion given in *The Archaeology of Knowledge*. After 1969, however, the notion of the archive virtually disappeared from Foucault's vocabulary, when genealogy emerges as the principal framing lens of his work. A similar argument could be made for the terms 'episteme' (which was central in *The Order of Things*) and 'historical a priori' (see Nealon 2014). The relationship between the terms archive, episteme and historical a priori is discussed in Roth 1981.
9. Gutting (1989: 236) discusses how Foucault employs this distinction in his archaeological analysis and provides an interesting example for the scope of this book. Looking at *The Order of Things* he highlights how that book showed in what ways the field of presence of the modern sciences of man 'corresponds to the distinctive set of statements about man that are accorded serious disciplinary consideration by psychology, sociology and literary analysis', where the field of concomitance includes the empirical sciences as biology, economics and philology that provide their models and, finally, their field of memory includes the disciplines of the Classical age that they have substituted.
10. It is worth to note here that, if Foucault clearly states in *The Archaeology of Knowledge* that he has not devoted a work to the specific task of a system of formation of strategies and its implicit rules (2002b: 72), as Dreyfus and Rabinow suggest (1982: 72), his systematisation of the analytic of finitude in *The Order of Things* (2002a) 'can, however, serve as an example of what such an approach can accomplish', when Foucault shows how, across two centuries, three strategies were explored and exhausted in the attempt to find out how to identify and overcome man's essential limitations. It is thus the analytic of finitude that 'sets up a space in which strategies can arise, embroil whole areas of research, and then be replaced by others' (Dreyfus and Rabinow 1982: 73), where the elements go through a certain number of intrinsic transformations but the general form of discursive practice is not altered in its regularity.
11. In *The Archaeology of Knowledge* (2002b: 177–79), Foucault powerfully uses his analyses in *The Order of Things* as example to clarify what does it mean to uncover the play of analogies and differences between discursive formations. To provide an example of *archaeological isomorphism*, he recalls how the concepts of General Grammar, like those of verb, subject, complement and root, were formed on the basis

of the same arrangements of the enunciative field – theories of attribution, articulation, designation and derivation – as the very different, radically heterogeneous concepts of Natural History and Economy. Within the same space, however, they had different *archaeological models*, in so far as General Grammar followed the order 'theories of attribution, articulation, designation, and derivation theory of derivation', whereas Natural History and the Analysis of Wealth regrouped the first two and the last two, but linking them in the reverse order. Coming to *archaeological isotopia*, Foucault recalls how the concepts of value and specific character, or price and generic character occupied similar positions in the ramifications of their respective discursive formations (the Analysis of Wealth and Natural History). As examples of an *archaeological shift* Foucault recalls, instead, the notions of origin and evolution, emphasizing how they had not the same role, place and formation in the discursive formations of the General Grammar and Natural History.

12. As Foucault recognizes (1997a: 316), 'it is true that we have to give up hope of ever acceding to a point of view that could give us access to any complete and definitive knowledge [*connaissance*] of what may constitute our historical limits. And, from this point of view, the theoretical and practical experience we have of our limits, and of the possibility of moving beyond them, is always limited and determined; thus, we are always in the position of beginning again'.

13. I want to clarify that there is not determinism here. Discursive practices culturally shape the fields within which actors enact their strategic conduct, contributing to the definition of both the possibilities of thought and the rules of the game. Moreover, they play a crucial role in the construction of the acting subjects themselves, shaping positional identities and power relations among the actors as well as the possible courses of action. In emphasizing this point, Ball (2006: 49) states that 'there are real struggles over the interpretation and enactment' of discursive possibilities, but 'these are typically set within a moving discursive frame which articulates and constrains the possibilities and probabilities of interpretation and enactment'. In these terms the effect of the discursive is to enable, limit and change the possibilities we have for thinking 'otherwise' and responding to change. The perspective proposed in this book acknowledges how enactments take place into social environments where alternative discursive formations 'clash and grate against one another' (ibid; Tamboukou 1999). The fields of validity, normativity and actuality are not univocally defined by any single discursive formation. Rather, Foucault's emphasis on discontinuity and on the processes of exclusion, co-option, subjugation and marginalisation offers an image of the discursive as a field of struggle where diverging discursive formations confront each other, where 'dominant discourses pre-suppose their opposite' and 'the existence of […] 'outlaw' discourses, always presents the possibility of some kind of 'disidentification' (Ball 2006: 49).

Chapter 2

Educational evaluation as an enunciative field

Suspending educational evaluation

This chapter describes educational evaluation as a contemporary practical domain and a field of possible experiences, unravelling the complex tangle between educational evaluation as a scientific domain, a political technology and a moral practice. This necessarily partial description will attempt to outline the main traits of a dispersed and heterogeneous globalised space made of relations between the material forms assumed by evaluative thought in education. These forms include scientific, policy, advisory or juridical texts, regulations, graphic formalisations, images, models, tables, figures, charts and maps.

Consistently with the overall frame of the *analytics of government*, the description of such a field is organised trying to figure out the main traits of educational evaluation as an ensemble of ways of being, thinking, reasoning, visualising, representing, acting, intervening and theorising. I will show how educational evaluation assumes today the form of a key governmental rationality in contemporary education on a global scale and how its material forms play a key role as means of visualisation for the objects, subjects, processes and outcomes of education. I will insist on how material forms of evaluative thought play a distinctive role in the codification of educators, students, policymakers and experts as forms of educational person, self and identity.

Thus this chapter stands as a first and preliminary move in the archaeological detachment from educational evaluation as immediate and familiar forms of unity (evaluation as a discipline, specific approaches to evaluation, distinct evaluative technologies and models). In treating, on the contrary, educational evaluation as an inexhaustible and never closed enunciative field, the following description will use the grid of the analytics of government to illuminate how these unities articulate themselves in our educational present and will prepare the terrain for their suspension and archaeological re-composition in terms of discursive regularities.

A long-standing and globalised social experiment to make education governable

Evaluation can be considered a distinctive trait of modern society, which is linked through a *fil rouge* to the founding categories of modernity. It is part of 'a larger societal trend that also includes activities such as auditing, inspection, quality assurance, and accreditation' and as such can be considered as a key pillar of 'a huge and unavoidable social experiment which is conspicuously cross sectional and transnational' (Dahler-Larsen 2012: 3). This societal trend has some historical depth, being rooted in the foundations of modernity and the modern liberal state and linked to the problems of government, rationality and autonomy. Governmentality studies show how evaluation has played, and still plays, the role of a key governmental technique in *the constitution of society as a governable domain*, according to a liberal and later on neoliberal political rationality whose project was to produce free subjects and, at the same time, shape the social sphere as calculable, predictable and amenable to the practices of government (Rose 1999; Miller and Rose 2008; Dean 2010). Evaluation as a form of rationality, technique and ethics finds its historical conditions in the rise of the problem of population in the 19th century and the related needs for techniques of population management (Foucault 2009). It is both an effect and instrument of the complex tangle of governmental processes developing through and around the interaction between: (a) the rise of biopolitics and the governmentalisation of the state, whose governing action turns to the administration of life; (b) the ongoing centrality of the positive sciences of economics, statistics, sociology, medicine, biology, psychiatry and psychology in producing the truths on populations, conceived as the bearer of an array of problematic conducts and capacities; (c) the related rise of expert figures, entitled to deploy a range of scientific and technical knowledges that allowed the possibility of exercising rule over time and space and (d) the rise of liberalism as a key political rationality in western modern societies, with the related shift towards the individual as the primary locus and actor of government (Ball 2012: 59).

Through these historical processes, 'rule becomes dependent upon ways of rendering intelligible and practicable [the] conditions for the production and government of a polity of free citizens' (Rose 1996: 44). Government increasingly focuses on the production of pedagogical machines. Mechanisms/Devices for the governing of the population, as education and schools, are made as key domains of knowledge (Ball 2012: 41–42; Hunter 1996). Rule starts to be based on the knowledge of the ruled subject 'in order to produce desirable objectives while at the same time respecting its autonomy' (Rose 1996: 44). The paradoxical relation between freedom and regulation that lies at the heart of liberalism as political rationality (Foucault 2009) is key to understand the historical rise of evaluation and educational evaluation. Evaluation as mode of regulation is a correlative of liberal freedom and the need to govern it at a distance, playing a role in the following governmental processes (Barry *et al.* 1996):

- the tying of government to the positive knowledges of human conduct developed within the social and human sciences, where the 'activity of government becomes connected up to all manners of facts, theories, diagrams, techniques, knowledgeable persons who can speak in the name of society' and knowledge production has the aim 'to render docile the unruly domains over which government is to be exercised' (Rose 1996: 44–45);
- the production of free individuals who will govern and care for themselves, being committed to make the most of their own existence by conducting their life responsibly (Rose 1996: 46);
- the creation and legitimation of instrumental forms of non-state but autonomous expert authority designed to govern at a distance;
- the translation into a mode of action of the liberal dissatisfaction with government and the will to diagnose failures to govern better (Rose 1996: 47).

Nevertheless, evaluation as we know it today becomes a key governmental technique in the late 20th century, as expression of a larger trend that actualises a formula for the relation between government, expertise and subjectivity which differs from classical liberalism. In fact, as a versatile and highly transferable technology for governing the conduct of population, evaluation has its roots, at least in part, 'in the success of welfare in authorizing expertise in relation to a range of social objectives, and in implanting in citizens the aspiration to pursue their own civility, wellbeing and advancement' (Rose 1996: 40).

In the attempt to explain the composite character of present-day evaluative activities, Vedung (2010) has identified four waves of evaluation diffusion that have deposited sediments in the Western world, where evaluation 'has been coupled to diverse, more general public sector governance doctrines' covering a wide political spectrum (ibid. 264). According to his historical and epistemological analysis, the 1950s have witnessed the rise of a *science-driven* evaluation. At this time, evaluation was prominently framed within radical rationalism and instrumentalism, that is as a means to render government more rational, scientific and grounded in facts. Evaluation research interacted with public and private decision-making according to an 'engineering model', a mode of inquiry that mainly worked through the scientific method in the form of randomised (or matched) two-group experimentations to provide neutral, reliable and objective knowledge of the effects of interventions. In the mid-1970s, this model of experimental evaluation was challenged by a *dialogue-oriented* wave, where a more pluralistic and dialogic form of evaluation was framed within a constructivist epistemology (Guba and Lincoln 1989) and rested upon a communicative rationality (Vedung 2010: 270). Here evaluation was promoted as a mode of inquiry employing hermeneutic-dialectic methods to 'generate broad agreements, consensus, political acceptability and democratic legitimacy' (ibid.). In a radical opposition to that, the late 1970s see also the rise of a neoliberal wave, within which evaluation turns into a permanent feature of New Public Management (as a public sector reform movement) and a doctrine of results-based management. Within marketisation policy, evaluation assumes new forms such as accountability assessments, performance measurement and consumer satisfaction appraisal, quality assurance or benchmarking. Vedung closes his analysis arguing that the 1990s are the decade of an *evidence* wave and a return of experimentation (ibid. 273), which tended 'to structure the field from a social science methodology point of view' and downsize the political, administrative or client-oriented orientations that inspired evaluation. The epistemological space where this conceptualisation and practice of evaluation emerge is the *evidence-based movement* (Hammersley 2013) and, relatedly, evaluation becomes a mode of inquiry with an aim to show 'what works'. In a sort of return to science-based evaluation, but in a new disguise, evaluation becomes based on a means–ends rationality and elects as its privileged methodological tools randomised experiments, quasi-experiments, meta-analyses and systematic reviews. Notably, this is the wave where in different policy fields (and education among them), international and national bodies began to be established to produce 'systematic reviews' of the learned evidence-based lessons (ibid. 273).

Thus, evaluation, as a technology of expert social government, arises as a grey science with a claim to truth on social and educational phenomena which, thanks to its technicality and expertise, carries with it the pretension 'to be simultaneously modest and omniscient, limited yet apparently limitless in their application to problems' (Rose 1996: 54). In this respect, the rise of evaluation can be interpreted also as part of a process of 'de-statization of government', that is of implantation of a particular mode of reasoning and calculation into agents who are invited to think at themselves as autonomous entities (enterprises, organisations, communities, professionals, individuals) who are the maker of their destiny and responsible for their successes and failures (Power 1997). The imperative for evaluation replaces the trust accorded to professionals and at the same time implies a process of responsibility devolution, with the entities that are called to evaluate and being evaluated that undergo a process of transformation thanks to the production of new grids of visibilities for the conduct of organisations and those who inhabit them. Within the contemporary governmental landscape, evaluation is a technology that installs and supports the multiple project of neoliberalisation of the social, by shaping and governing the capacities, competencies and wills of subjects, who are apparently cast outside the formal control of the public powers and are asked to conduct themselves establishing an entrepreneurial relation to the self (Simons 2002: 621). Being entrepreneurial means here 'to maximize their quality of life through acts of choice, according their life a meaning and value to the extent that it can be rationalized as the outcome of choices made or choices to be made' (Rose 1996: 57). The role of evaluation is to help active and enterprising individuals to relate to reality in the position of a 'permanent learner' and to look at the self 'from the perspective of actualization, development, a personal project and governing ourselves accordingly' (Simons 2002: 620).

Of course, the institutionalisation of evaluation as a long-standing societal trend is marked by significant historical and spatial discontinuities and variations across different sectors, types of organisations and levels of administration. In many countries, evaluation has become an obligatory passage point and a social obsession in public and private sectors, although this has occurred with differences in paces and intensity. However, as Dahler-Larsen (2012: 17) observes, 'no societal type has previously evaluated so willingly and so frequently as our own' and this is a particularly a cogent argument if we restrict our focus to the field of education.

Educational evaluation and assessment

In the field of education, the raise of evaluation and assessment can be located within this general historical trend, as a specific inflection of the problem of government. Evaluation and assessment as tools to monitor students' progress towards preestablished objectives have been since the 19th century an integral part of teaching and learning. This has implied, for instance, 'the development of a longstanding tradition of psychometric testing – predominantly achievement testing – that is unparalleled in other domains' (Ryan and Cousins 2009). This has preceded and, later on, paralleled and interacted with the introduction in the field of education of the evaluative tools and techniques coming from the field of scientific management and social sciences to evaluate educational systems, organisations and professionals according to the logics of effectiveness and efficiency.

Thus, evaluation and assessment have acted and still act as two of the 'many and varied capillaries of power' through which governmentality of schooling takes place. As Ball has argued, the history of the modern school and of contemporary education policy can be understood as a history of classifications and exclusions (Ball 2012: 55), which has developed through the intertwining of two distinct techniques and politics for the management of populations, the disciplinary and the regulatory. Here evaluation and assessment participate to the disciplining of schools, breaking down classrooms, teachers, learners, their movements, times, actions and operations into components that can be seen, analysed, classified by ability and effectiveness and modified (ibid. 46). They have provided a technical repertoire for managing, knowing, classifying, positioning and comparing the educational population, a scientific mode of identification of groups and categories and their divisions as deserving and undeserving, productive and unproductive in relation to a social norm (ibid. 68). As governmental techniques, they also have historically responded to the need to identify and act on specific problematic cases, through the production of judgements on deviant particular conducts. Through evaluation and assessment, education is 'anatomized by experts, rendered calculable in terms of norms and deviations, judged in terms of [its] social costs and consequences and subject to regimes of reformation' (Rose 1996: 49) and the modern project of perfection.

Today, in the scientific and political discourse on education, evaluation is increasingly framed as a universal good, as knowledge and practice that cannot be rejected or opposed, because of its promises of enlightenment, improvement, social betterment, increased efficiency, democracy, transparency and responsibilisation. Unsurprisingly, evaluation is a transversal milestone and a recurrent issue in what Sahlberg (2014) has termed the *Global Education Reform Movement* (GERM), that is the core set of education policies and reform principles that have been epidemically employed at the global level to improve the quality of education and education systems, within the window of possibilities created by the problematisation of welfarist education. Worldwide, public education has been profoundly redesigned through the enforcement of external and self-evaluation systems that are functionally tied to outcome and standards-based education policies. Moreover, evaluation has become a necessary and obvious symbolic device and technique for the management and development of educational organisations and administrations. It acts as an interlocking element between the adoption of standard and outcome-based accountability policies for schools, the institutionalisation of standard-based and externally driven processes of accrediting, promoting, inspecting, rewarding or sanctioning and the introduction of corporate management models. In particular, the ongoing establishment of a global frame of values, including efficiency, entrepreneurship, market-based reform, rational management and performance-based accountability is laterally but extensively influencing the articulation of the field of educational evaluation. Educational evaluation is more and more tied in its development as a field to the neoliberal project to rewrite the state as a market-maker and the creation of enterprising and entrepreneurial individuals (Peters 2001; Carlson 2009). It plays the role of an 'environmental technology' (Foucault 2008: 259) that operates around and on the individuals within their fields of game, changing the rules and variables that govern them.

Evaluative ideas, recipes, models and forms flow and are mobilised across scales and places (Madaus and Stufflebeam 2002: 18). They travel across local, national and global settings, moving along complex and continuously evolving network relations among multilateral agencies, supranational and national governments, evaluation agencies, think tanks, consultancy and EdTech firms, philanthropies, policy entrepreneurs, academic experts and associations. These actors and institutions combine in different and heterarchical

Educational evaluation as an enunciative field 59

forms, constituting a globalised space made of interlocking policy and epistemic communities, which are both horizontally related and hierarchically scaled (Normand 2016). Those communities share a global imaginary (Rizvi and Lingard 2010) about evaluation that connects evaluative concepts and moral values to a distinctive set of techniques and technologies and envisages a clear causal relation between evaluation and educational improvement. Their relations assume multiple, material and durable forms through funding relations, partnerships, cross-referencing, dissemination, best practices codification and transfer and other forms of exchange (Ball *et al.* 2017: 31). Figure 2.1 represents a necessarily partial attempt to map a section of this globalised space, showing the connections and the evaluative forms linking some of these policy and epistemic spaces and communities.

The 2013 OECD report *Better Synergies for Learning*, in reviewing the main policy trends in evaluation and assessment in the field of education in several

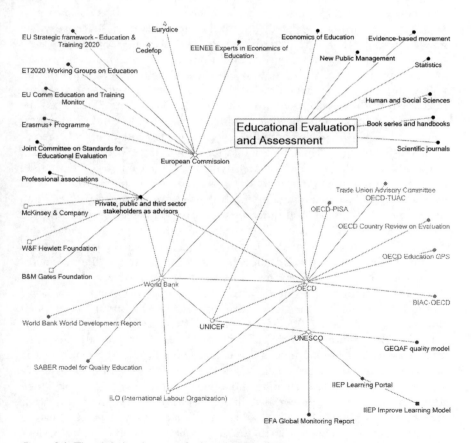

Figure 2.1 The globalised space of educational evaluation.

countries around the world, offers a detailed account of the ongoing centrality of the category of evaluation (and assessment), as linking improvement, accountability, capacity building, decentralisation and autonomy and social change. It shows how pervasive evaluation has come to be as a mode of inquiry, a mode of ordering and valuing educational things and beings and as an ethic. Whereas it is becoming the necessary empirical strategy to knowing school systems and characterising/classifying its constitutive elements, at the same time, it is having and has to perform a key role in constituting the educational subjects and in shaping their modes of being, acting, thinking and speaking, according to the imperative of improvement.

As a result of this global trend, at the individual scale, as teachers, educators, students, parents, researchers or administrators we are continuously evaluated. National or regional systems, organisations, communities and individuals are continuously put under scrutiny within the spectacle of comparison at different scales and within interlocked fields of visibility, in order to produce judgements on their quality, their value and their capacity to match the standards and, relatedly, to fulfil their function in the delivery of a good education (ILO 2011; World Bank 2011a; 2011b; OECD 2007).

However, as Ryan and Cousins (2009) note, if educational evaluation is part of this global imaginary and operates according to and through similar policy and governance structures, at the same time it is remarkably unique in relation to the heterogeneity, internal differentiation and plurality of the field. The mobilisation of evaluative ideas, recipes, models and forms across scales and places involves continuous processes of translation, intermediation, reassembling and recontextualisation (Peck and Theodore 2012: 24; Grek 2009). In this complex spatial dynamic, global but recontextualised evaluation policy and practices are to be found in 'local' spaces, where global evaluative agendas come up against existing practices and priorities (Ozga and Jones 2006: 2). This internal differentiation can be related to the distinctive and yet ambiguous link existing between means and ends in the field of education (Biesta 2007; Hunter 1994). If evaluation and assessment are regarded as indisputable universal goods and they are both related to the indisputable goal of improving student learning, the field has historically developed through differentiation around the right problematisation and evaluative solutions to be adopted to achieve this objective (see for instance Campbell and Stanley 1963; Cook 2002; Cronbach et al. 1980; Eisner 1994; Guba 1969; Stake 2003). It is not by chance that the 2013 OECD report also accounts for a growing diversity in the conceptualisations and uses of evaluation, calling at the same time for the generalised adoption of a holistic approach in 'developing an effective evaluation and assessment framework' that gives due attention to 'achieving proper articulation between the different evaluation components' (system and school evaluation and staff appraisal) and 'situating education system evaluation in the broader context of public sector performance requirements' (OECD 2013: 22–23). Thus, there is a paradox here, with an apparently unitary and dominant global orthodoxy (the imperative for evaluation) which is marked by a sensible heterogeneity, proliferating in the diverse spaces where the games of truth of educational evaluation unfold. Whatever is the semantic, geopolitical and intellectual space we refer to, and the scale of education we take into consideration, evaluation represents an omnipresent category. At the same time, it is also a milestone around which intense games of truth develop, in and across political, scientific and public spaces. Those spaces co-opt, enrol and engage each others.

As introduced above, this book addresses this complex landscape as an enunciative field, in search for rules, that is fields of coexistences, effects of series and successions, a distribution of functions and roles and regularities in such a dispersion. In the attempt to identify the contours of the archaeological territory that I will explore in the rest of the book, in the next sections of the chapter I will focus on educational evaluation as a form of rationality, a set of ways of seeing and perceiving education and its objects/subjects, an array of techniques and a form of identity formation.

Educational evaluation as a form of rationality

The globalised epistemic and policy scape portrayed in Figure 2.1 shows how educational evaluation assumes today the form of a global governmental rationality in contemporary education, thanks and through the influential and pervasive action of global public and private players (international institutions and organisations, global consultants, philanthropies, networks of expertise). It stands as a set of distinctive ways of thinking, reasoning and theorising educational reality and value, its practices, subjects, means and ends (Simons 2002: 618). What emerge within this global assemblage and circulate across its connections are evaluative thoughts, forms of knowledge, expertise, strategies, programmes and means of calculation that are employed in and inform the practices of government in the field of education.

The 2002 OECD *Glossary of Key Terms in Evaluation and Results Based Management* provides an influential and shared definition of evaluation within such a globalised space:

> The systematic and objective assessment of an ongoing or completed project, program or policy, its design, implementation and results. The aim is to determine the relevance and fulfillment of objectives, development efficiency, effectiveness, impact and sustainability. An evaluation should provide information that is credible and useful, enabling the incorporation of lessons learned into the decision-making process of both recipients and donors. Evaluation also refers to the process of determining the worth or significance of an activity, policy or program. An assessment, as systematic and objective as possible, of a planned, on-going, or completed development intervention. (OECD 2002: 21)

As a systematic and objective mode of knowing education, evaluation is related to the definition of appropriate standards, the examination of performance against those standards in terms of effectiveness and efficiency within an accountability frame. Within such rationality, the direct referent of evaluation is performance, intended as 'the degree to which a development intervention or a development partner operates according to specific criteria/standards/guidelines or achieves results [that is output, outcome or impact] in accordance with stated goals or plans' (OECD 2002: 29). As an assessment of actual and expected results and as a tool for the identification of relevant generalisable lessons, it represents a pivotal device of a project of modernisation of education which is based on the assumption that an evidence-based, result-oriented, systematic and preferably calculative evaluation is necessary to knowing whether an education system or organisation is delivering good education and to providing feedback for improvement (ILO 2011; World Bank 2011b). In a proliferation of labels, evaluation is mainly inflected as program, process or project, ex-ante, mid-term or ex-post, self-, internal or external, joint, participatory or independent, Meta or impact, formative, summative or thematic. Within this frame, as a mode to express a judgement on educational action, evaluation represents the main link between policy and educational realisation and a tool for modelling the form and the direction of education (Borer and Lawn 2013: 50; Felouzis and Hanhart 2011: 16).

Interestingly, the power of this form of rationality manifests itself in its capacity to generate a vast array of global and local policy agendas where such a way of thinking and reasoning about evaluation is embodied into policies and tools to evaluate, assess, monitor, calculate, compare, position in a commensurable space and rank education systems, organisations, subjects and practices. Evaluative tools and strategies paradoxically become both the means to modernise and improve education and aims/objectives in themselves. Global and local policies increasingly adopt a comprehensive approach, enacting a peculiar logic of scaling that identifies as effective evaluation framework a concentric assemblage of evaluative policies and tools that addresses five levels: system evaluation, policy evaluation, school evaluation, staff appraisal and student assessment (OECD 2013).

Yet, policies mobilise and are mobilised by bodies of evaluative knowledge that can be related to specific fields of theoretical and empirical investigation, in a process where the borders between science and policy are constantly renegotiated (Gambardella and Lumino 2015). The globalised policy space mapped in Figure 2.1 can also be described as an epistemic space, a totality of dispersed statements that constitutes a discursive space (Bhola 2002) in which people, objects, activities, organisations, systems or the diverse combination of them 'emerge and are continuously transformed' as objects and subjects of evaluation (Foucault 2002a: 36). A space that has, moreover, a certain style, that presupposes 'the same way of looking at things', the same practices of division, the same analytical strategies, the same modes to make things visible (ibid. 37). Here, evaluation has progressively acquired an authoritative voice as a distinct and powerful discipline in the space of the social and economic sciences, that employs scientific procedures to produce knowledge on education.

This epistemic space is extremely heterogeneous and contested. The apparently cohesive global evaluative frame promoted by international players like OECD, World Bank, ILO, UNESCO or European Commission (Bhola 2002) stands out against a background of intense debates in the academic/ intellectual space on the adequacy, limits and possibilities of a vast array of evaluative theories, models and methods. This is a field of struggle between epistemic subcommunities and is the space where, since the early 20th century a body of knowledge named as *evaluation* has attempted to establish itself as a science.

In the attempt to introduce some analytical order, it is possible to portray evaluation as a heterogeneous field of theoretical and empirical investigation (Scriven 1991) with different sub-fields, drawing 'concepts, criteria, and methods from such other fields as philosophy, political science, psychology, sociology, anthropology, education, economics, communication, public administration, information technology, statistics, and measurement' (Stufflebeam and Coryn 2014: 6). According to Alkin (2011: 8), we can distinguish between *Product Evaluation*, when an appraisal is made about the value of a product, *Personnel Evaluation*, where evaluations, again, require the making of judgements about relative value of individuals, *Policy Evaluation*, where the judgement regards policies as general directions for actions that not necessarily refer to a particular programme or plan and finally *Program Evaluation*, where the interest is in using multiple information 'to better understand the program in which participants or products are involved' (Alkin 2011: 6–7). In the field of education, these assume the forms of programme evaluation, school personnel evaluation, school accreditation and curriculum evaluation to student assessment, measurement and testing (Kellaghan *et al.* 2003: 1). Yet, the heterogeneity of the field, the plurality of the perspectives and the intensity of the confrontation are significant and sometimes result in apparently incompatible positions (see Scriven 1991; Stufflebeam *et al.* 2002; Rossi *et al.* 1999 Ryan and Cousins 2009; Alkin 2011).

These bodies of evaluative knowledge have multiple spaces of materialisation. Since the early 1970s, scientific and professional journals and other types of publications (handbooks and book series issued by the major global publishers), dedicated exclusively to evaluation scholarship and practice, began to appear to communicate and disseminate developments in, thinking about, and critiques of evaluation theory, methods and practice (see Figure 2.1). Moreover, many evaluation scholars and practitioners 'disseminate their work in discipline-specific journals in education, health and medicine, philosophy, psychology, and sociology [and] in subject-specific areas, such as measurement, research, and statistics' (Stufflebeam and Coryn 2014: 5). Together with the ongoing establishment of evaluation as a globalised form of rationality, the number of professional associations with an education section started to increase. As Stufflebeam and Coryn observe (2014: 5), in '1995 there were only five evaluation organizations worldwide' (the American, Canadian, Australasian, European and Central American evaluation societies), whereas 'by 2006 there were more than fifty national and regional evaluation organizations throughout the world' with also their university interdisciplinary training and PhD programmes. At the same time, every global association of educational research (e.g. the American or the European Educational Research Association) has a section dedicated to evaluation and assessment.

This ongoing institutionalisation and professionalisation of evaluation as a disciplinary field and professional practice/service has been also reinforced by the development of internationally recognised standards for evaluation services, and most notably the Joint Committee on Standards for Educational Evaluation's standards for evaluating programmes, personnel and students (Stufflebeam and Coryn 2014: 5).

Educational evaluation as a way of seeing and perceiving

The globalised space sketched in Figure 2.1 is also a space of educational world making (Borer and Lawn 2013: 51), where evaluation as a form of rationality enables the emergence and is embodied into specific forms of visualisation (Latour 1986) of the educational reality. The material forms of educational evaluation become means of visualisation for the objects, subjects, processes and outcomes of education and 'enable them to be identified, classified, ordered or sorted' (Williamson 2016: 127).

Policy documents, scientific texts, websites, online videos and public speeches circulating across the connections of such a space are all dispersed centres of visualisation where models, tables, figures, charts, maps and graphs displaying and reporting evaluative data (often numbers) are mobilised as ways for visualising educational fields and objects to be governed. Fields and objects are made 'seeable', intelligible and amenable to deliberation and decision-making (Miller and Rose 2008). Those forms are mobile but also immutable, presentable, readable and combinable means of visualisation and cognition (Latour 1986: 7). They create and legitimise 'a common cognitive space' and illuminate 'certain facets of [educational] reality while hiding others or placing them in shadow' (Borer and Lawn 2013: 49–50). As Williamson (2016: 131; see also Kitchin *et al.* 2015) notes, 'they are configured according to a realist epistemology' which assumes that the educational world can be represented as visualised facts and those facts can be employed to create arguments and generate explanations.

Evaluation as measurement and the drive towards quantification (Sauder and Espeland 2009) are central here, together with the 'performance–evaluation' nexus (Clarke 2009). A vast array of figures appearing into international reports such as the OECD Education at a Glance, the World Bank World Development Report or the UNESCO Global Education Monitoring Report mobilise evaluative data to visualise the qualities of these entities and practices (Lawn and Segerholm 2011), producing 'a global grid of visibility' in which educational activity and entities (through the lenses of performance) are made 'comparable and, importantly, public through seemingly scientific and non-political modes of technical expertise in statistical measurement and graphical presentation' (Williamson 2016: 130–31).

Those graphical presentations involve the use of multiple forms, such as diagrams, charts, tables, plots and infographics that make education intelligible to a wide variety of audiences. Through tabular forms, evaluative data are visually organised into a graphic representation that breaks down and classifies practices, entities and performance into units and subunits and 'make meaning out of the data' (Williamson 2016: 129). More often, evaluative data are presented through dynamic and diachronic forms of representation (scales, trends, factorial analyses, determinants of educational processes and outcomes) which construct the performance and the capacity to improve the visualised educational entities through time. Evaluative data become the units assembled into different graphical accounts, which take alternatively the form of dashboards, monitoring accounts, comparison and rankings, which respond to multiple functions such as classifying, diagnosing and ranking. They also constitute the informational infrastructure of different digital tools of data processing and search engines (e.g. the OECD *Education GPS*) that can be used to generate graphical displays and create customised visualisation, enabling 'a particular view of [educational] reality as enumerable and calculable by its in-built statistical formulas and models' (Williamson 2016: 129).

As Lawn (2013a: 9) observes, here 'seeing' becomes viral. A dystopic turn, with the related flows of data and technologies of measurement, creates 'a series of new mental, social and physical spaces [...] across education', which in turn are interconnected with the decoding and governing of education. Through such an activity of decoding, the education space is fabricated as a space of commensuration governed by numbers (Ozga 2009; Rose 1999), within which comparison for constant improvement against competition comes to be the standard by which education systems, practices and subjects are judged (Grek *et al.* 2009). Regulation through benchmarks and targets and the politics of quality act as the pillars of a 'softer' governance turn, where self-regulation is conceived as the best basis for constant improvement (Ozga et al. 2011).

Educational evaluation as a governmental techne

Material forms of evaluative thought, as policy or scientific texts and forms of visualisation, are constitutive elements of diverse techniques and modes of intervention deployed to govern contemporary education, globally and locally. As already discussed, evaluation is co-opted by multiple political rationalities as an instrument of economic and social knowledge to serve different political purposes and programmes of control. It is part of the reinvention of the governmentality of education through the establishment of new governmental modes that reflect a liberal, neoliberal or neoconservative conception of the relations between the state, the market, the profession and rational action (Power 1997). Within this scenario, specific technologies have become obligatory passage points, thanks to and through the mundane and pervasive work of multifaceted transnational epistemic communities and the power of key nodal global actors such as the OECD or the World Bank.

In fact, in the space of problematisation opened by evaluation as a form of rationality and the ontological work of the evaluative forms of visualisation, a set of evaluation and assessment policies and techniques are used to govern education in most of the Western countries. The main policy trends include an increasing prominence of evaluation and assessment in education policy, the creation of dedicated agencies to govern evaluation and assessment, the rise of educational measurement and indicators development, an increasing variation in the uses of evaluation and assessment results as tools for multiple accountability purposes, greater reliance on standards and a growing technological sophistication of evaluation procedures and data analysis (OECD 2013: 45). More generally, countries are 'developing more comprehensive evaluation and assessment frameworks with more resources devoted to evaluation components other than student assessment' (ibid. 38).

Table 2.1 presents a necessarily incomplete attempt to summarise the main policies and techniques that are epidemically enacted in the education systems of most of the Western countries as part of modernisation projects that aim to improve the quality of education and education systems (of course, with different intensities and inflections and great variation).

Through the enactment of such a capillary governmental evaluative techne, national and regional education systems, districts, educational organisations and communities, individuals are continuously put under scrutiny within the spectacle of comparison at different scales and within interlocked fields of visibility. Judgements are produced on their value and their capacity to match the standards and, relatedly, to fulfil their function. In this respect, evaluation and assessment play also a major role in the process of identity formation in the field of education.

Table 2.1 Educational evaluation as a governmental techne

| **Educational evaluation and assessment** As a recurrent issue in the *Global Education Reform Movement* (GERM) As a set of governmental techniques epidemically employed in most of the OECD countries to improve the quality of education and education systems | **System evaluation** The aim is to monitor the quality and equity of the education system, bringing together evidence from the evaluation and assessment of different objects at different levels, in order to inform policies for system improvement. The unit of evaluation can be either a national education system or a subnational education system.

This results in the enforcement of evaluation systems that are functionally tied to outcome and standards-based education policies.

Different forms of evaluation used in education system evaluation:

• the use of indicator frameworks to monitor key information on school systems;
• the use of tools to monitor student outcomes (national assessments, longitudinal research and surveys, international assessments);
• the use of qualitative reviews of particular aspects of the education system (evaluative information generated via external education system reviews);
• the evaluation of specific programmes and policies.

Policy evaluation The aim is the monitoring of the impact of given policy initiatives or educational programmes. Policies and programmes are typically submitted to evidence-based evaluation to judge their results (with randomised controlled trials as the dominant model).

School evaluation School evaluation refers to the evaluation of individual schools as organisations. It typically involves:

• external school evaluation (school reviews, school inspections);
• school self-evaluation;
• the use of comparative school performance measures as means to pursue school improvement.

School evaluation is increasingly mobilised as a governing tool to orient decision-making and resource allocation, especially in systems where reforms have granted further autonomy to schools, introduced market forms of accountability and delegated to the school the key responsibility for improving student learning.

School external evaluation is typically conducted by an external agency and involves a sequence of activities which may begin with self-reflection by the school, includes a visit by an external evaluator or team of evaluators and leads to a summative report which may be published and may require a follow-up process. Schools may also be held accountable on the basis of evaluation standard criteria and comparable measures of student results. International comparison shows a remarkable degree of convergence on three areas addressed during school evaluation: educational practices; outcomes; and compliance with rules and regulations. |

(Continued)

Table 2.1 Educational evaluation as a governmental techne (*Continued*)

Staff appraisal

Staff appraisal refers to the evaluation of teachers and school leaders to make a judgement and/or provide feedback about their competencies and performance. It aims to support professional development and/or career advancement, and also serves to hold professionals accountable for their practice. It is possible to detect three main types of staff appraisal:

- appraisal for the completion of a probationary period;
- appraisal for performance management, i.e. formal appraisal processes employing performance indicators and designed to ensure that individual and organisational goals are met;
- reward schemes, i.e. appraisal designed to identify high-performing staff to acknowledge and reward their competence and performance through rewards or one-off salary increases.

Teachers' and school leaders' appraisal procedures vary considerably across countries and often involve the establishment of reference standards to appraise. Formal schemes are often complemented with more informal school-level practices of feedback to teachers.

Student assessment

Student assessment refers to the processes in which evidence of learning is collected in a planned and systematic way in order to make a judgement about student learning for summative and formative purposes.

Different forms of and trends in student assessment include:

- national and international (full-cohort or sample-based) standardised student assessments, with diagnostic and monitoring purposes;
- teacher-based and within-the-school designed and implemented summative and formative student assessments;
- definition of assessment criteria and scoring rubrics.

Source: Our elaboration from OECD 2013.

Education evaluation as identity formation

Material forms of evaluative thought play a distinctive role in the codification of educators, students, policymakers and experts as forms of educational person, self and identity. At the individual scale, teachers, educators, students, parents, researchers or administrators are continuously evaluated and asked to evaluate. This involves the formation of ways of being, thinking, reasoning and acting. Material forms of evaluative thought participate in the definition of the 'statuses, capacities, attributes and orientations' assumed of those who exercise authority and are to be governed in the field of education, the forms of conduct that are expected from them and the set of duties and rights associated to their identities. In this respect, educational evaluation can be interpreted as a moral practice, a governmental activity through which educational people become subjects of a permanent evaluative tribunal and are 'interpellated' to establish a specific relation to the self in order to be accountable and governable (Simons 2002: 619). The evaluative rationality, modes of visualisation and techne are constantly related to a distinct ethico-political frame, where the political priority of economic growth produces an unprecedented attention on the quality of education systems and the need to continuously monitor and improve education, which in turn calls for effective quality assurance and evaluation systems covering all education levels (e.g. European Commission/EACEA/Eurydice 2015; OECD 2011; UNESCO 2016; World Bank 2011b; UNICEF 2010). This implies ethical work. As the European Commission emphatically declares, 'we need to foster a culture that strives to constantly improve the quality of teaching and learning' and 'to ensure transparency of quality assessment [and evaluation] outcomes [...] by promoting mutual learning in the field' (European Commission/EACEA/Eurydice 2015: 3).

Despite the great variability in the local design and enactment of the educational evaluation and assessment techniques described in this chapter, in most of the OECD countries the daily life of educators, students, heads and teachers is characterised by immediate recurrences in terms of evaluative practices and bureaucratic correlatives. These recurrences imply the enactment of a distinct set of related subjectivities, increasingly produced as free subjects acting, thinking and judging in meticulously regulated environments.

Through system and policy evaluation, school evaluation, staff appraisal and student assessments, schools, professionals and students are, on the one hand, asked to act as evaluands. Their educational and administrative activities are continuously given rhythm and organised by evaluative mechanisms that judge, examine, sort out, classify, select, hierarchise and rank them, their practices and performance, their capacity to meet the goals, to add value, to improve student learning. Externally evaluated or self-evaluating schools, appraised professionals and assessed students are requested to forge themselves as bodies docile to evaluation as a mode of inquiry and dividing practice. They are asked to make them inspectionable, accountable, quantifiable and comparable and rework ethically themselves as valorous fabricators of evaluable performance (Ball 2003) and responsible performance ascetics (Nicoli 2015). On the other hand, depending on the evaluative procedures and their institutional design, they are positioned as evaluators (of themselves in self-evaluation procedures; of their teachers in the case of headteacher-lead staff appraisal; of their communities and peers in the case of internal evaluation boards and committees; of their students in the various forms of assessment; and so on). As objects and subjects of evaluation, they encounter and are coached by a heterogeneous universe of facilitating figures (external inspectors and evaluators, institutional, academic or private experts and consultants, facilitators, mentors) and enter into a distinct kind of contractual relation with public authority at the national and local levels, with the policymaker that reframe itself as contractor, evaluation commissioner and rational decision-maker.

This is a sort of institutional obsession with evaluation, where evaluation and assessment techniques act as ways to organise freedom and assume educational subjects who are required to become experts of themselves, to adopt 'an educated and knowledgeable relation of self-care' (Rose 1996: 59) in respect of their minds and forms of conduct and that of the members of their educational communities. Such an educated and knowledgeable relation of self-care makes of learning (and of the disposition of learning to learn) a crucial dimension of an ethical life. As Simons (2002: 627) put it, learning to learn become crucial:

> in order to meet needs, in choosing goals and adequate learning activities and strategies, in making use of tools, in controlling one's own concentration and motivation and in assessing one's own progress and results. [In doing so] it delivers individuals who see themselves as positioned in an environment, who objectify life as a collection of different needs and who try to meet these needs in managing the production and the learning process.

This is a 'deeply penetrating, consciousness-moulding and thus serious business of constructing new categories of [...] thought and action' and evaluation and assessment techniques inculcate responsibilisation and self-steering as positive norms and values 'that transform the conduct of organisations and individuals in their capacity as 'self-actualizing' agents, so as to achieve political objects through 'action at a distance' (Grek et al. 2009: 129).

Conclusion

If educational evaluation can be interpreted as an enunciative field, this chapter has attempted a first move in the detaching work of suspending its immediate forms of unity. I have identified a set of recurrences in a dispersed and heterogeneous but globalised governmental domain where scientific knowledge, political technologies and moral practices are inextricably tangled. Of course, this does not imply that educational evaluation and assessment as rationality, modes of visualisation, techne and ethical practice can be interpreted as a totalising frame, despite the stunning recurrences.

The affirmation of a global evaluation and assessment hegemonic framework has stimulated intellectual and political struggles that oppose its champions to communities of critical scholars and professionals from different fields. Increasingly, dominant evaluation and assessment knowledges and techniques are accused to be epistemologically reductionist, practically inadequate and politically undemocratic. Key points of critique are related to the increasing mathematisation of evaluation and the neoliberal and neomanagerialist underpinnings/uses of evaluation as a tool of governing and control. At the same time, an increasing number of scholars are concentrating their efforts in critically analysing the uses of evaluation (i.e. the governing by numbers) or the features of the epistemic communities and networks through evaluative knowledges, and techniques circulate and become obligatory passage points. Moreover, the academic and intellectual debate on evaluation, in the fields of evaluation, education and beyond, develops around the political, epistemological and methodological nodes, in the effort to identify more democratic and socially accountable, or more rigorous, or less reductionist, or again more useful evaluation models.

This archaeological exercise, as a form of double distancing from the evaluative truth and from ourselves as evaluand and evaluators, intends to contribute to this academic, intellectual and public debate and to allow the folding on the limits of validity of the educational world that we inhabit. As a first move in this exercise of historical criticism, the analysis carried on the chapter in terms of 'recurrences within the plurality' can be considered as propaedeutic to the identification of the contours of the archaeological territory that I will explore in the rest of the book, showing how and to what extent it is possible to identify a complex form of positivity that encompasses a set of statements about educational evaluation concerning the commonalities and differences between educational beings, their visible structure, their specific and generic characters, their possible classification, discontinuities, separations and connections (Foucault 2002b: 198).

Chapter 3

The epistemic space of educational evaluation

In this chapter I discuss educational evaluation as strictly related to the complex tangle of governmental processes that develops around the interrelationship between the problem of the government of population, the foundation of the modern state, statistics and expertise (Foucault 2008; Rose 1999). Looking specifically at the epistemic dimension, the chapter recognises the inescapable relation that educational evaluation has with mathematical formalisation and numbers and the tension towards the application of quantification to education as empirical domains. In doing this, I engage with criticism of educational evaluation as part of governing by numbers, data and standards (Ozga 2009; Grek 2009; Lawn 2013a; Landri 2014; Ball 2015). However, the chapter invites the readers to reflect on the hypothesis that the historical a priori of educational evaluation is not identifiable in its relation to mathematics and numbers and the project of mathematical formalisation of education as an empirical domain. Rather, the constitutive possibility for educational evaluation is related to the rise of human sciences as an answer to the problem of governing the population and, later on, the problem of controlling (and reducing) the uncertainty inherent in human activity.

Recalling Foucault's analysis in *The Order of Things* (2002a), the chapter frames educational evaluation as belonging to that space of epistemic possibilities 'that takes as its object man as an empirical entity' (ibid. 375) and opens the empirical fields of life, labour and language. Consistently, I propose to interpret evaluation as a mode of inquiry that proceeds through models and/or concepts transferred from biology, political economy and the study of language and, moving from that, pursues the project to establish itself a mathematical formalisation and explores some distinctive empirical manifestations of 'that mode of being of man which philosophy is attempting to conceive at the level of radical finitude' (ibid. 379).

Educational evaluation and the project of a mathematical formalisation

The analysis of evaluation as a long-standing and globalised social experiment to make education governable sketched in the previous chapter has already identified a relation between educational evaluation and a complex tangle of governmental processes that developed around the rise of the problem of population management, liberal (and later on neoliberal) reason, the central role assumed by positive sciences of population and statistics among them. It is possible to identify a *fil rouge* connecting evaluation as a mode of inquiry and intervention with (a) the rise of biopolitics and the appearance of population as a governmental problem that is at once scientific and political (Foucault 2003: 245), (b) the knowledge possibilities offered by statistics, quantification and the language of numbers and (c) the need to establish centres of calculation and action such that events in distant educational places could be known and regulated by political decisions (Rose 1996: 38).

Evaluation nowadays increasingly takes the form of the systematic production of evidence, where 'evidence' often takes the form of numeric and comparative accounts (Gorur and Koyama 2013: 634). Evaluative numerical data play a key role in contemporary government as powerful and widely transposable inscription devices (Latour 1986). They circulate easily, are abstract, concise and portable, and because they decontextualise so thoroughly, they travel widely and are easily inserted into new places and for new uses (Sauder and Espeland 2009: 72).

Vedung (2010: 274) describes contemporary evaluation as a field influenced by an evidence wave, a field structured from social science methodology and based on means–ends rationality, where the task of evaluation is to produce and disseminate objective, stable, non-negotiable and predictive knowledge. This is what Dahler-Larsen (2012: 171) defines as cultural neorigorism. Evaluation becomes a form of knowledge production with an aim to eliminate the sense of contingency and plurality of perspectives and produce a kind of knowledge which is functional to the representation of a trustworthy social order (ibid. 175). Within such a rational and scientised frame, evaluation becomes part of an endeavour of social engineering, within which quantitative methodologies are the privileged means to obtain reliable, empirically tested and validated knowledge (Sanderson 2002: 6). Objectivity is said to be achieved through the systemic enumeration, or technicisation, of complex processes (Gorur and Koyama 2013: 634–35). Here quantification plays the role of a tool of coordination of government (Desrosieres 2011: 76) and a key mechanism of discipline (Shore and Wright 2015a: 22). As Desrosieres (2010) has argued, the production of such an order develops through three different stages: the making of numbers from social phenomena, the uses and reworking of numbers as variables and the inscription of variables into more complex models. Modelling allows the disaggregation of complex social and cultural situations into neatly formalised and calculable problems that can be addressed through computational means. Through that, governable entities are distributed into fixed physical spaces and dynamic analytical spaces, and quantification acts as criterion of factuality and reality reflection (Desrosieres 2011: 70). Normand (2016: 90) has argued how, nowadays, the flexible and contextualised use of numbers is key for a 'politics of standards' that has considerably restructured the governance of education systems, their modes of knowledge and evaluation. In evaluation and quality assurance, numbers are essential for structuring modes of knowledge production imposing 'a normative definition of education in terms of classification, criteria, procedures and indicators' (ibid). Ozga has underlined how evaluative numerical data function in the neoliberal mode of governance: 'data and standards, benchmarks and indicators serve to manage some of the tensions that arise between centralised and decentralised levels of governance, deregulation and (re-) regulatory instruments of governance' (Ozga 2016: 71).

However, this is not at all a recent story. Rose's brief social history of numbers emphasises how the 'dreams of democratic potential that numbers held for politics', and the idea to develop a political arithmetic emerge with Enlightenment (Rose 1999: 202). This relates to the Enlightenment belief in progress and the capacity of the individuals to master their own fate. It is also based on the faith that physical sciences methods 'which employed mathematical laws, measurement quantification' and were based 'on a metaphysic of atomism, reducing complex physical phenomena to its smallest component particle' could be used in the same way to study the social world (Olssen 2014: 218). Within this frame, since the second half of the 18th century, as the analysis of Hacking (1975) has shown, the collection of statistics is enmeshed in the formation of a great bureaucratic state machine, part of the technology of power of the modern state. Statistics, in enabling the taming of chance, in turning a qualitative world into information and rendering it amenable to control and in establishing the classifications by which people come to think of themselves and their choices, appears to be bound up with an apparatus of domination (Rose 1999: 203).

It is the combination between the need to guarantee the productivity and docility of the population using the norm as a grid of intelligibility and the possibilities opened by statistics that made possible the measurement of social phenomena, the description of groups, the calculation of gaps between individuals and their distribution in a given population (see Foucault 1995: 190).

Thus, in advanced liberal societies, numbers and politics are in a relation of reciprocal and mutual constitution, and numerical technologies perform the power to disclose the realities of our societies, making them representable in a docile form and, in the name of objectivity, de-politicising vast areas of political judgement (Rose 1999: 198). As Ball has recently shown in detail, evaluation and assessment arise as a response to the need to govern the school population, to manage it as a resource and to sift the good and bad. Statistics and numbers have played a key role in the production of evaluation as a governmental disciplinary and regulatory technique, providing the notions of normal distribution and distribution of normality as a technical means to establish the norm and the related key inscription devices (Ball 2012: 57–58). Evaluation as a performance measurement, comparison and ranking is a key governmental technique that reveals the historical depth emergence of a type of governmentality based on objectification through calculus and an instrumental, results-based and target-driven normative order that governs by numbers and, more importantly, through numbers (Shore and Wright 2015b: 430). The entities which populate the field of education (the nation, schools, teachers and individual students) 'are captured in a matrix of calculabilities […] addressed to improvements in quality and efficiency' and numbers become part of a method of government that combines optics, objectivities and productivity by making those entities legible (Ball 2012: 103–4).

Within this type of governmentality, numbers act as key black-boxing devices in a spiral of technicisation of politics creating a mathematically formalised field of visibility for political and educational facts where conflicts can be settled or diminished, guaranteeing at the same time a strategic position in the epistemic battlefield to the technical expertise entitled to gather and interpret them (Normand 2016). They create and legitimate new sites of truth (Ball 2012: 74).

In liberal and advanced liberal political problematisations, programmes and evaluation, numbers perform four functions: (a) operate as diagnostic tools; (b) make possible modes of government, making up their domain of objects as intelligible, delimited, calculable and practicable through numerical representation; (c) play a key part in the mechanism of conferring legitimacy; and importantly (d) are linked to evaluation of government (i.e. to measure quantitative changes in what it seeks to govern) and make judgeable modes of government, in so far as 'rates, tables, graphs, trends, numerical comparisons have become essential to the critical scrutiny of authority in contemporary society' (Rose 1999: 197–98). As Shore and Wright (2015b: 430) observe, the seductive power of numbers relates to 'their association with science and the pure and constant rules of mathematics'. Thanks to that, measurement acts as the privileged way to scrutinise the inner worlds of organisations and render different individuals, institutions and objects commensurable and controllable. Numbers act as material devices for a set of disciplinary governing techniques: comparison, differentiation, hierarchisation, homogenisation and exclusion. As the language of comparison, they contribute to reinforce the idea that educational entities belong to a distinct set of homogeneous classes of objects, opening also the possibility of commensurate performances and producing differences through the application of common metrics.

Numbers are functional to the creation of a single norm for excellence and a related evaluative regime based on measurability and standards. In a zero-sum game, qualities and values are turned into quantities, and the difference is expressed as an interval and is hierarchised. Through the organisation of numbers into rankings, difference becomes value-laden and functional to homogenising and conforming pressures (Sauder and Espeland 2009: 73).

Interestingly, Rose (1999: 214) also emphasises how numbers and the related techniques of calculation need to be understood not only as technologies of domination that make individuals calculable, but also as technologies of autonomisation and responsibilisation, that 'turn the individual into a calculating self endowed with a range of ways of thinking about, calculating about, predicting and judging their own activities and those of others'.

Through evaluation and the production of evaluative numbers to represent reality in terms of quantifiable and manipulable domains, 'individuality is created and recreated as sets and categories which describe and explain', demarcating the valuable and the worthwhile, the productive from the residual (Ball 2012: 74). There is a relation here between disciplined subjectivity, numeracy and democracy (Rose 1999: 224–25), a subtle but profound link between numbers, statistics, the formation of the political argument and democracy as a political rationality, a technology of rule and a form of ethics. As Pettersson et al. (2016: 184–85) nicely put it in relation to the epistemic power of numbers:

> Numbers seem technical, objective and calculable and embodying the idea of giving all equal chances and representation. Numbers standardized the subject of measurement and assessment but also the act of exchange so that they were no longer seen as dependent on the personalities or the statuses of those who performed the measurements or assessments. The faith in numbers in social affairs today is so markedly part of common sense that it is possible to talk about «transparency» in governmental social affairs and even personal relations can be discussed through statistical charts and graphs. Making government «transparent» have become an act of democratic modes of acting for ensuring that everybody «knows» how decisions are made. In that sense, numbers have become part of a discourse about guaranteeing democracy.

Through a pedagogy of numbers, self-controlling democratic citizens are made as calculating subjects who employ numeracy to act in a numericised space (Rose 1999: 200). They are asked to behave as 'if numeric representation had the greatest gravity, density or solidity' (Gannon 2013: 20) and, according to that, to use targets, indicators, performance measures, monitoring and evaluation 'to govern their conduct while according them a certain autonomy of decisional power and responsibility for their actions' (Rose 1996: 57).

Educational research and evaluative numbers as a technology of government

In the last decades, drawing on the literature on governmentality and governing by numbers, educational researchers have devoted a significant attention to evaluation of numerical data as a technology of government, providing critical and insightful analyses of their effects.

Focusing on social epistemology, Normand (2016) has extensively discussed government by numbers in relation to the politics of quality in the European education area and its evidence-based epistemology, documenting the building of a European and common space of measurement, the role of standards and the changing relationship between science, expertise and policy. He observes how in the field of education, trust in numbers and quantification has been reinforced inside states and international organisations particularly through the technology of benchmarking and comparison. In relation to that, Grek (2009: 25) has analysed statistics and numbers as forms of knowledge which elide the local and are key to the construction of education and education policy as a globalised commensurable field, where education becomes legible for governing at different scales (Novoa and Yariv-Mashal 2003). Ball (2012: 104) has argued that the contemporary regime of numbers defines for governments, teachers, educational professionals and students a moral economy of educational value, within which educational subjects are positioned as standing in front of a permanent economic tribunal (Simons and Masschelein 2006). These authors signal how numbers and quantification produce a field of new realities, a space within which the process of educating is rendered into an input-output calculation and 'performance indicators become the principle of intelligibility of social relationships' (Ball 2012: 138). Similarly, Shore and Wright (2015a, 2015b) have documented how the work of schools is increasingly regulated through numerical score sheets and competitive rankings within regimes of accountability inspired by the holy principles of efficiency and transparency. Within these regulatory regimes, performance indicators are devised as the dominant 'measures of the quality, efficiency, and value for money' for education and quantification and scientific management marry a performative ethics of accountability' (Shore and Wright 2015b: 425).

Goldstein and Moss (2014: 260) label as striking the rise to prominence of numerical data in education policy, emphasising how they now set public debates on the quality of national education systems and their worth and act as the means of auditing ever more closely the complex social processes of teaching and learning. In relation to the production of evaluative numerical data and the use of massive numerical information generated by national examinations in the practices of control and steering, Piattoeva (2015: 322) has emphasised their relatively new public nature, highlighting how these undergo popular usage. In her analysis, Piattoeva shows how the 'ongoing circulation of numbers enhances their legitimacy and power as they move upwards in the hierarchy of command and accumulate new networks of constituents, technologies and things' (Piattoeva 2015: 318).

Evaluation and performance measurement have been studied from the perspective of governance and the strengthening of more and more pervasive accountability frames, showing how they are key devices in the shift towards forms of soft, heterarchical or networked governance (Ozga *et al.* 2011; Meyer and Benavot 2013) and the production of new de-regulated regulatory regime that relies very heavily on numbers, data and data flows (Lawn 2013a; Lingard *et al.* 2012). Here evaluative numerical data are analysed as a powerful resource that make possible the pedagogical and political rethinking of education as a governable domain at a distance (Goldstein and Moss 2014). Ozga (2009: 150) underlines how 'evaluation data fill the space between the state and the new consumer-citizen'.

Lawn (2013b: 11), in his analysis of the internationalisation of education data, has shown how the measurement of education, in the form of budgetary elements, costs of teachers, testing and selection results and comparisons and productivity audits, has become a defining element of the governing of education and a powerful explanatory strategy throughout the 20th century. He relates the increasing use of numerical data to the action of powerful international organisations like the Organisation of Economic Cooperation and Development (OECD) and 'the ability of measuring tools to be standardised' and the consequent possibility for reproducing the production of data in different places, according to different demands (see also Grek *et al.* 2009; Lingard and Sellar 2013). In relation to this, Simola *et al.* (2011) present a detailed analysis of contextual differences in the operationalisation of data and highlight some key differences in the systems in their experience of the new 'calculative rationality' in education.

Despite these contextual and historical differences, Lingard *et al.* (2012: 316) highlight how numbers, data, statistics and national statistical systems take on greater significance in the neoliberal project of state restructurings and how this is pushed forward by and through digital technologies. In relation to this, Van Dijck *et al.* (2018: 7) has highlighted how datafication is one of the main drivers of the reorganisation of education as a societal sector, with large quantities of numerical data that are collected (often automatically) in national evaluations or in-house forms of monitoring through the digital devices and services that students, teachers, parents and school administrators use. Data are changing school curricula and pedagogies. Selwyn (2015), Williamson (2016) and Landri (2018) have extensively discussed how educational evaluation and assessment are increasingly quantified and learning predictive analytics, grounded in large numbers of students' online behavioural data, pave the way for the emergence of 'real-time' and 'future-tense' techniques of digital education governance.

Locating educational evaluation in a tridimensional epistemic space

Critical scholars are right in criticising the colonisation of evaluation by the pure sciences of the mathematical order and the related processes of quantification. No doubt that educational evaluation has an inescapable relation with numerical data. The tension towards the application of mathematical formalisation to the empirical domain of educational evaluation can be regarded as a constant of its history as a discipline and policy technology. Mathematical formalisation has established, paradoxically, the clearest and the most untroubled relations with educational evaluation. It has provided evaluative knowledge, especially within the positivist and neo-positivist epistemological paradigms, a set of instruments to claim for itself a scientific style, a form and a justification as a reliable disciplinary knowledge (Foucault 1995). However, the perspective I adopt here invites to complement and go beyond such a critique, in search for a different *historical a priori* for educational evaluation.

In his writing about governing by numbers, Rose has warned against the risk of thinking of numbers and quantification as devices with some intrinsic characters (for instance their capacity to reduce complexity or establish an order). He advises how quantification occurs only within political rationalities and regimes for the production, delimitation and authorisation of truth and value (Rose 1999: 206). Similarly, Pettersson *et al.* (2016: 178) observe that 'numbers enter into cultural realms that are never merely numbers but codifications and standardization of what are to constitute reality and planning', that is, a set of rules through which experiences are classified, problems are settled and legitimate procedures are provided for thinking, seeing, acting and intervening. In their emergence on the surface of history, numbers embody diverse cultural theses about differences and historically specific styles of scientific reasoning (Hacking 1992). Relatedly, Rose invites to study the role of numbers in the link between government and knowledge within different epistemic traditions and, more specifically, the symbiotic relations between numericisation of human sciences and 'their relations with the practical domains of their deployment within human technologies' (Rose 1999: 209).

Foucault's analysis in *The Order of Things* (2002a: 264–70, 321–27) is illuminating in this respect. It shows how the modernity distinction between the analytical (mathematical) and the empirical disciplines creates the epistemological possibility (and the urgency) for 'the endeavour to purify, formalize, and possibly mathematicize the [empirical] domains' reconstituting 'a unified epistemological field' (ibid. 267). These are attempts that face with the affirmation of an impossibility, as manifested in all the critiques that rehearse the problem of methodological reductionism. As Foucault (ibid: 268) puts it:

> in this double affirmation [...] of being able and not being able to formalize the empirical, perhaps we should recognize the ground-plan of that profound event which, towards the end of the eighteenth century, detached the possibility of synthesis from the space of representations. It is this event that places formalization, or mathematicization, at the very heart of any modern scientific project.

Moreover, Foucauldian analysis illustrates how the dream of perfect mathematicisation, the positivist obsession for objectivity and more generally all the attempts to establish techniques of formalisation to represent reality in its *natural mode of being* are in a mutually constitutive relation with the methods of interpretation and all the exegetical analyses that flourished since the late 19th century. This was the consequence of a distinctive epistemic change, the 'demotion of language to the mere status of an object' and its continuous re-emergence 'on the side of the knowing subject' (ibid. 323). Such a paradoxical trait of language in modernity produced a returning concern that explains the positivist dream, that is, 'the wish to neutralize [...] scientific language to the point at which [...] it could become the exact reflection [...] of a non-verbal knowledge', purifying it from the contingencies of any verbal knowledge (ibid). According to Foucault, human sciences are entrapped in such a dual space of knowledge and, then, they are 'naturally' shaped by the pendulum between the two main forms of analysis of our time: the attempts of formalisation and the interpretative approaches. Nonetheless, as Foucault observes, formalisation and interpretation are two correlative techniques which find their common ground of possibility in the being of language, as constituted in modernity (ibid. 326).

If we reframe the relation between educational evaluation, mathematics and the project of a pure science in these terms, then we should recognise that the distinctive epistemic trait of the evaluative endeavour, in its positivist or anti-positivist emergences, is not its relation to mathematics but its pretensions of knowing 'man in so far as he lives, speaks, and produces' (Foucault 2002a: 383). If we assume this perspective, we should work through the hypothesis that if one wants to understand the epistemic conditions of possibility for evaluation as a form of knowledge, one needs to situate it 'in the vicinity, on the immediate frontiers, and along the whole length of those sciences that deal with life, labour, and language' (ibid. 383).

It is not by chance that much of the debate about evaluation and its positivity as a form of knowledge is still centred on the dualisms between explanation and comprehension, positivism and relativism and all the related oppositions. It is polarised around an apparently radical ideological and epistemological (more than methodological) opposition between 'those advocating positivistic/quantitative approaches to evaluation and proponents of phenomenological/qualitative approaches' (Madaus and Stufflebeam 2002: 16).

The formation of educational evaluation as an enunciative field through transferences

Following Rose's invitation, in the rest of the book I will argue that it is not in its relation to numbers and mathematical formalisation that educational evaluation acquired its autonomy and defined its particular positivity. Drawing on Foucault's analysis in *The Order of Things*, the chapters will address evaluation and educational evaluation as a specific domain that found its constitutive possibility when, in relation to the problems of governing, controlling and reducing the uncertainty inherent in human activity, the empirical fields of labour, life and language were opened. Problems of educational evaluation and its possibility of emergence will be framed as being in-between sciences of life and mathematics and concerning the relations between the empirical contents of knowledge, the domain of empiricity and the transcendental anthropological foundation of knowledge (Foucault 2002a: 269).

Addressing the archaeological level, the positivity of educational evaluation will be described as positioned within the interstices of the tridimensional epistemological space described in Figure 3.1. I will argue that educational evaluation rests upon a specific set of transferences of categories or constitutive models from the sciences of life, production and language, that 'make it possible to create groups of phenomena as so many objects' (Foucault 2002a: 389) for an evaluative knowledge.

My argument here is that as an enunciative field, educational evaluation defines its objects of study and modes of inquiry and intervention in a complex and yet specific way:

- through transference from *biology* it has adopted the category of man as a living being possessing functions, receiving stimuli from the external environment and reacting to them, a being who is able to adapt, evolve and submit himself to the demands of an environment, but also comes to terms with the modifications it imposes, a being who acts in accordance with regularities and is keen to 'finding average norms of adjustment which permit him to perform his functions' (Foucault 2002a: 389);
- from *political economy* it assumes man as its object of study as a being who has needs and desires, and tries to satisfy them, as a subject having interests who lives in a perennial situation of conflicts and creates rules in order to limit/control these conflicts (although the rules produce new conflicts);

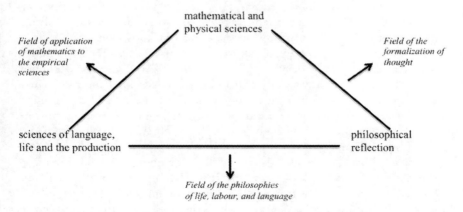

Figure 3.1 The tridimensional epistemic space of educational evaluation.

- from the *study of language* it has imported the problem of meaning, the understanding of man's behaviours/conducts as signifying something, and the idea that everything the man arranges around him forms a coherent system of signs.

I will argue, in particular, that *life, labour* and *language* can be considered the *historical a priori* for evaluative knowledge, or to put it differently, what made it possible to think the objects of evaluation is the appearance, at the archaeological level of modernity in the Western world, of three figures, that soon became fundamental in the general space of modern knowledge:

- the figure of *life* makes it possible to think about the evaluation of objects in terms of the relationship between character and function, and makes available the general method of the comparative search for analogies. It suggests, in turn, the idea to study specific objects as living systems with their internal organisation and to translate the analytical strategies of comparative anatomy;
- the figure of *labour as production* makes possible the appearance of value, worth and merit as objects of knowledge, and creates the necessity for economy-oriented concepts and methods such as the cost/benefit analyses, or the SWOT analyses in the field of evaluation;
- the figure of *language* makes it possible to think about the objects of evaluation as historical systems of signs and meanings, whose understanding requires the employment of a whole set of interpretative strategies of inquiry.

Throughout the analyses in the next chapters, I will try to argue that educational evaluation can be understood as an intermediary discipline that finds its epistemic space in the field of knowledge of man outlined by the linking and opposition of three conceptual pairs of function and norm, conflict and rule and signification and system translated from biology, political economy and the study of language. As a form of knowledge that finds its historical roots in the problem of government, in fact, educational evaluation has a clear familiarity with what Foucault defined as the sociological region (ibid. 388) and is basically a study of man in terms of conflict and rule, which can be interpreted time by time as rooted in needs, desires and the attempts to satisfy them, or as derived from functions, as if men under evaluation were individuals who are organically bonded to each other, or starting from systems of signs/meanings.

In fact, Bhola (2002: 389) describes the development of the discourses on evaluation showing how they find their driving force in the dialectic between numbers and meanings. He outlines an epistemic triangle formed by systems thinking, constructivist thinking and dialectical thinking as heuristic to characterise evaluation's struggles to reject linearity, include multiple causality and mutual shaping, and develop methods of making meanings, where numerical assertions become one specific type of construction (Bhola 2002: 390). A specific example to show the relevance of this argument could be the case of *School Effectiveness Research* and *School Improvement* models, an influential and authoritative subset of statements in educational evaluation as an enunciative field. Some of the *School Effectiveness Research* most renown exponents define its conceptual and epistemological basis as reported in Box 3.1 (Scheerens and Creemers 1989: 691, 696) and Box 3.2 (Scheerens and Demeuse 2005: 374).

The cases of *School Effectiveness* and *Improvement Research* are an interesting demonstration of how, despite the specific objects of evaluation, what characterises educational evaluation as an enunciative field, is exactly the fact that

---

Box 3.1

The case of school effectiveness research

School effectiveness research has its roots in quantitative sociological input-output studies and economic research on educational production functions [...]. The second wave of school effectiveness research emphasised 'process' rather than 'input' correlates of school output and employed in general more in-depth investigation of relatively small samples of schools [...].

The way effectiveness is defined in the main stream of school effectiveness research conforms to the notion of organisational productivity and its theoretical background of economic rationality. The productivity view of effectiveness sees output of the organisation's primary process as the criterion to judge goal attainment and emphasises the search for organisational characteristics that maximise output. When the constraint of 'least costs' is added to the maximisation of output, effectiveness is transformed into the more demanding notion of efficiency.

[*Then the authors present some alternative models of organisational effectiveness that use other effectiveness criteria and that are summarised in the following table*].

Models of organisational effectiveness

Effectiveness criteria	Level of analysis	Focus of interest	Theoretical background
Productivity	Organisation	Outputs and its determinants	Economic rationality
Adaptability	Organisation	Input requirement	Open systems
Commitment	Individual members	Motivation	Human relations
Continuity	Organisation/ individuals	Formal structure	Theory of bureaucracy
Responsiveness to external constituents	Subgroups within organisation	Dependencies power	Political theory

> **Box 3.2**
>
> **The case of school improvement and its relations to economy and biology**
>
> Scheerens and Demeuse (2005: 374, 382) identify in the micro-economic theory and public choice theory, cybernetics and theories on learning organisations and the concept of autopoiesis originated from biology three of the basic theoretical strands influencing school effectiveness research and school improvement models.
>
> [They continue arguing how] with respect to school improvement and school effectiveness, the perspective of autopoiesis can be seen as a basis for explaining resistance to change and less "intrinsic" interest for enhancing effectiveness. It could also be seen as a philosophy that underlines the importance of available concepts and cultural preferences of key actors enforcing the status quo in organisations, which defy "easy" transformations. [...] Autopoiesis offers a more evolutionary perspective than rational planning.

the setting of problems and the search for solutions occur within the epistemic space outlined through these three different transferences. The coordinates of this epistemic space define the limits of thought for educational evaluation.

Conclusion

In the rest of the book, I will analyse educational evaluation as an enunciative field in search for regularities as rules and relations, focusing on the processes of transference of the three fundamental figures of life, labour as production and language, and their implications. I will start from educational evaluation in its manifest deployment as a rationality, a family of disciplines, a techne, a mode of visualisation and a mode of identity formation to describe archaeological positivities that are continuously emerging on the surface of history in our educational present (in educational practice, scientific disciplines, political decisions, legal and policy texts, media discourse and in statements made and opinions expressed in daily life).

Thus, what follows is a work of rewriting that starts from practice and the material to suspend and reconstruct the self-evident unities of educational evaluation. It is a regulated transformation of what is written, said, visualised and done through a systematic description of an enunciative field as an object. Such a rewriting is intended to propose an archaeological analysis that takes as its point of attack the threshold of epistemologisation – the point of cleavage between educational evaluation as a discursive formation defined by its positivity and epistemological figures that are not necessarily all scientific. It has the ambition to reveal the 'profound' compatibility of the different and apparently opposed evaluative models, approaches, theories and methods that emerge at different points in space and time within the field (Foucault 2002b: 67–68). The next chapters analyse the transference of the epistemic figures of living systems, labour as production and system of meaning as conditions of possibilities for the emergence of educational evaluation as an enunciative field. Such an analysis will be functional to describe how:

- the different evaluative theories and techniques can be ordered; and what forms of succession are possible between system, policy, school, teachers and head teachers evaluation and student assessment. I will attempt to show how these orders and successions 'are laid down by the relations of dependence that may be observed between' the theories of life, labour and language;
- educational evaluation defines a domain of validity, normativity and actuality for itself, with its own criteria to establish the truth or falsehood of a proposition, to exclude certain statements as irrelevant, inessential, marginal or non-scientific, and to define present problems, acquired solutions, situating concepts and obsolete affirmations;
- educational evaluation forms itself in a regular space where it is possible to identify a distinctive set of relations (transference of concepts, their modification and alteration between one domain and another) between educational evaluation itself and mathesis as a project of a general science of order, the biological problems of characterisation and taxonomy, the analysis of wealth and exchange;
- the various conceptions of educational evaluation become simultaneously or diachronically possible under the form of alternatives, transformations or substitutions, where those figures make possible analogies but also show a certain number of differences and set the space of possibility and difference.

Chapter 4

Living systems

In this chapter, I present the archaeological analysis of educational evaluation as an enunciative field in search of its regularities as rules of formation and relations between statements. The focus will be on those regularities that, I argue, can be understood as the effects of a distinct set of processes of transference from biology through organisational theory as concomitant enunciative fields. The chapter initially concentrates on the formation of objects and concepts, using this as a starting point to present a distinct set of points of articulation of educational evaluation on those two discursive formations. I attempt to map a field of coordination and subordination in which educational evaluation objects, concepts, enunciative modalities and strategies appear are defined, applied and transformed. Such an analysis should be carried on using the foucauldian tree of enunciative derivation and an analytics of interdiscursive configurations as heuristics.

System as a grid of specification

The enunciative field of educational evaluation is characterised by a series of definitions and visualisations of the evaluative endeavour that make actual a field of particular kind of evaluative objects and a related domain of evaluative concepts. A comparative analysis of these definitions and visualisations reveals a first regularity: any educational evaluation deals with an *evaluand*, or a field of visible objects to be evaluated; some *criteria* orient the assessment of the objects under evaluation, or an evaluative rationality; an evaluative techne, or a systematic *methodology* that allows to collect information on the performance of the *evaluand* on those criteria and, finally, a *purpose* or intended *use*, that is an evaluative ethic (see Dahler-Larsen 2012: 9), which generally relates to the formulation of a judgment of overall social utility or value (House 1978). Interestingly, despite the great variety of inflections, almost all the contemporary definitions and visualisations seem to find their conditions of possibility in the establishment of a distinct relation between the two figures of 'system' and 'organisation'. Grasping and clarifying the generative effects of such a relation is fundamental to understand how the enunciative field of educational evaluation is articulated.

The formation of the evaluand

The formation of the *evaluand* as a form of being through the figure of 'system' is a regular occurrence in educational evaluation (Scheerens *et al.* 2003: 2; Williams and Imam 2007). It is a *governing statement*. In a whole package of texts, visualisations, speeches, projects, programmes and explanations, what educational evaluation deals with is defined as a system, a bounded volume made of parts or sub-units horizontally and hierarchically connected through communication. Figure 4.1 provides a graphical representation of the form assumed by this regularity and how it makes possible a whole field of concepts and objects to appear in the enunciative field of educational evaluation.

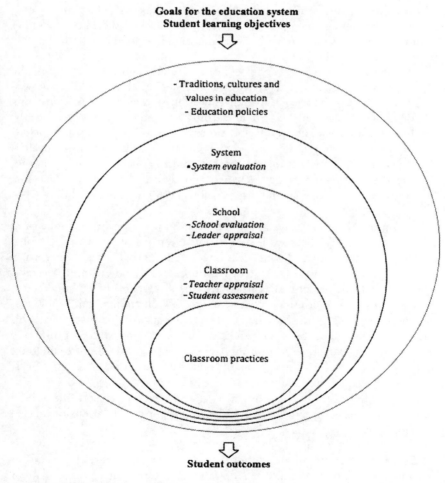

Figure 4.1 Living system as a grid of specification.

One of the most schematic, clearest and influential visualisations where it is possible to recognise such a regularity is probably the *Evaluation and Assessment Holistic Framework* proposed by the OECD in its 2013 report, *Better Synergies for Learning*, that represents a sort of pivotal material form of evaluative thought in contemporary education policy at the global level (p. 60).

System stands here as a *grid of specification* according to which a multi-layered domain of distinct and possible educational objects to be evaluated (the education system, the district, the school, the classroom, the school leader, the teacher, the student and all their activities) are hierarchically grouped within a scalar structure, divided into concentric units, connected through relations of dependence, causation and communication and derived from one another. Through the grid, system levels and sub-units are made as observable structures which are alternatively functionalised by a goal or objective. The same governing statement can be recognised in the way in which the World Bank defines its evaluative offer to sustain and orient education reform at the global level:

> To generate knowledge about education reforms and interventions, the Bank will provide: system assessment and benchmarking tools, along with data, to assess the capacity of an education system to improve learning outcomes; assessments of student learning and achievement that cover the basic competencies of reading and numeracy, as well as other skills, including critical thinking, problem solving, and team skills; and impact evaluations and other analytical work that can inform policies and interventions, together with knowledge exchange and debate that facilitate learning across partner countries and organizations (World Bank 2011a: 8).

The figure of system plays a key role in the formation of the *evaluand* as a form of being also because it makes possible to think about educational reality on the basis of the distinction between an internal and external space. Each level and sub-unit of a system has an external and an internal space, where the external is defined as an environment made of influencing factors such as traditions, cultures, policies, resources, constraints and opportunities and established goals, but also of objectively appraisable outcomes. This opens up a field of possibilities for the conceptualisation of different modes of evaluation and evaluative positioning (system, policy and school evaluation, staff appraisal and learning assessment, but also internal and external evaluation, self-evaluation, ex ante, in itinere and ex post). The 2015 Eurydice report on School Evaluation in Europe offers an exemplary account of how these modes can be discursively articulated and put into relations of mutual functionality:

> In 31 education systems, schools both carry out internal evaluation and are examined by external evaluators. One widespread form of interdependence between the two processes is the use that external

evaluators make of internal evaluation findings. In two thirds of the education systems where external and internal school evaluation coexist, internal evaluation findings are part of the information analysed during the preliminary phase of external evaluation. Together with other sources of information, internal evaluation findings often enable external evaluators to elaborate on the profile of the school to be visited and better focus their work. (European Commission/EACEA/Eurydice 2015: 12)

Interestingly, the duality internal/external is a point where the figure of system articulates itself with two *methods of characterisation*. When the internal is concerned, the *evaluand* is regularly said to have an organisational structure to be taken into consideration. The concept of *organisation* characterises and gives a form to the internal space of each sub-unit of the system as a set of observable structures: more or less defined boundaries, sites and facilities, a timing, a target, programmatic or functional collaborations with other organisational entities, a distinct set of activities with more or less expected and actually observable effects and outcomes (Rossi *et al.* 1999: 50–51). The plurality in the field of educational evaluation and the variety of models proposed to unveil the organisational textures of educational systems parallel the debate in organisational theory and the ways in which organisation is conceived alternatively as a rational, learning or institutionalised form of coordination (see Dahler-Larsen 2012: 26).

When the gaze is projected towards the external, the *environment* acts as a second *method of characterisation*. Systems and organisations are positioned within ecological spaces populated by other systems and organisations as stakeholders and regulated by established goals, objectives, needs and demands (goals for the education system, education policy, learning objectives; Simons 2002: 628). This is a scalar characterisation, with systems being the external environment of their sub-units and organisations and so on.

Educational systems, sub-units and organisations are constituted as adaptive, responsive and learning entities within an ever-changing and unpredictable environment. Standing in a relation of adaptiveness, they are required to respond to a set of pre-established needs. At the same time, they are capable of generating knowledge in their relation to the environment and rethinking/acting back/correcting themselves, their plans and procedures via feedback after actions. As learning systems and organisations, they have a history of experience and knowledge depending on prior actions, and a limited information capacity that 'react to the feedback they register as a result of their own actions' (Dahler-Larsen 2012: 44). Learning is here a cyclical and potentially never-ending process of knowledge acquisition and conversion into action, which is articulated into a detecting stage, a comparison with standards and a reparatory action/intervention (ibid. 39).

The interpretation of the evaluand

Given this ontological formation, educational evaluation is established as an activity of interpretation, a way to relate the history of an entity to an act of meaning production that designates this entity as valuable. As such, the focus of evaluation becomes the capacity to act as coordinated with the environment and the other entities, to learn from them and – using various instruments and procedures – to adapt and respond to their needs.

In fact, when it comes to the issue of the *criteria* that orient the assessment of the objects under evaluation, the archaeological gaze recognises the regular occurrence of a distinct *conceptual form of derivation* that connects the notions of value, worth, context, purpose, need, outcome, treatment and evaluation. If evaluation is recursively defined as an activity of value assessment or determination, value itself is articulated as worth (extrinsic value) and merit (intrinsic value) on the basis of another inflection of the dualism between the internal and the external. In Chapter 5, I will analyse the chain of conceptual derivation within which the notion of merit is positioned. Here, I want to address the chain involving the concept of worth. Notably, in a vast array of policy and scientific texts worth is conceptualised as the value of an entity 'within the context of a particular culture and its associated needs, costs, and related circumstances' (Stufflebeam and Coryn 2014: 8; Joint Committee 1994; Scriven 1991). The 'extrinsic' value of a system, organisation or sub-unit as worth is related to their capacity to be functional to environmentally defined clear but continuously changing needs. Need in turn derives from the existence of a 'defensible purpose', being defined as something necessary to fulfil such a purpose. Within this chain of derivation, functionality (or effectiveness) stands as the capacity to fulfil a purpose, addressing the related need. In turn, addressing a need means to provide an excellent and high-quality service (a treatment need) or to obtain an outcome/level of achievement (outcome need) (see Davidson 2005). Ultimately, such a capacity becomes the actual referent of the evaluative judgement, which assumes the trait of a systematic investigation of an entity's ability to meet treatment or outcome needs. Clear examples of how such a chain of derivation connects to the definition of the *evaluand* through the grid of specification of system and the concept of organisation can be recognised by the OECD, World Bank and Eurydice texts quoted so far, but also by the following academic text:

> By a need, we refer to something that is necessary or useful for fulfilling a defensible purpose, without which satisfactory functioning cannot occur. We define a defensible purpose as a legitimately defined, desired end that is consistent with a guiding philosophy, set of professional standards, institutional mission, mandated curriculum, national constitution, or public referendum, for example. Other terms to describe defensible purposes are legitimatized mandates, goals, and priorities. In the middle

school illustration, presumably the state curriculum requires that all students in the state be well educated in designated areas of history. This 'defensible purpose' requires further that school districts employ competent history teachers. In this case, a competent history teacher fits our definition of an entity that is necessary or useful for fulfilling the defensible purpose of sound history instruction – that is, a need. [...] In reaching judgments of something's worth, evaluators should identify needs, then determine whether they are being met, partially met, or unmet in the context of interest (Stufflebeam and Coryn 2014: 10).

Moreover, the formation of the evaluand as adaptive entities positioned within an environment where they respond to a need/purpose makes it possible for another chain of derivation which further qualifies its form of being. Relations of adaptation and responsiveness are intrinsically dialectical and diachronic. Thus, systems, organisations and sub-units have a history that is made of their transformations in relation to their environment and the 'defensible purposes' they are called to respond to. This implies that no two evaluands are identical in their organisational structure and environmental, social and political circumstances, even when they fulfil the same purpose. The distinctive structure and circumstances of an evaluand constitute major focuses for evaluation and this makes possible to think about the life of an evaluand as 'a developmental progression in which different questions are at issue at different stages' (Rossi *et al.* 1999: 44).

The empirical analysis of the evaluand

This formation of the evaluand opens up a space of epistemological possibilities where to search for systematic *methods* to collect information on the performance of the *evaluand* and establish the foundations for the evaluative judgement on the basis of the criteria of value/worth. As already discussed in Chapter 2, educational evaluation as an enunciative field distinguishes itself for the recurrence of particular forms of description and perceptual codes with the related analytical strategies. At the archaeological level, it is possible to identify two main regularities in relation to that.

The first one relates to the derivation between system as a grid of specification and the concepts of purpose (or plan), need, outcome and indicators. In this respect, Rossi *et al.* (1999: 50) argue how in the enunciative field of educational evaluation it is recurrent to observe descriptions of the evaluative activity as an attempt to deal with 'the distinctness and explicitness of [the evaluand] plan of operation, the logic that connects its activities to the intended outcomes, and the rationale provided for why it does what it does'. Relatedly, when the issue of methodology comes to the fore, a key archaeological regularity is the attempt of educational evaluation to search for levels of functionality to a plan (or effectiveness) at the analytical level, turning also those relations into a norm, a standard. This is coupled with a distinct mode of reduction of the complexity of educational reality (and of the judgement on the extrinsic value of its entities) through the use of treatment/realisation and outcome indicators. Treatment or outcome indicators become the starting focus of educational evaluation and its preferential way to establish entities' worth. Here, the obsessive employment of test scores, performance indicators and evaluative rubrics finds its conditions of possibility. The case of OECD Programme for International Student Assessment (PISA) is probably the most well-known example of such a regularity (Grek 2009; Sellar et al. 2017). More generally, in his work on evaluation ideologies, Scriven (2002: 261) identifies four basic logical relations in evaluation: grading, or the allocation of objects to a set of classes that are ordered by merit or worth in relation to an external standard; ranking, or the allocation of individuals to some position in an ordering by merit or worth; scoring, or the ascription of a quantitative measure of merit or worth to each entity in a system under evaluation and apportioning, or the allocation of a finite valuable resource in varying amounts to each individual as a means of expressing an assessment of merit or worth. The relation of derivation between system, purpose, worth, functionality and indicators creates here the possibility for standardisation as a process of attribution of empirically testable properties to independent entities, a substantialist reduction of the evaluand to a purpose/plan and its objectives (Thévenot 2009: 809), with effectiveness becoming nothing more than conformity to the formulation of the standard and its evaluation.

There is a second regularity; however, that has to do with the recurrence of the attempts to disarticulate into analysable units, the systems/units/individuals, under judgement, search for lateral correlations and establish hierarchical orderings. In fact, if outcome and treatment are the observable effect through which it is possible to evaluate and assess the functioning (and worth) of the evaluand, then evaluation and assessment assume the objective to relate to each other's educational outcomes and educational/organisational processes (defined in terms of factors) through causal reasoning. In most of the policy and scientific texts, visualisations, speeches, projects, programmes and explanations emerging in the field, educational evaluation is characterised as both the appraisal of the educational outcomes of a system and the unveiling of its organisational texture. Unveiling means here analysing the forms of effective or ineffective coordination of the system units' different actions in relation to their intention and capacity to contribute to the fulfilment of common purposes (what is defined as functionality or effectiveness). House (1978: 4) in his late 1970s historical discussion of the major evaluation model in liberal society has identified one of them in what he named as *Systems Analysis*, an approach which 'assumes a few quantitative output measures, usually test scores, and tries to relate differences in programs to variations in test scores', relating outcome measures to actions via correlational analyses and employing experimental design. These are the underpinnings of comparison as an evaluative style of reasoning that creates differences in kinds of educational entities through their hierarchical ordering. Correlational analyses linking outcomes to actions are a second main mode of empirical characterisation that finds here its conditions of possibility.

This is done in order to reflect, judge and intervene on the capacity of the evaluand to be functional and value them comparatively. Comparison becomes an act of examining similarities and differences among entities in relation to their functionality/effectiveness and, on the basis of that, a way to establish equivalence in terms of worth/value. Within this tree of derivation, three different kind of comparisons become possible: (a) between the present and the past of the same entity; (b) between different entities which are functionally equivalent; or (c) against a norm or standard (Pettersson *et al.* 2016).

The World Bank's *System Assessment and Benchmarking for Education Results* (SABER – see http://saber.worldbank.org/index.cfm) model offers an interesting example, using the metaphor of evaluation as a contextualised and deepening diagnostics of strengths and weaknesses of a system and its sub-domains against standards:

> [To generate knowledge about education reforms and interventions] consists of applying a system approach in which a conceptual framework, analytical methods, and measurement and monitoring tools are developed for the different policy domains of an education system. [SABER] assesses a country's institutional capacity and policies related to specific dimensions of its education system; diagnoses its strengths and weaknesses against global standards, best practices, and the performance of comparator countries; and guides reforms aimed at improving learning for all. The framework, analytical methods and measurement tools will not be applied in a one-size-fits-all manner. Rather, the approach will be applied contextually, with diagnostics and interpretations that are appropriate to each country's starting point and constraints. Country-specific diagnostics and performance reports will make it possible to obtain simple, objective, up-to-date snapshots of how a system functions, how well it is performing, and what the system can do to achieve measurably better results. (World Bank 2011a: 61)

The SABER collects information, classifies and analyses them to diagnose in a view to improve the effectiveness of the operating entities within the system and identifies those who do and do not support a better alignment to the system goals. As the World Bank (2011a: 6) declares, 'by investing in [evaluation and assessment] the Bank will help its partner countries answer the key questions that shape educational reform: Where are the strengths of our system? Where are the weaknesses? What interventions have proven most effective in addressing them?' Evaluation as system diagnostics is also the core of the UNESCO *General Education System Quality*

Analysis/Diagnosis Framework (GEQAF – see http://www.ibe.unesco.org/en/general-education-system-quality-analysisdiagnosis-framework-geqaf), with its '15 Analytical Tools covering all key aspects of an education system' that take into account the interdependencies and linkages between those aspects. GEQAF aim is to 'strengthen both the qualitative and quantitative knowledge base required to design and implement responsive, targeted and timely quality improvement interventions'.

Analysing the effectiveness of the evaluand and the use of educational evaluation

As the recurrence of the concept of diagnosis reveals, these modalities of detection and possibilities of comparison open the way for a domain of conceptual coordination and coexistence. Further ordered enunciative series emerge where the governmental function of educational evaluation is defined as an analysis of the effectiveness of system-like entities that is functional to a normative 'revise, fix and repair' strategy.

In fact, it is possible to observe the regular occurrence of enunciative series where the evaluand is historicised as a potentially ineffective (non-functional) entity that needs evaluation as a form of diagnosis which is preliminary to intervention. If evaluands are thought as entities that have a plan and function to respond to an environmental purpose/need, then the possibility arises for thinking about the success and failure of that plan or functioning in relation to the purpose/need. The dualism success/failure is a key reference point for any scientific and policy text on educational evaluation (see Stufflebeam *et al.* 2002 for an overview). The OECD *Glossary of Key Terms in Evaluation and Results Based Management* (2002: 18–19) defines the conclusions of any evaluation as the identification of:

> [...] the factors of success and failure of the evaluated intervention, with special attention paid to the intended and unintended results and impacts, and more generally to any other strength or weakness. A conclusion draws on data collection and analyses undertaken, through a transparent chain of arguments.

A relevant example of these recurrent series is the chain 'organisational plan-program process theory-implementation failure-theory failure', where: (a) the plan is defined as the functions and activities the evaluand is expected to perform through the mobilisation of its resources and (b) failure is conceived as an inadequate performance of the expected activities or as the incapacity to produce the expected effects and achieve the planned benefits in the environment (Rossi *et al.* 1999: 78; Rogers 2002: 210; Stake 1983: 292). Failure as the incapacity to respond to a need can be related to the issue of coordination and the degree of consensus, conflict or confusion among the parts of the systems about the values or principles, its mission and goals. It can be also attributed to a limited capacity of the evaluands to control and intervene on their environment, make plans, manage alternatives, foresee consequences of their actions and, finally, know themselves. In sum, failure is a permanent and probable risk and possibility which is inherent in the relationship between the evaluand, the plan and its environment.

In the classificatory space opened by the dualism failure/success, evaluands are organised into tables, graphs and other forms of comparative and hierarchical visualisation by functionality/effectiveness. They are disarticulated 'into a cellular arrangement of divisible segments', populated by entities with different gradients of capacity to fit, to perform, to success with different speeds of achievement (Ball 2012: 100). Their continuums are structured by breaks, and are organised around a norm and around the divergence from the norm. Such a representation of the evaluand sets the scene for a differentiated 'fix and repair' intervention, which case by case can be focused on cognitive, cultural, organisational or relational factors. As Ball has argued (2012: 101), 'an optics of truth is linked in very practical and mundane ways to the production of objectified' entities, which are organised for improvement purposes and are encouraged to view themselves in terms of the paradigm of performance and its normal distribution. Educational evaluation becomes here the production of natural histories of the evaluand, which in turn represents/creates an order, with all the entities becoming visible, classified, each defined by a set of essential characters and separated from one another by their performative differences. The norm or standard through which such an order is established are defined at the outset, they cannot be modified and 'character and differences are made visible by a heady combination of classical observation and modernist testing' (ibid.).

Thus, evaluation is framed as a strategic enterprise whose aim is to compare the evaluand against a standard of effectiveness (House 1978: 8) within a developmental history. Another recurrent enunciative series where it is possible to observe such a positioning in terms of strategic 'use' is the chain 'Governance-Design-Implementation-Evaluation-Capacity building-Use of results' (see Figure 4.1). Here, educational evaluation and assessment act as central pillars of a governing process that acts back on the system and its subunits. As hierarchical and functional distributions of elements, evaluand systems can and have to be governed through evaluation. The preferential mode of this regulatory control is through design, which is the configuration and articulation of system's main components and the establishment of the key principles on which its procedure have to rely and align to the system goal. Implementation as the functioning of the system through the strategic work of its components (factors) stands as the focus of the evaluative knowledge endeavour, whose aim is to build the capacity of the system's components to learn and use the results to adapt/respond/perform better in relations to their intrinsic or extrinsic needs. In the scientific literature on educational evaluation, it is common to find description of what is termed as 'comprehensive evaluation' similar to the following:

> [...] evaluating something requires that pertinent dimensions of its performance or characteristics be described and then judged against appropriate standards or criteria. Program evaluation generally involves assessment of one or more of five program domains: (a) the need for the program, (b) the design of the program, (c) the program implementation and service delivery, (d) the program impact or outcomes, and (e) program efficiency (cost-effectiveness). In some circumstances, an evaluation of a social program may encompass all these program domains; evaluations that do so are termed comprehensive evaluations. (Rossi et al. 1999: 22)

In terms of government, evaluative knowledge becomes functional here to a regulatory process of continuous design and re-design of systems and components. Design assumes the form of the planning of a milieu, that is a space of uncertain events or series of events or possible elements linked through nexus of cause and effect (Foucault 2009: 20–21). Again, the 2013 OECD report, *Better Synergies for Learning* offer an interesting example, among many, of the possible declinations of this chain when, for instance, student assessment is at stake:

> Many diagnostic tools are designed specifically to uncover the causes of students' learning difficulties. The results of diagnostic assessment are typically used to inform future programme planning, design differentiated instruction and deliver remedial programmes for at-risk students. The distinctive feature of diagnostic assessment, vis-à-vis formative assessment more generally, is its greater focus on the use of results for individualised intervention and/or remediation. (OECD 2013: 213)

If the diagnosis produces the need for individualised programmes of intervention that fix and repair the anomalies with respect to standards, and for the work of evaluators/therapists of various kind, at the same time comparison against a standard of effectiveness makes of evaluation a necessary learning enterprise to identify dysfunctions and correct the functioning of the evaluand via feedback after actions. Two further and clear examples of this are the already quoted World Bank SABER model or the UNESCO GEQAF that aspires to act as a diagnosis framework 'for conducting systemic analyses of critical constraints hampering the achievement of education quality goals', on the basis of the recognition that 'despite all the efforts, the education quality challenge persists, and the EFA quality goals are dauntingly off track' because of the lack of systemic evaluative tools (http://www.ibe.unesco.org/en/general-education-system-quality-analysisdiagnosis-framework-geqaf).

Biology, organisational theory and educational evaluation as fields of concomitance

Dahler-Larsen's analysis of the 'organisalisation' of evaluation (2012: 34) shows insightfully how modern evaluation 'embodies organisational thinking' and to what extent organisational theory can be considered as an enunciative field whose statements act as points of analogy, general principles, accepted premises and transferable models for many of the evaluative statements that we have analysed above. The objects and the subjects of evaluation are regularly thought as organisations and organisationally thinking entities, having their own dynamics, motives and relations. Moreover, some of the most recurrent evaluative concepts have been transferred from organisational theory, under the general idea that evaluation 'must look inside organizations' and consider their environments (ibid. 35). At the same time, the analysis of the enunciative tree of derivation of educational evaluation has shown the recurrence of a grid of specification and methods of characterisation that present significant points of analogy with the field of modern biology.

Through a lateral rapprochement, I briefly attempt to depict the *play of analogies (and differences)* between educational evaluation, organisational theory and biology in the attempt to highlight how the former finds, at least in part, its conditions of possibility in the transference from the latter. My thesis is that these three fields share a similar archaeological model. My aim is to show how the concepts of educational evaluation, like system, organisation, environment, value, worth, function, goal, plan, outcomes, effectiveness, governance, design, implementation, comparison, diagnosis, use and capacity building (and their chains of derivation), have been formed on the basis of the same epistemic essential functions as the very different, radically heterogeneous concepts of organisational theory and biology (Figure 4.2). Because of space limits, in the following pages I directly draw on Dahler-Larsen's insightful analysis of the relation between evaluation and organisational theory in *The Evaluative Society* (2012) and Foucault's archaeological analysis of modern biology in *The Order of Things* (2002a). In my discussion, I focus, in particular, on the *archaeological isotopia*, to show how some concepts occupy a similar position in the ramification of the three enunciative fields.

First, there is a striking similarity on the position occupied by the notion of *system* as a grid of specification to produce a field of visibility. As in the case of biology (Foucault 2002a: 287) and those organisational theories that construct organisation as learning entities (Dahler-Larsen 2012: 43), the objects of analysis or the entities whose value and worth have to be defined, whatever the level is, are always thought as *living systems* or as *organs* of a living system, where different organs and their dispositions are subject to the sovereignty of a *function*, defined in terms of an *effect* to be obtained. For example, as it happens for the educational evaluand, the learning organisation is theorised as adaptable to the demands of an ever-changing environment, having

98 Living systems

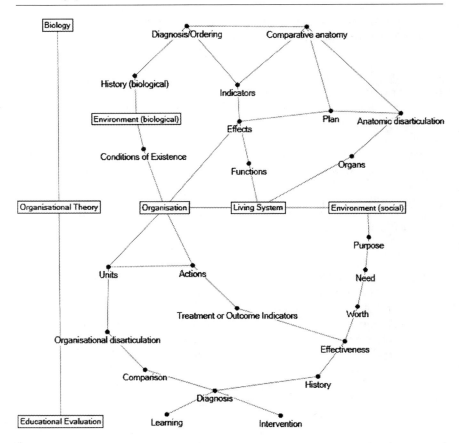

Figure 4.2 Biology, organisational theory and educational evaluation as fields of concomitance.

a memory and a structure, and as moved by a stake, or motivational factors within a system of external demands. It learns through feedback. Moreover, in all the three enunciative fields, *function* and *effect* are key nodes in the tree of derivation, whereas analytical strategies tend to identify a limited but necessary number of functions and to define organs and units of the entities under evaluation starting from them. In the field of educational evaluation, this is the case of the function of leadership, its centrality in every evaluation checklist and the role it plays in the definition of the value of any activity/ organisation/subject. Moreover, *functions* and *effects* become the locus where all the efforts to produce knowledge are directed.

Second, the concept of *organisation* plays a key role as well, as a method of characterisation to conceive the internal principle of the living system which is out of the field of visibility and need to be enlightened. Despite the diversity of inflections, in the three enunciative fields the concept ultimately refers to: (a) a hierarchy of characters that can be conceived as more or less important in so far as they are linked to the existence of functions that are essential to a living being and (b) a multi-layered disposition of the elements/organs that constitute the organisation/living system. As such, it operates subordinating characters one to another, linking them to functions and arranging 'them in accordance with an architecture that is internal as well as external, and no less invisible than visible' (Foucault 2002a: 251).

This conceptualisation implies that the knowing activity requires 'to be able to apprehend in the depths of the [living system] the relations that link superficial organs to those whose existence and hidden forms perform the essential functions' (Foucault 2002a: 248). Knowing (and evaluating) becomes 'to relate the visible, to the invisible, to its deeper cause, as it were, then to rise upwards once more from that hidden architecture towards the more obvious signs displayed on the surfaces' of the living systems/organisations and evaluands.

A further form of *archaeological isotopia* is that the kind of *diversity* between living systems/organisations/evaluands that become visible (and which is worth to make visible) is not a diversity defined in terms of a set of variables, but that of the 'functional units capable of being realized and of accomplishing their aims in various ways' (Foucault 2002a: 288). This is clearly recognisable in much of the evaluative approaches and analyses where units and entities under evaluation become comparable (and can be related to each other or be said to be similar) mainly on the basis of the *effect they produce*.

It is the centrality of the categories of *living system* and *function* which in turn determines the kind of relationships that knowledge endeavours in the three fields are naturally brought to search for at the analytical level and to establish at the normative level:

- *lateral correlations* that establish relationships of coexistence between elements of the same level that are rooted in functional necessities;
- *hierarchical orderings*, where functions (and relatedly units) are ordered along a hierarchical pyramid of importance responding to a knowledge need. Such a knowledge need arises from the constitution of the objects of analysis as living systems that are reciprocally arranged and determine each other. In this way, evaluative, organisational or biological analyses attribute to themselves the task to establish distinctions and similarities on the background of a table of functions (defined in terms of effects to be obtained) that each living system or functional unit accomplishes to;
- the *functionality of a plan*, here the conception of the objects of analysis/ *evaluands* as living systems and the centrality of the category of *function* as the task the living system has to accomplish to, together with the heuristics through which the living system can be known, invite to imagine that each living system obeys to a *plan*. The plan here is intended

as a hierarchical principle that 'defines the most important functions, arranges the anatomical elements that enable it to operate, and places them in the appropriate parts of the body' (ibid. 290).

In this sense, *life* as something that has non-perceivable, concealed and purely functional aspects, lays down the external possibility for bodies of knowledge that classify and order hierarchically their objects on the basis of a judgement about value or worth. In relation to educational evaluation, it is such a transference of categories drawn from biology through the mediation of organisational theory in the formation of the evaluand that explains the already mentioned constant recurrence of two analytical strategies and techniques:

- the exploration of the ways in which the units that accomplish to a function (i.e. the production of an effect) are 'broken down, spatialized, and ordered in relation to one another' (ibid. 293) and the description of their correlation to explain the accomplishing of a function. In its underlying logic, this is a strategy of 'anatomic disarticulation' (ibid. 294) of an object/entity intended as a living system, which in turn allows evaluation to produce a kind of knowledge that orders entities along a scale of decreasing complexity and/or on the basis of the perfection/effectiveness of the functional units;
- the use of visible elements as indicators of something which is hidden in the living system, of something that it conceals at a superficial glance, but it is fundamental in so far as it has to do with its *plan, main function (effects)* and the capacity of the living system to accomplish them (*effectiveness*). This is a key analytical strategy employed by educational evaluation, which again becomes thinkable because of the transference of the figure of system as a grid of specification to constitute the evaluand and its characterisation in the terms of the 'organisational'. This is what explains the conditions of possibility for those evaluative strategies that pretends to make inferences about the overall functioning of an evaluand from a single element (think of the use of testing or the logic underlying the controlled randomised trials, or on a different ground the evaluative analysis of leadership processes as the key indicator of the effectiveness of an educational organisation) or a limited set of elements (think of the multiplicity of evaluation agendas/rubrics and checklists).

The widespread obsession for the relationship between the objects of educational evaluation and their contexts, the resources they can rely on, the threads and the opportunities they have to confront or face can be also understood as a further consequence of those processes of transference. These analytical strategies and techniques for classifying and ordering (grouping by performance, ranking, hierarchical ordering) are functional in all the three enunciative fields to a form of diagnosis, learning and intervention.

Importantly for my overall argument in the book, the process of transference I am discussing here can also explain, at the archaeological level and at the cross-roads on the encounter between political economy and biology (see the next chapter), the recurrence of the dualism between success and failure as a key feature of the enunciative field of educational evaluation, and in particular what appears to be as the assumption of the fallibility of the evaluand and its activity. The formation of the objects of evaluation as living systems, in fact, implies that any of them can be (and should be) conceived as organisational systems that 'maintains uninterrupted relations with exterior elements that they utilizes [through the exercise of a specific function, i.e. to produce an effect] in order to maintain or develop their own structure' (Foucault 2002a: 298). This generates the analytical and normative idea that the *production* of an *effect*, which means the capacity of an *organisation* to fulfil its function, depends on determined *conditions of existence*. Here the 'double space' of the internal and the external becomes, respectively: (a) the space of the coherence and coordination of the functional units, the space of the anatomy of the organisation that can be judged as close or far from perfection (effectiveness; *internal*) and (b) the space of the elements that constitute the environment, the context of an organisation as living system and represent the resources it can draw on (but also the threads it has to confront with; *external*). As we have seen, in the field of educational evaluation the constitution of this double space provides an analytical distinction that at the same time segments the objects/entities under evaluation, identifying different but interdependent foci of analysis and reorder them under the unitary logic of the *conditions of effectiveness*.

This is exactly the background against which the idea of fallibility is established. The idea that there is a discontinuity/distinction between the living systems and their conditions of effectiveness makes thinkable, and somehow invites to think at, a historicity of living systems as a declination of the historicity of life. The idea that living systems can be known as organisations that fulfil a function, which in turn can be analytically defined as an effect to be produced, makes thinkable the existence of forces that drive towards the fulfilling of a function which struggle against the threads of ineffectiveness in a dialectical but never ending dynamics. The place of such a historicity is exactly in the conditions of effectiveness. In the field of educational evaluation, this biological perspective is transferred into a somehow pessimistic evolutionary mode of thinking that, despite the apparent diversity of the evaluative approaches, lies at the very foundations for most of the evaluative knowledge. The struggle of the evaluand as object/subject of (self-) evaluation against his perennial ineffectiveness and failure to meet his needs recalls here the war between life and death which is at the basis of biology and constitutes the historicity of life. Living entities are limited and unable to escape from death. It is here that evaluation finds his possibility as a curative experimental and diagnostic knowing enterprise.

It is not by chance that a well-known and influential evaluation scholar as Scriven (2002: 28), in his recent defence of the place for evaluation among science, employs a biological/medical metaphor to make a case for it: 'Evaluation seeks only to determine and describe certain aspects of the world – those aspects referred to by the vocabulary of value, i.e., in terms of merit, worth, or significance and their cognomens. [...]. The connection to action and survival is a good reason to respect efforts to improve it, just as we respect efforts to determine causation or to provide accurate classifications of medications and poisons'.

Conclusion

The analysis carried out in this chapter allows the identification of an archaeological quadrilateral (Figure 4.3), where it is possible to visualise the relations of concomitance between the enunciative fields of educational evaluation, organisational theory and biology. It shows how educational evaluation forms its objects, concepts and strategies through transferences from the latter.

Here, the ontological formation of the evaluand through the transference of the figure of system establishes an uncertain world populated by living entities responding to a plan and whose internal space (an organisation) is made of functions. As functional entities, the evaluands/systems are located within an environment (an ecological space) and then have a developmental

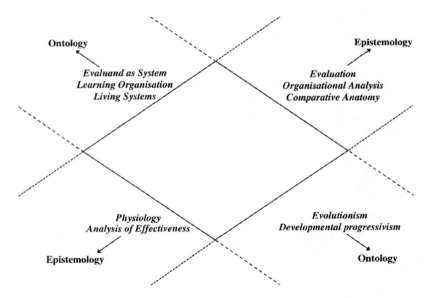

Figure 4.3 The archaeological quadrilateral of educational evaluation, organisational theory and biology.

history, which is a history of functions and dysfunctions, successes and failures, life and death. Epistemologically, evaluation stands as an 'organisationalised' mode of knowing (Dahler-Larsen 2012: 34) that assumes the form of an anatomic disarticulation of the evaluand and of its diagnosis through the definition of its worth (effectiveness), that is its capacity to respond effectively to intrinsic or extrinsic needs. If evaluation as anatomic disarticulation is a mode to unveil the invisible in the life of the evaluand, then the analysis of effectiveness as diagnosis becomes a means for the caring of the evaluand through learning, that is its governing as adaptive, responsive, functional and performative entity within a developmental and evolutionary historical time. The time of development and learning is 'both evolutive and cumulative, stable, linear and oriented towards a terminal point, but also serial and progressive' (Ball 2012: 49) and, within it, the present becomes always a matter of an externally driven progress.

The formation of such a specific space-time nexus is linked to the establishment of a particular kind of norm, which is the basis for any judgement on the value (and grouping by performance) of the entities populating such a space-time. As Foucault (2003: 239) has argued, the basic governmental phenomena of the 19th century were power's hold over life. The biological came under state control, biopower related to man as living being (the population-biological processes-regulatory mechanisms-state series, ibid. 250) and the norm, and in particular, the normal curve became the key element circulating 'between the disciplinary and the regulatory power' (Ball 2012: 60). It is in the transference of the figure of living system as a grid of specification that is possible to recognise, at least in part, the epistemic foundations of this link between biology, biopolitics, statistics and the governmental role exerted by evaluation in modern societies as a technique for the management and classifications of the modern population as deserving and undeserving, worth and worthless, functional and dysfunctional entities (Ball 2012: 68).

Here the nature or, better, naturalness of the biological (the organism) as 'a set of constants and regularities – patterns of behaviour – distributions' (ibid. 59) and as something that is constantly accessible to agents and techniques of transformation is transferred to the educational evaluand. This occurs 'on condition that these agents and techniques are at once enlightened, reflected, analytical, calculated and calculating' (Foucault 2009: 71). Evaluation as disarticulation, comparison, measurement, effectiveness analysis and numerical visualisation of all of this, is made available as governmental 'technique to produce domination and responsibilisation and construct calculating selves and centres of calculation' (Ball 2012: 58) in the field of education.

In relation to political rationality, such a form of biologising naturalism (Boltanski 2011: 33) relates clearly to liberal and neoliberal individualism, with their tendency to: (a) think development as a consequence of inner mechanisms and capacities logically distinct from social processes and (b) understand living entities as unitary rational units which are affected by environmental factors but whose derivation and development is determined by internally shaped drives (e.g. behaviours, attitudes, emotions, language and dispositions) (Olssen 1999: 164).

Thus, within an epistemic space where evolutionary thinking plays a pivotal role as a bundle of notions that provided a way of conceiving the relations between the living entities and their environment, the normal curve becomes possible, with its 'deep assumptions of unity by which [individual entities] could be compared on the same conceptual space to the entire population' (Olssen 1999: 165). Educational evaluation as a scientific analytics and judgement stands as a technique through which living entities 'could be categorized and compared in relation to one another, and in relation to the national interest, and the management of the population as a resource' and 'be fit on a moral, economic and biological sense' (Ball 2012: 61). It becomes an expertise of subjectivity and a technique for the calculated management of subjectivity as the central task for the modern educational organisation, which fills the space between the private lives of educational subjects and the public concerns and objectives of education systems (Rose 1989: 2).

Chapter 5

Forms of production

In the uncertain world produced within the epistemic space outlined in the previous chapter, the analysis and management of living entities become key problems. If the evaluand is objectified through the system as a grid of specification, then a multiple correlational space opens up for the concept of management. The correlate of management can be established as an organisation within an environment. At the same time, in the enunciative field of educational evaluation, it is possible to identify the regular occurrence of further grids of specification and methods of characterisation that allow valuing, diagnosis and ordering as practices functional to the management of the educational evaluand.

In this chapter I expand the archaeological analysis of educational evaluation as an enunciative field looking at those grids and methods that can be understood as the effect of a distinct set of transferences from political economy through the mediation of management theory as a 'concomitant' enunciative field. As in Chapter 4, I initially concentrated on the formation of objects and concepts, and then on the mapping of a field of conceptual coordination and subordination.

Production as a grid of specification

Within the dispersion of statements that define evaluation as an empirically based judgement on the value of educational things and entities, it is possible to recognise another recurrent governing statement: the regular occurrence of the figure of *production* acts as a way to objectify educational processes as evaluands and turn them into observable objects and structures. This regularity can be observed in a great deal of definitions or visualisations of the evaluative endeavour, when the formation of the evaluand, the establishment of the criteria to value it, the search for a methodology and the definition of the purpose of evaluation are at stake. As in the case of the figure of system, exploring the generative effects of such a regularity is fundamental to further understand the articulation of the enunciative field of educational evaluation.

The formation of the evaluand

In a vast array of policy texts, forms of visualisation, speeches, projects, evaluative tools and explanations, education as *evaluand* is specified as *production*, that is a rational process that starts from the definition of (externally defined) goals, occurs within a context regulated by natural or institutional arrangements, responds to distinctive laws and necessities, develops through a linear time and is expected to produce a result, that is some outputs, outcomes or impact (Madaus and Kellaghan 2002: 23). A clear and influential example where *production* (Figure 5.1) acts as a *grid of specification* in the field of educational evaluation is the well-known and widely used Stufflebeam's (1972) *Context-Input-Process-Product* (CIPP) model. The CIPP evaluation model is today a key reference for policymakers, institutional evaluation designers, evaluators, schools and professionals in many countries and is defined as 'a comprehensive framework for guiding evaluations of programs, projects, personnel, products, institutions, and systems'. Its underlying assumption 'is that evaluation's most important purpose is not to prove, but to improve' (Stufflebeam 2003: 31). It has been recalled and expanded, as in the case of Scheerens *et al.* (2003) *Monitoring and Evaluation (M&E) in Education* framework.

As an OECD report has recognised (Faubert 2009: 17), in many countries the definition of aspects to be assessed in the course of educational evaluation is regularly done using the CIPP model, and '*context* is usually related to readiness to learn, public attitudes to education, and the role of school in the community. *Inputs* include facilities and equipment, educational choice,

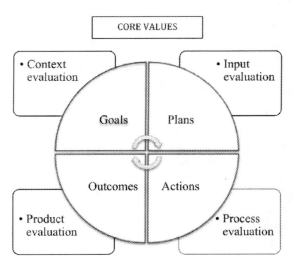

Figure 5.1 Production as a grid of specification. The *Context-Input-Process-Product* evaluation model.

financing, teaching characteristics and classroom characteristics. *Processes* are related to expectations and attitudes, learning measures, teaching arrangements, parental and community involvement. Finally, *products* include student academic performance and post-schooling outcomes' (Faubert 2009: 17). Other examples are the goal-based evaluation, the experimental or field trail model for evaluation and the various decision-oriented or management-oriented evaluation models, that 'embody many of the concepts underlying the production/technological metaphors used to describe schools' and function through the making of 'causal inferences about the efficacy of treatments' (Madaus and Kellaghan 2002: 23).

Interestingly, in a distinct set of influential visualisations of educational evaluation as a policy framework, *production* as a grid of specification emerges within a relation of concomitance and articulation with that of *system*, as in the case of the OECD *Evaluation and Assessment Holistic Framework* (OECD 2013: 91), where production is specified through the series 'input, processes, outcomes'. This occurs when, within a system-oriented understanding of the education system and its units, the problems of 'what to evaluate', 'what elements to assess' and 'for what scope' are considered.

In all these cases, through the grid of specification of *production*, a field of objects is made actual, together with a domain of conceptual coordination and coexistence organised into ordered enunciative series. Any evaluation endeavour is associated with a sequenced series of evaluative foci: goals, plans, actions and results (Stufflebeam 2003: 32). The evaluative foci are positioned within a linear, unitary, nonreversible but cumulative time, made of implicit assumptions about multiple nexus of dependence and causation between them. Within those series, output, outcome or impact are always the final result of a linear but reproducible cycle, that can be segmented and analytically approached from different starting points.

At the same time, goals, plans, actions and results are made into distinct and isolable evaluative domains, where further processes of objectification/ disarticulation and causal linking become possible. The setting of defensible goals is located into a space of educational target groups and their needs. The evaluand resources and constraints act as basis for that setting. Within this conceptual chain, through the concept of 'goal' educational entities are made as forms of beings: (a) responding to a target population with a set of needs and preferences; (b) capable to define goals that can be judged as reflecting or not the needs of target groups; (c) enabled by internal and external resources (material and cognitive resources, budget, institutional arrangements but also forms of commitment) and (d) constrained by barriers to the achievement of their goals. Given such initial characterisation, planning is the space where educational entities elaborate a strategic work plan to respond to the perceived needs. Through the concept of 'plan', educational entities are, thus, constituted as rational systems made of coordinated elements having capabilities and strategies, but also the capacity to choose among strategies and design the implementation of the chosen strategy. It is the succession between goals and plans that makes possible to think of 'actions' as the plan implementation, that is as a set of strategic and managed activities put in place to realise the goal and respond to the needs of the target population. As Bhola (2002: 390) notes, these are 'purposive actions' which are in instrumental (means-ends) relation with planning (as a script for implementation) and implementation (as anticipation of evaluation).

Here, the entities under evaluation are constituted as 'systems that loyally implement plans decided after description of objectives and calculations of alternatives' (Dahler-Larsen 2012: 39). As such, they are assumed as naturally focused on achieving important results and committed to meet targeted needs through feasible and cost-effective actions (Stufflebeam 2003: 50). At the end of the chain, the concept of result qualifies the intended/unintended, or positive/negative output, outcome or impact of the linear process that links 'goals setting, planning and implementation' as a process of production. Here, result as output/outcome and impact is the product of the causation between the capacity to set appropriate goals, design an effective plan or choose the right strategy and implement efficiently the work plan (see Stufflebeam 2003: 40).

Interestingly, production as a grid of specification makes it possible again to think about educational reality on the basis of a distinction between an internal and an external space. This distinction opens the possibility for the articulation between production and two *methods of characterisation*: organisation and the market. Production, in fact, has an organisation, that is commonly referred to as a division of labour, a specific mode to arrange human, material and symbolic resources into productive rational procedures with the aim to achieve a preestablished goal. This internal space, characterised as a 'rational and productive organisation' (Dahler-Larsen 2012: 31), is objectified as both an activity (managing, teaching, leading as processes or set of actions) and a combination of individuated factors (specific resources, goals, plans, teachers, leaders, students and their characters/properties/commitments/motivations/experiences). As a set of activities and factors, the rational organisation is constituted through a linear temporality, a time of efficiency and effectiveness in the production of value. As such, its history is that of a particular form of activity, outputs and outcomes, and changes in the organisational arrangements and mode of activity (a division of labour), which are related to specific capacities to define goals, establish plans, implement them and, in the end, produce value.

However, production as evaluand implies also an external space, a space which in the linear temporality of the productive process both preexists and is subsequent to the productive/implementing actions. This is the space of the target educational populations with their predetermined needs that have to be recognised and responded to. It functions as a *market-like* environment populated by rational and strategic entities, where the supply of the education service is expected to match a (potentially ever changing) demand (see, for instance, the debate around the *consumer-oriented* or *producer-oriented* evaluation as a result of such an epistemic positioning – Scriven 2002). The core values of the CIPP model, that is the foundations/criteria for evaluation as the determination of the value of educational things, are located in this external space. As Stufflebeam (2003: 33) argues:

> Essentially, evaluators assess the services of an institution, program, or person against a pertinent set of societal, institutional, program, and professional technical values. The values provide the foundation for deriving the particular evaluative criteria. The criteria, along with questions of stakeholders, lead to clarification of information needs. These, in turn, provide the basis for selecting and constructing the evaluation instruments and procedures and interpreting standards. Evaluators and their clients must regularly employ values clarification as the foundation of their evaluation activities.

Put in a constant relationship to this space, evaluands are characterised as in a permanent condition of responsiveness or contractual obligations with plural external demands, where the stakeholders can be institutional actors, contractors or consumers. Finally, this external space is the subsequent space of the product, the result of the productive process, which is positioned as the key reference for the judgement on the value of the evaluand as merit and worth.

The interpretation of the evaluand

In Chapter 4, I have discussed how educational evaluation is regularly defined as 'the systematic and objective determination of the worth or merit of an object' (Joint Committee on Standards for Educational Evaluation 1994: 205). In relation to the *criteria* that orient evaluation, I have also shown how *system* as a grid of specification opens the space for a distinct and regularly occurring *conceptual form of derivation* between the notions of value and worth, which qualifies educational evaluation as a peculiar activity of interpretation of the evaluand and defines educational evaluands as valuable. I want to complement that analysis showing how *production* as a grid of specification allows the deployment of a further chain of conceptual succession where value as merit stands in a relation of derivation with the concepts of quality, performance and excellence.

In a vast array of policy and scientific texts, the ontological formation of the evaluand as production and the related modes of description and characterisation make it possible to conceptualise value as merit as 'the excellence of an object as assessed by its intrinsic qualities or performance' (Stufflebeam and Coryn 2014: 8; OECD 2002). Educational objects are positioned as assessable in terms of their intrinsic value or quality, which is made observable/appraisable through the equation between quality and performance (the realisation of a task, the provision of a service or the making of a product). When quality and performance are to be ordered along a hierarchy of merit, then the concepts of excellence and levels of excellence regularly provide a classificatory tool to organise such an ordering. Importantly, within this chain, the concept of performance becomes the node of a specific kind of articulation between the intrinsic value/quality of the educational evaluand as object of assessment (the input and process of the CIPP model) and the evaluand external space (the core values, the context and the product). In fact, if performance is the observable correlate of quality, what is the ultimate element in relation to which the merit/value of a performance is determined? Despite the variety of inflections, the interpretation of the evaluand in educational evaluation is regularly conceptualised as an attempt to reply to the following question: 'does the object do well what it is intended to do?' (Stufflebeam and Coryn 2014: 9). Here the ontological formation of the educational evaluand as production creates the possibility for further forms of derivation, which make actual an instrumental form of educational evaluation, where the relations means-ends and objective-results act as pivotal coordinates (Bhola 2002: 390). If the quality of an evaluand can be judged on the basis of the empirical appraisal of its performance, then the need arises to define a reference against which to judge the 'doing well' on the part of the evaluand. Similarly to what we have seen in the case of transferences from biology, within this tree of conceptual derivation, accepted standards of quality regularly play the role of such a reference. They are the switches to two further derivations. As a judgement on the capacity of the evaluand to perform well/meet a standard, merit assessment both precedes and follows educational things, with quality of the evaluand migrating 'from the thing to the processes of production of the thing, or to their control' (Pinto 2012: 124). Standards precede the empirical appraisal of performance and the interpretation of the evaluand becomes dependent on an external recognition of value. They act as both the objective to be pursued and the criteria to be used to judge the goodness of the evaluand, as a form of activity and as an entity.

The interpretation of the evaluand is formed as a way to relate the history of an entity to an act of designation of this entity as valuable through the following conceptual form of derivation: production-goals-intrinsic value-merit-quality-excellence-performance-standards/criteria. A further articulation has to be noted here. The operationalisation of merit in terms of levels of excellence establishes educational evaluands as inherently competitive objects, that is as comparable more and less performative evaluands. In this respect, performance is positioned within this recurrent conceptual chain as something that can be assessed through the reference to an institutional or market-originated standard of quality or against competitive objects of the same type. In the first case, the space of the evaluative judgement is a competitive space where, however, all the evaluands have the potential to meet externally established goals/standards and reach excellence. In the second case, the evaluative space assumes the shape of an external market of products and productions, with permanent traits such as the comparison with competitive objects and a hierarchical ordering among better-performing and underperforming entities.

The empirical analysis of the evaluand

The formation of the evaluand as production and productive entities makes available a distinct set of epistemological possibilities to perform evaluation as an empirical investigation that uses techniques from the social sciences (Scriven 1991). When educational evaluation is at stake as an empirically based judgement on the merit of educational entities, two regularly occurring enunciative forms of succession prescribe the modalities of empirical description and the perceptual codes in the field. They have the function to define the employable methods to shed light on: (a) the internal space of educational production, that is its rational and productive organisation as activity and combination of individuated factors and (b) the relations of determination, adherence, contractual responsiveness and competitiveness between the evaluand and its external space.

The first enunciative form of succession constitutes educational evaluation as a mode of empirical analysis through the following conceptual chain: Evaluation-Context-Input-Process-Results (what is often termed as the *result chain* – see OECD 2002: 33). This, in turn, allows the derivation of four different kind of evaluations and evaluative positioning. As argued above, the figure of production establishes a linear temporality, a history of particular forms of activity, labour and results and changes in the organisational arrangements (a division of labour) to produce value through the meeting of externally established standards/goals. The conceptual series under examination offers a way to segment such a linear history into empirically knowable domains. When the *context* of educational production is taken into consideration, educational evaluation becomes a form of empirical investigation with the aim to identify existing (hypostatised) needs, diagnose barriers, assess resources, judge whether the established goals reflect the identified needs and, finally, establish criteria to judge outcomes (*needs assessment* – Rossi et al. 1999: 119). Context evaluation is regularly associated with methods that range from system analysis to diagnostic tests, checklists, secondary data analysis, surveys, document and literature reviews, interviews, focus groups and expert visits. When the evaluative gaze is projected on the *results*, then empirical investigation turns into the collection of descriptions and judgements of outputs, outcomes or impacts 'to relate them to goals and to context, input, and process information' in order to interpret their merit and worth (Stufflebeam 2003: 40). This act of relating is linked to methods such as measurement, judgement or comparison of intended and unintended outcomes (*product evaluation* – Scriven 1991). On the contrary, when the evaluative gaze is projected towards the internal space of production, *input* evaluation is defined as the identification and assessment of system capabilities, strategies, design, staffing plan, schedule and budget. Such a definition opens the space for the identification of visits, panel reviews, pilot trials, inventory and feasibility or cost analysis as functional methods for the empirical characterisation of the evaluand (Madaus and Kellaghan 2002: 27). Finally, *process* evaluation is established as the stage of the evaluative empirical investigation with the aim to record and judge the actual work of the educational system/organisation/entity and identify or predict defect in the work plan or its implementation (Stufflebeam 2003: 40). This investigation is related to the employment of methods like observation, interviews, document review, monitoring and recording. This chain constitutes the condition of possibilities of a vast array of characterisation of educational evaluation as method, as in the case of Rossi et al. (1999: 63) or Alkin (2011: 62), who argue that what any evaluation endeavour should know about an evaluand is: '(1) what the [evaluand] intends to accomplish, (2) who it serves, (3) what are the services provided and their sequence for potentially achieving those accomplishments, and (4) what people and materials are required for providing these services'.

In the tree of derivation of educational evaluation, each of these forms of empirical investigation acts as a point of articulation for further conceptual chains that characterise the evaluand more in details. Input, process and outcomes are regularly characterised, respectively, in terms of 'infrastructure, staff and students intake', 'teaching, learning, leadership and administration' and 'level, distribution and equity of students results' (see OECD 2013: 91). Generally speaking, the overall trait of those characterisations is that education as a rational process is made up into an instrumental activity involving people, materials and organisational structures having a particular objective (what Alkin 2011: 60 defines as program components). The evaluand components have to be analysed through a classification of tasks, units, structures and skills in the attempt to describe (and judge) in detail the instrumental functionality of each of them, in order to make them manageable and improvable. The concept of organisation as a mode to structure production comes here to the fore in qualifying a specific way to approach the empirical analysis of the evaluand, as it happens within this example from program evaluation literature:

> [The evaluand] involves people, but the focus is not on evaluating the people – that would be personnel evaluation. It involves materials, but the focus is not on evaluating the materials – that would be product evaluation. These people and materials are structured in a way that they interact. That is, there is an organizational structure governing how people and materials jointly interact in trying to do something for program recipients. People do things with materials. There are sets of prescribed

activities involving the people and the materials that indicate what is to take place. In a program, we prescribe what materials will be used, often in conjunction with people, and when this will take place. Programs also have identifiable audiences – clients of the program. (Alkin 2011: 60)

Around the projection of educational evaluation as a gaze towards the internal space of production's organisational structure, a second series of regular conceptual derivations emerges which prescribes the forms of empirical description and the perceptual codes in the field: evaluation-program-monitoring-organisation-personnel-materials-implementation-mechanisms. Evaluation becomes the monitoring of a production process. Monitoring (or process evaluation) is focused on the form of such a process of production, that is on the way in which a set of interactions between personnel and materials that have been planned to respond to a programme actually occur within an organisational structure (what is referred to as implementation – King et al. 1987). In Rossi et al. (1999: 191), it is possible to find an interesting example of this chain:

> An important *evaluation* function, therefore, is to assess program *implementation*: the program activities that actually take place and the services that are actually delivered in routine program operation. Program *monitoring* (*process evaluation*) and related procedures are the means by which the evaluator investigates these issues. Program monitoring is usually directed at one or more of three key questions: (a) whether a program is reaching the appropriate *target population*, (b) whether its service delivery and support functions are consistent with *program design* specifications or other appropriate *standards*, and (c) whether positive changes appear among the program participants and social conditions the program addresses. Monitoring may also examine what *resources* are being, or have been, expended in the conduct of the program. Program monitoring is an essential evaluation activity. It is the principal tool for formative evaluation designed to provide feedback for program improvement and is especially applicable to relatively new programs attempting to establish their organization, clientele, and services.

Educational evaluation stands a mode of knowing and assessing a procedure, in the attempt to formalise an effective mode of ordering and coordinating abstract elements (what are commonly defined as evaluand elements, that is the things that are supposed to happen within the evaluand activity) and mechanisms (what are commonly defined as program mechanisms, that is the kind of connections between the elements of an activity with specified outcomes – see Alkin 2011: 133) in time and space.

Organisation, personnel and materials as elements of the production process are further specified as observable objects of description. Personnel can be known by analysing number, appropriate qualifications, understanding of the program and attitudes. Materials can be known through the appraisal of their potential and use. Organisational structure can be known by looking at the activity plan, coherence and sequencing of the intended activities, administration, facilities and budget. Finally, the empirical analysis of mechanisms is established as the assessment of the linkages between the program, the organisational structure, personnel, materials and the output/outcome of the production process (see ibid. 138).

Mechanisms are the point where the chain articulates itself regularly with two further concepts, performance and indicator, through which the space that is external to the production process comes under the evaluative lens. Performance is the concept that gives back unity to the distinction between elements and mechanisms, process and product evaluation, monitoring and measurement, being defined as 'the degree to which a development intervention or a development partner operates according to specific criteria/standards/guidelines or achieves results in accordance with stated goals or plans' (OECD 2002: 29). Performance is conceived as analysable through performance indicators, that is quantitative or qualitative variables that 'allow the verification of changes in the development intervention, show results relative to what was planned' or help assess the performance of a development actor (ibid.). This is the epistemic space where educational evaluation meets statistical and econometrics techniques and the related 'methods of regression or [...] randomised experiments' led by 'the question of the pure effect of a variable or the causal effect in order to evaluate the effects which can be expected to result from this or that action' (Desrosieres 2011: 77) (see, e.g. the works of the *European Expert Network on Economics of Education,* their 2009 paper *Methods for Causal Evaluation in Education* and the discussion of controlled experiments, lotteries of oversubscribed programs, instrumental variables, regression discontinuities, differences-indifferences, and panel-data techniques as evaluative methods – http://www.eenee.de/eeneeHome/EENEE.html).

Analysing the performance of the evaluand and the use of educational evaluation

In addition to what I have highlighted in Chapter 4, the exploration of educational evaluation as enunciative field shows the recurrence of a further domain of conceptual coordination and coexistence that articulates itself on the ending point of the chain evaluation-context-input-process-results. It further characterises the function of educational evaluation in the governing of education.

Production as a grid of specification and the related methods of empirical characterisation are regularly coordinated with further enunciative series where the evaluand as context, input, process or result is respectively historicised as potentially: (a) misaligned to the target population needs; (b) provided with inadequate capabilities, the wrong strategy, plan, design, staff or budget to implement the plan; (c) having work plan or implementation defects and (d) being of poor quality in relation to a standard or a benchmark. We have here a production or market-oriented rearticulation of the dualism success/failure that I have discussed in Chapter 4. Educational entities and processes are positioned in a state of continuous need for change and improvement, being permanently a potentially failing enterprise. Failure here is naturalised as a twofold possibility: (a) the failure to match the process or output standards, as defined within a contract-like (or principal-agent) relationship and (b) a competitive failure (e.g. not reaching the benchmark or being below the average) which is defined as failure through the competitive dynamics of a market and clients/consumers choices (see as examples Rossi et al. 1999: 26–27; Patton 1997; Scriven 1991). This is the archaeological point where the empirical analysis of the productive performance of the evaluand becomes functional to a normative *use* of evaluation that is fourfolded:

- determining the setting to be served, the target group, the goals, the priorities and the evaluation criteria to judge the results of education, on the basis of the empirical analysis of the beneficiaries' needs;
- determining the sources of support, strategies, procedural design, staffing plan and budget that are needed to structure the (change) activities;
- refining the work plan and record/control the implementation process, to identify defects and improve the process;
- deciding to continue, terminate, modify or refocus the activities, recording intended and unintended, positive and negative results (as output, outcome and impact) and comparing them with needs and goals (Stufflebeam 2003: 40).

Here, learning and change to improvement complete the enunciative chain of production. What emerges is again a developmental process where production as a grid of specification offers a whole reality to be known through learning and intervened on, in order to fix, ameliorate, prevent failure and change to improve. An example of this conceptual derivation can be found in the 2015 *Eurydice Report on School Evaluation* in Europe:

> Quality assurance in education can be understood as policies, procedures, and practices that are designed to achieve, maintain or enhance quality in specific areas, and that rely on an evaluation process. By 'evaluation', we understand a general process of systematic and critical analysis of a defined subject that includes the collection of relevant data and leads to judgements and/or recommendations for improvement. The evaluation can focus on various subjects: schools, school heads, teachers and other educational staff, programmes, local authorities, or the performance of the whole education system. (European Commission/EACEA/Eurydice 2015: 13)

116 Forms of production

In the enunciative field of educational evaluation is possible to identify multiple visual statements where such a developmental process is articulated into measurement, monitoring and evidence-based intervention on the mechanics of the educational process through the use of evaluative data. Figure 5.2 summarises the structure and elements of those visual statements. One of the clearest examples can be found on the UNESCO *International Institute for Educational Planning Learning Portal* (see http://www.iiep.unesco.org/en/join-e-forum-towards-global-framework-measuring-learning-3324).

If failure is a natural and permanent possibility, the success as its contrary becomes an ethical imperative. Evaluands are ethically positioned within a world where it is always possible and desirable to improve. As Rossi *et al.* (1999: 25) emphatically argue, if the purpose of human activity 'is in some way to improve the human condition, the purpose of evaluation, in turn, is to improve' this activity, providing answers to 'questions about what the [an activity] is doing but, more important, about how well it is being done and whether it is worth doing'. In this frame, evaluation is conceptualised as user-oriented and finalised to capacity-building (Christie and Alkin 2008). The subjects of evaluation inhabit a field of strategic choices. The kinds of reasoning they are expected to perform range from cost-benefit analysis to calculating advantages and disadvantages of certain alternative actions, testing of alternatives under controlled conditions, feedback, follow-up and so on (Dahler-Larsen 2012: 41). They are established as pragmatic, entrepreneurial and problem-solving knowledgeable entities (Popkewitz 2000: 21). Their knowing activity is conceived as evidence-based and instrumentally oriented towards the strategic, mechanic and performative aspects of the

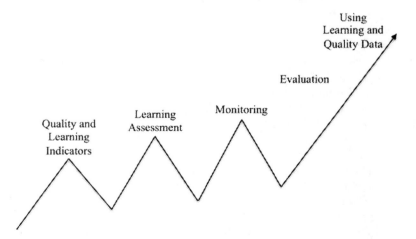

Figure 5.2 Measuring, monitoring and intervening on the mechanics of the educational process as production.

real-educational world and the functionality of those performative aspects to the achievement of preestablished or market-oriented goals. For those subjects, objectified as enterprises operating in a historically changing configuration of management, quality and the management of its heterogeneous components appear as permanent concerns (Simons 2002: 624). As entrepreneurs, they need 'information' about the quality of their actions and modes of being in order to choose, manage and empower themselves (ibid. 628).

Here, evaluation as a mode of knowing is framed as a rational-instrumental learning technique for the mastering of an uncertain world which is prone to failure and, as such, needs to be turned into a predictable space. Within this conceptual chain, evaluation as learning is objectified as an important characteristic of entrepreneurship (ibid. 626). Investments in evaluation and self-evaluation and the will to produce better results are positioned as an ethically necessary practice of knowledge to meeting the needs of others intended as contractors/customers but also to self-realisation and self-development (Rose 1989).

At the same time, as an instrumental knowledge endeavour, educational evaluation is established as a separate classificatory and ordering function in the complex division of labour of an organisation/system. As a function, it is intended to outline a continuum of value through which evaluand value (adequacy, capability, competence, performativity, standardisation, competitiveness) is constructed, ranked and benchmarked. It is an activity of map-making which establishes relations of inclusion/exclusion, telling us 'symbolically how to order the objects of the world for scrutiny and practice' (Popkewitz 2000: 22). Through the judgement on merit, educational evaluation organises the territories of education by producing boundaries between the productive and the unproductive, the deserving and the undeserving. It qualifies or disqualifies the evaluands ordering, dividing and normalising their inner capabilities and characteristics on the basis of an external (standardised or competitive) reference. At the intersection between evaluation as capacity-building and evaluation as classificatory and ordering technique, the individual is positioned within a paradox. On the one hand, evaluation takes the individual as a unitary rational actor and as the primary object of investigation (Olssen 1999: 164). The single case is abstracted from context, process and product. If these are all important and influential factors, educational evaluation attempts to isolate the value of the individual from contaminating factors (as in the case of the added value of a component measured through regression). On the other hand, the individual is regularly evaluated as instrumental, as relay or condition of a mechanic that needs to be 'properly managed, maintained, and encouraged' for obtaining something at the level of the production process and its results (Foucault 2009: 42).

Political economy, management and educational evaluation as fields of concomitance

In his 1978 historical work on the major evaluation models, House highlighted the relationships of concomitance between liberal epistemology or empiricism, management theory and a distinct family of evaluative approaches:

> With or without the historical connections, the similarity of the managerial evaluation models to Mill's epistemology is strong. Perhaps the leading proponent of the systems analysis model has been Alice M. Rivlin. She was in the group that introduced cost benefit analysis to education and other social programs in the Department of Health, Education and Welfare in the 1960s. Most of the large federal evaluation efforts were based on the systems analysis logic (McLaughlin 1975). The key ideas in Rivlin's (1971) approach were these: – Key decisions will be made at higher governmental levels. – The end of evaluation is efficiency in the production of social services. – The only true knowledge is a production function specifying stable relationships between educational inputs and outputs. – The only way to such knowledge is through experimental methods and statistical techniques. – It is impossible to agree on goals and on a few output measures. – There is a direct parallel between production in social services and in manufacturing. The same techniques of analysis will apply. (House 1978: 7)

There are clear relations between the tree of derivation of educational evaluation I have presented so far in this chapter and some of the key concepts and conceptual chains of scientific management, with the aim to formalise through bureaucracy and standardisation the problems of production and the related solutions in order to make the world of production manageable. House (1978: 7) observes that 'scientific management bears a strong resemblance to the systems analysis and behavioural objectives models of evaluation' and 'the managerial orientation to evaluation has long historical roots'. Rose (1989: 95–96) has discussed the relationship between the rationality of production, management theory and human and social sciences as the kind of knowledge 'providing a vocabulary and a technology for rendering the labour of the worker visible, calculable, and manageable, enabling it to be integrated into the rational economic calculus'. This is the epistemic terrain where educational evaluation articulates itself with both a formal rationality, inspired by the principles of calculability, predictability and efficiency, and an abstract and instrumental rationality that claims a separation from any substantive value in the name of efficiency and predictability, laws and universal rules of production (Dahler-Larsen 2012: 40). If the organisation of the mode of production is conceived as an instrument, at the same time and through a paradoxical move, the actualisation of distinctive social forms of this organisation becomes a purpose in itself, independent of any substantive value.

Within the same line of reasoning, in the following pages I want to deepen my analysis of the enunciative tree of derivation of educational evaluation showing how the regularities I have identified so far present significant points of analogy with management theory (Dahler-Larsen 2012: 37) and the field of political economy. Through a lateral rapprochement I will explore the *play of analogies (and differences)* between educational evaluation, management theory and political economy. My aim is to highlight how the former finds, at least in part, its conditions of possibility in the transference from the latters, and how these three fields share a similar archaeological model. In this respect I will show how the chains of derivation linking the concepts of educational evaluation (production, goals, plan, actions, output, outcome, context, input, process, product, results, merit, effectiveness, efficiency and performance) have been formed on the basis of the same epistemic essential functions as the very different, radically heterogeneous concepts of management theory and political economy (Figure 5.3). Since I have not enough space to present in detail the trees of enunciative derivation of both management theory and political economy, in the following I directly draw on literature analysis of the relation between evaluation and management theory (House 1978; Dahler-Larsen 2005) and Foucault's archaeological analysis of political economy in *The Order of Things* (2002a; see also De Lima 2010; Kologlugil 2010).

As in Chapter 4, I focus on the *archaeological isotopia*, with the aim to show how some concepts occupy a similar position in the ramification of the three enunciative fields. The first significant similarity relates to the positioning of the figure of production as a grid of specification that creates a field of visibility and intervention. The formation of the evaluand through the chain goals-plan-action-results finds its conditions of possibility in the transference from political economy of a basic feature of the figure of *production*: the distinction between labour as 'energy, toil, and time that are bought and sold' within a market relation between the worker/producer and a contractor, and 'the activity that is at the origin of the value of things' (Foucault 2002a: 276). It is through the transference of this concept of labour as production that the human being as evaluand is formed as a being/object of study who has needs and desires, and tries to satisfy them, as a subject having interests who lives in a perennial situation of conflict within the environment and creates rules in order to limit/control the conflict.

Both the distinction between labour as energy/time and activity, fully developed in the economic thought of Ricardo, and the idea of *labour* as a producing activity [that] is 'the source of all value' (ibid. 277) make thinkable educational evaluation as a mode of empirical inquiry that produces judgements about the value of things or entities analysing value/merit as a product of specific *forms of production*, as in the case of the chain

120 Forms of production

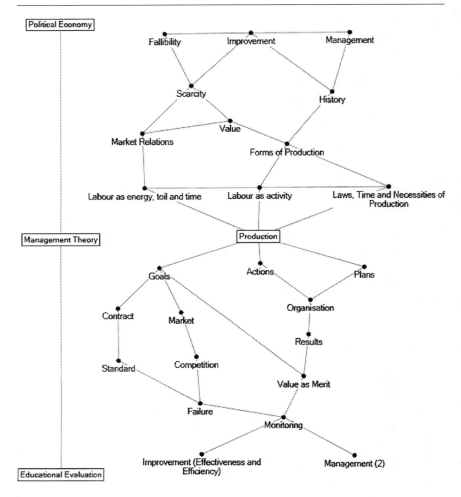

Figure 5.3 Political economy, management theory and educational evaluation as fields of concomitance.

context-input-process-results. Educational evaluation shares with political economy (and specifically the analysis of production) the assumption that value is not a sign. It does not belong to the realm of representation, but is a *product/result* of labour/activity. This is the epistemic basis for the causal series that underpins much of the educational evaluative models employed in the formation of judgements about the value of outputs/outcomes, personnel, organisations or programmes in education: it is the form of production that determines the quantity of work needed to obtain an educational output/outcome (product), which in turn determines the value of that output/outcome.

In this way, educational evaluation thinks the history of the individuals or organisations to be evaluated as a history of forms of production (rational organisation as a method of characterisation) and products/results and changes in the forms of production, which are related to specific capacities to produce value. The economic idea that value is a product of specific forms of production can be considered as the epistemic basis for the causal series that underpins much of the evaluative models discussed in the chapter. This is the point of articulation where educational evaluation meets scientific management as efficiency and effectiveness engineering (House 1978: 7) and the managerial polity of value based on effectiveness (Boltanski 2011: 167). Such an historical and mechanic formation of the evaluand opens up the space for the ideal of the mastery of the world, which is constitutive of management as an enunciative field. The rationale is the making of the world as a predictable space through rational organisation and management. Through management as a field of concomitance, educational evaluation establishes itself as a mode of instrumental intervention in the world that, once a set of objectives has been established, uses diagnostic tools to know which are the best arrangements that guarantee a probable (and predictable) achievement of those objectives through time (see Dahler-Larsen 2012: 38).

Educational evaluation transfers from political economy another key mode of reasoning, which again is related to the epistemic figure of production and its consequences. Whereas in political economy, what makes economic activity possible and necessary is a perpetual and fundamental situation of scarcity, and the *homo economicus* is a being who lives in a continuous confrontation with death, educational evaluation finds its possibility and necessity in a discourse of *fallibility* that locates the educational beings as evaluand in a perennial state of potential failure (see Saltman 2010: 126 on 'educational economism', which 'refers to the framing of educational issues, practices and policies through restricted or scarcity-based economics'). The *homo of evaluation* (hereafter HoE) appears as a special inflection of the *economicus*, living his life in a perennial struggle against failure, a peculiar form of man's finitude or limitation. Evaluation, as political economy, is then strictly related to a discourse of human's finitude and to 'an anthropology that attempts to assign concrete forms to [this] finitude' (Foucault 2002a: 280).

This transference makes it possible for evaluation the distinction between the needs that the individuals under evaluation represent to themselves and the true conditions that determine the game/struggle against failure. As political economy and management theory, educational evaluation is based on an anthropology that problematises the essence of the human being, his fallibility (as a peculiar declination of his finitude), his constitutive relation with time, the imminence of failure 'and the object in which he invests his days of time and toil [that is the pursuing of value/merit as effectiveness and efficiency] without being able to recognize in it the object of his immediate need' (ibid. 244). As such, it constitutes itself as a field of knowledge that talks about mechanisms that are external to human consciousness, whose time is the time of a form of production, an 'organic structure which grows in accordance with its own necessity and develops in accordance with autochthonous laws' (ibid. 245) – the time of effectiveness, efficiency, merit and value.

Conclusion

As I have done in Chapter 4, I draw on the analysis carried on so far to present a second archaeological quadrilateral (Figure 5.4). It visualises the relations of concomitance between the enunciative fields of educational evaluation, management theory and political economy and shows how educational evaluation forms its objects, concepts and strategies through transferences from the latters.

The ontological formation of the evaluand through the transference of the figure of production as labour and the notion of scarcity makes it visible a mechanic and developmental world. This world functions and can be understood in terms of network of causalities connecting entities and forces (individuals, resources, needs, actions, plans, strategies). The effects of these networks of causalities can be experienced, identified and stabilised by means of instruments of categorisation (preferably through counting operations) and management (Boltanski 2011: 34). The time of these educational entities is a history of changes in the forms of production. Those changes can allow productive entities to win the struggle against failure. In educational evaluation,

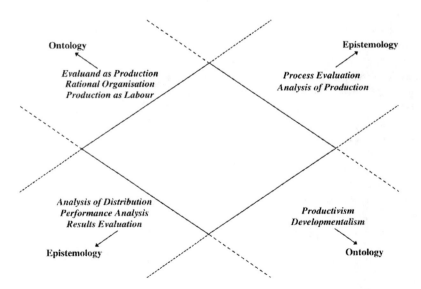

Figure 5.4 The archaeological quadrilateral of educational evaluation, management theory and political economy.

this assumes the form of the utopia of continuous development and improvement, which stands as a peculiar mode of navigating the relation between the historical and the anthropological poles of this epistemic space. The more evaluands exert their agency and improve, understanding and intervening on their activities, the more they come to confront with finitude, in the form of the increasing difficulty to further improve and the related higher probability to fail. Educational evaluation shows a double: whereas its empirical/positivist techne makes always visible the anthropological finitude of the human being, or his fallibility, the utopia of improvement represents its teleological, revolutionary promise. Such an ambivalence and logical *aporia* can be detected both in the economicist and positivist approaches to evaluation as well as in the attempts to introduce more democratic and interpretative (phenomenological) logics in the field (as I will show in the next chapter).

As it happens with the figure of production, the formation of this specific space-time nexus is linked to the establishment of a particular kind of norm, which again acts as a basis for: (a) the judgement on the value/merit of the entities inhabiting such a space-time through their process analysis and (b) for the classification/management of the educational entities as deserving and undeserving, productive and unproductive resources, through results' analysis (Ball 2012: 68). An epistemological and governmental double emerges here, in relation to educational evaluation as a governing tool to prevent failure. On the one hand, evaluation as empirical mode of characterisation of educational processes and results becomes functional to a disciplinary system of controls, constraint and permanent supervision which is standard-based and focused on events that is necessary to prevent before they become reality. On the other hand, it stands as a regulatory mechanism. Evaluation, in fact, is functional and acts as a stimulus to the autonomy, reflexivity and freedom to evaluate, manage and organise responsible enterprising entities. As in political economy, result and process evaluation act as a further point of integration between education as a moment of production, the educational environment as a market where educational results are established as competitive objects and finally the educational behaviour of self-governing educational producers and consumers (Foucault 2009: 41).

This is another epistemic terrain where educational evaluation relates clearly to liberalism and neoliberalism through the mediation of management theory and political economy. As House (1978: 5) has observed, the epistemology, politics and ethics of most of the evaluative models 'derive from the philosophy of liberalism' and the liberal 'attempt to rationalize and justify a market society which was organized on the principle of freedom of choice'. Educational evaluation shares with liberalism a descriptive, moral and political individualism, or what in essence is 'a metaphysic of individualism' (Olssen 2014: 217). Choice acts as a key idea in educational evaluation models 'although whose choice, what choices, and the grounds upon which choices are made are matters of difference' (House 1978: 5).

As emerged throughout the chapter, there is a link between the liberal objectivist epistemology and educational evaluation through the mediation of political economy, management and their emphasis on empiricism to the exclusion of theory (House 1978: 7). As in liberal objectivism (and in the stream of neoliberal epistemology that can be related to Friedman 1953), evaluation information has the pretension to establish itself as 'scientifically objective' and such objectivity is achieved by using 'objective' and preferably measuring and experimental methods. These methods allow a calculative and inductive reasoning and a temporally linear cause-effect and means-end representation of the world. As Madaus and Kellaghan (2002: 21–22) put it:

> The factory metaphor, and its close cousin technological production, have embedded in [most of the educational evaluative models] instrumental rationality. [...] In this world view, reality is based on empirical knowledge and is governed by technical rules; we can make predictions about physical or social events; we can manipulate and control the environment; no part of the work/curriculum process is unique and each part is reproducible; everything in the curriculum can be analysed into constituent, interdependent parts; and a worker's/teacher's activity can be evaluated in quantifiable terms. [...] Such a mind set tends to view education as a means to an end, e.g., as producing an educated workforce or making the country more competitive. Further, teaching and learning are seen as means to desired ends, elements in a system that can, in principle, be controlled. In this world view, teaching is regarded as a skilled craft based on technical expertise; problems with student learning can be dealt with by applying appropriate techniques; and education can be improved by a more complete mapping of cause and effect relationships in the teaching learning process.

Liberal and neoliberal politics are at stake here as well, with their methodological individualism. Educational evaluation models partake of the ideas of a competitive, individualist, market society, where the most fundamental idea is freedom of choice. The external space of any evaluand is conceived as a marketplace in which entities pursue their own individual goals in market or contract-like kind of relationships. This is intended to guarantee the common good, where the common good tends to be identified with the free initiative and the increased knowledge of those entities. Using the model enterprise-customer, evaluation contributes to subjecting the production/education process to a permanent quality tribunal (Simons 2002: 622). But evaluation also participates to the core political paradox of neoliberalism, acting as a regulatory technique with the aim to 'develop a more clear understanding of the enterprising self and of its relation to (quality) management' (ibid. 621), to increase/deepen intervention and control and, finally, to render free individuals governable in order to make them productive (Olssen 1999: 164).

Finally, on the terrain of ethics, the HoE is a version of the liberal individual who is proprietor of his/her own capacities, fate and destiny. He/she is not only the master of his/her destiny but more crucially is morally and legally responsible for himself/herself. He is naturally self-interested and desiring to produce and improve (Ball 2012: 59). Responsibility means here to know/learn to gain evaluative information which in turn serves to make informed and responsible choices for learning, development, productiveness and self-actualisation. Evaluation stands as a peculiar neoliberal technique of government, that acts as a tool for governing through freedom and competition, autonomisation and responsibilisation or, to put it another way, through the establishment of an entrepreneurial relation to the self. Simons (2002: 620) offers an illuminating description of the evaluative life of the HoE:

> Life is about making choices everyday and everywhere, turning oneself into a project, improving oneself, one's relations and professional life and about choosing 'lifestyles' [...]. People are responsible for the 'production' of their own wellbeing and self-actualization and therefore, a specific kind of self-knowledge ('experts of the self', e.g. therapists, can sell their expertise) and self-mastery is required. In a rather general way we could characterize the freedom and autonomy of the enterprising self as a subjection to a 'permanent economic tribunal', i.e. the judgment and characterization of one's life as a producer-consumer with needs and human capital in a (market) environment where everything has an (economic) value.

The autonomous, responsible and enterprising HoE is in a paradoxical relation to failure, which is conceptually split into two levels. On the one hand, the individual can get rid of failure by a sort of de-centred self-regulation through evaluation as a form of analysis and reparatory intervention. On the other hand, the individual confronts with the necessity of failure as something to be espoused, as something that generates reflexivity and generates improvement and, as such, must not disappear, if we want to pursue economic growth and social welfare.

Chapter 6
Meanings

In Chapters 4 and 5, I have discussed how educational evaluation establishes itself as a mode of inquiry that studies the evaluand alternatively as living systems and forms of production. In both cases, the archaeological analysis has pointed out the ways in which educational evaluation analyses them empirically as entities possessing functions in relation to a plan or appearing in a perennial situation of conflict for scarce resources. Moreover, it has highlighted how educational evaluation interprets their value (a) in terms of their capacity to find/adhere to average norms of adjustment which permit them to perform their functions within an environment or (b) establishing a body of rules which permit to account for their performance and escape or dominate conflict for scarce resources in a market-like space.

In this chapter, I continue the archaeological analysis of educational evaluation as an enunciative field showing how it is possible to recognise a further set of secondary regularities where the evaluand is studied as pertaining to the domain of meaning. These secondary regularities emerge in the interstices of the paradoxes produced by the dominance of the transferences from biology and political economy. They can mainly be observed in scientific literature, debates and research on school-based and self-evaluation, but rarely appear in policy statements. Within this epistemic space and its plays of opposition, educational evaluation looks at systemic thinking, where the concept of system assumes a different emphasis with respect to the biological transference. Or, in a different direction, a constructivist 'counter-educational evaluation' emerges, which is sensible to interpretation and the discovery of meaning. It is the case of those evaluative approaches generally referred to as *naturalistic* or *responsive* (see Guba and Lincoln 2004 and their *Fourth Generation Evaluation*). They flow in the opposite direction to dominant mechanistic models and turn evaluation to its epistemological basis, continuously attempting to 'unmake' the kind of evaluand whose positivity is created and re-created through evaluation, up to the reach of a ground where evaluation seems to lose its specificity as knowing endeavour (Dahler-Larsen 2012: 116). In both cases, comprehension is opposed to explanation as the key technique to approach the evaluand and say something on its value. The evaluand is located within a paradoxical time made of discontinuity and continuity. Scriven's (2002: 258–59) discussion of the recent controversies in the field of program evaluation offers a first and indicative insight into this oppositional space:

> Whereas the positivists were committed to the view that there was some kind of definite external world about which we learned through our senses and through experiments, more recent philosophy of science has tended to move away from this 'realistic' or 'external world' commitment towards the view that everyone has his or her own reality, all equally legitimate. And evaluation has been very much influenced by this movement in the philosophy of science. [...] in articles by the most distinguished workers in evaluation, one finds not only a shying away from the notion of objective determination of worth [...] but also a shying away from even the notion of objectively correct descriptions of programs.

In this chapter, I analyse those regularities, arguing that they can be understood as the analogical and differentiating effect of a distinct set of transferences from the study of language through the mediation of sociology as concomitant enunciative field. As in the previous chapters, I first analyse a section of the tree of enunciative derivation of educational evaluation and then map a field of coordination and subordination, discussing a distinct set of points of articulation of educational evaluation on the study of language and sociology.

System of meanings as a grid of specification

The regular occurrence of the enunciative series deriving from the formation of the educational evaluand as living system or form of production generates a field of oppositional discursive possibilities in the enunciative field of educational evaluation. On the one hand, educational evaluation links itself to system thinking (Bhola 2002; Scheerens and Demeuse 2005) to avoid what are considered the reductionisms of the production/factory metaphors (Madaus and Kellaghan 2002: 23). On the other hand, it embraces a subjectivist epistemology to challenge positivist and post-positivist objectivism (House 1978; Guba and Lincoln 1989).

These divergent options find their conditions of possibility in the recurrence of another *governing statement*. It establishes the evaluand as a *system of meanings*, which in turn can be empirically addressed as processes of meaning-making and whose value can be judged on the basis of its capacity to establish a coherent whole and an effective system of signification (*significance* – see Bhola 2003: 400). This statement opens the way for different modalities to objectify educational processes as evaluands and turn them into observable objects and structures. This regularity can be mainly observed in a good deal of scientific evaluative models and texts, whereas is marginal (if not marginalised) in the policy space. As in the previous chapters, I explore here the generative effects of such a regularity for the articulation of the enunciative field.

The formation of the evaluand

In scientific and professional texts, models and speeches on school-based and self-evaluation that explicitly opposes themselves to positivist epistemology and productivism, it is possible to recognise two kinds of enunciative series where the evaluand is formed as a *system of meanings*, which develop respectively in the epistemic regions of system thinking (Williams and Imam 2007) and constructivist thinking (Lincoln 2002). I use here two renown evaluative approaches, Patton's *Developmental Evaluation* (Patton 2011) and Guba and Lincoln's *Fourth Generation Evaluation* (1989) as examples to show the specific forms of enunciative derivation that *system of meanings* as a *grid of specification* make possible in relation to the nature of the evaluand, the evaluative criteria, the methods and the use of educational evaluation (see also Leonard et al. 2016; Kuji-Shikatani et al. 2015; Ryan et al. 2007; Scheerens and Demeuse 2005; Hopkins and West 2002; Russell and Willinsky 1997; Finger and Russell 1994).

In Patton's *Developmental Evaluation*, the evaluand is indirectly defined as a *situation*, a *complex and dynamic system/environment*, which has in uncertainty and unpredictability two of its constitutive traits. Complex and dynamic systems are told to have elusive and dynamic boundaries and change according to system-driven dynamics, which are the driving forces of intervention. Systems-change-driven dynamics produce specific emergent outcomes or effects, which are largely unanticipated. Emergent and unanticipated outcomes/effects are established as the fundamental evaluation focus (Patton 2011: 23–26). Complexity acts here as a *method of characterisation*. Complex systems have the following characteristics (the sensitising concepts that inspire developmental evaluation): (a) nonlinearity (sensitivity to initial conditions and small actions can stimulate large reactions); (b) emergence (patterns emerge from self-organisation among interacting agents and the whole of the interactions cohere); (c) adaptation (interacting elements and agents respond and adapt to each other, and to their environment); (d) uncertainty (processes and outcomes are unpredictable, uncontrollable and unknowable in advance); (e) dynamical systems change (changes seem to be spontaneous, but they are driven by the internal dynamics of the system itself) and (f) coevolution (agents evolve together within and as part of the whole system, over time) (ibid. 150–51). On the basis of this characterisation, *Developmental Evaluation* ultimately defines the evaluand as 'human systems with real, live, interacting human beings'. On this basis, it establishes itself as 'particularly attuned to human factors as the source of complexity' and keen to raising consciousness 'about the realities of real-world uncertainties' through meaning production (ibid. 149).

Guba and Lincoln's *Fourth Generation Evaluation* is a site of emergence where the grid of specification '*system of meanings*' makes possible a different kind of enunciative series. In this case, the biology/political economy-inspired series 'goals/needs-objectives-plans-process-results' is paralleled and opposed by a different one which situates itself at the level of meaning 'claims-concerns-issues-values' (Guba and Lincoln 1989: 72). Here problems addressed, interventions themselves and their meaning and importance are all social constructions that inevitably differ case by case. As a consequence, the evaluative focus shifts from objectives, decisions, outcomes and the like to the diverse claims, concerns, issues and values put forth in a situation. The concept of construction acts as a *method of characterisation* and, through it, educational evaluation becomes an act of eliciting from entities their 'construction about the evaluand, and range of claims, concerns and issues they wish to raise in relation to it' (Guba and Lincoln 1989: 72).

Although the significant differences between the two evaluative approaches, in both the series the evaluand is objectified as an activity or a practice signifying something and which is based on its own cultural premises. In the formation of the evaluand as a field of objects, the focus shifts from function or purpose to meaning, with the evaluand becoming the interpretative processes through which interests, goals, functions, actors and the end point of actions are socially constructed by reflexive subjects/entities within educational situations that have a logic of their own (see Dahler-Larsen 2012: 59). Goals, needs, purposes and plans are the products of meaning-making processes, and they follow actions. Subjectivity is established as the only reality, although it is often positioned as unfolding as a part of a wider logic. The only way the unknown can become known is through individual belief systems (Christie and Alkin 2008: 134). Evaluands 'attain to existence only in so far as they are able to form the elements of a signifying system' (Foucault 2002a: 416). Educational evaluation as a hermeneutic endeavour becomes constitutive of its very object.

Another enunciative area where it is possible to observe the recurrence of this grid of specification is the *School Improvement and Effectiveness* approach (Scheerens and Demeuse 2005). Here system thinking and, in particular, the metaphorical translation of the biological concept of *autopoiesis* through organisational science are playing a significant role in the recent evolution of the approach, as an alternative to those organisational images based on rational planning and the idea of open systems. The concepts of closure, autonomy and self-reference come to the fore to characterise the mechanisms of organisational functioning (Scheerens and Demeuse 2005: 381).

Another relevant example where it is possible to recognise the emergence of conceptual chains similar to those recognised in the case of *Fourth Generation Evaluation* is Stake's *Responsive Evaluation* (Stake 2003: 63):

> Responsive evaluation is an approach, a predisposition, to the evaluation of educational and other programs. Compared to most other approaches it draws attention to program activity, to program uniqueness, and to the social plurality of its people. [...] A responsive evaluation is a search and documentation of program quality. The essential feature of the approach is a responsiveness to key issues or problems, especially those recognized by people at the site. It is not particularly responsive to program theory or stated goals but more to stakeholder concerns. Its design usually develops slowly, with continuing adaptation of evaluation goal-setting and data-gathering in pace with the evaluators becoming well acquainted with the program and its contexts. Issues are often taken as the "conceptual organizers" for the inquiry, rather than needs, objectives, hypotheses, or social and economic equations. Issues are organizational perplexities or complex social problems, regularly attendant to unexpected costs or side effects of program efforts. The term "issue" draws thinking toward the interactivity, particularity, and subjective valuing already felt by persons associated with the program.

A further site of emergence of these conceptual chains is constituted by those evaluative approaches that adopt an understanding of the evaluand as institutionalised organisation (Dahler-Larsen 2012: 39). Here, the organisation acts again as *method of characterisation* to form a field of objects/evaluands as 'loosely coupled systems of metaphorical understandings, values, and organisational recipes and routines that are imitated and taken for granted, and that give legitimacy' within normative fields 'held together by agencies [...] that have common interactions and connections' (Dahler-Larsen 2012: 60).

In all these examples, the combination between system of meanings as a grid of specification and the methods of characterisation of complexity and construction (or institutionalised organisation) defines an educational reality where the distinction between the evaluand internal and external space tends to be blurred through the notion of system itself. The evaluand is established as something whose boundaries are objects of construction in themselves and, as such, become objects of knowledge. As an entity to be reconstructed, the evaluand is thought as facing contingency but in search for stability, equilibrium or consensus in a space of multiple interconnections and perspectives (Williams and Imam 2007). This is the space of 'contexts in the plural', rather than of context, where instability, contradiction, inconsistency and conflict become the threats and risks to be avoided (see Dahler-Larsen 2012: 63–64).

As such, the evaluand is immersed within and constituted through a discontinuous time, a time of contingency, where social order is fragile, relations and determinations between elements could always be otherwise and there is the risk and the expectation that existing social arrangements can be turned on and off (Dahler-Larsen 2012: 128). This is a time in which there is no logical end to contingency and, as a consequence, development as innovation, adaptation or significance become the ideal to be pursued. Madaus and Kellaghan (2002: 23) use the metaphor of the travel and the traveller to define the traits of the educational evaluand constructed throughout those evaluative approaches: a travel where variability and unpredictability are inevitable and desirable, but which is the object of 'a great effort [...] to plot the route so that the journey will be as rich, as fascinating, and as memorable as possible'. Such a mode of conceiving the entities to be evaluated has important consequences in relation to the establishment of the criteria according to which educational evaluation establishes itself as a judgement on the value of the evaluand.

The interpretation of the evaluand

Bhola (2003: 400) observes how system thinking and constructivism open the space for a definition of value not as worth, neither as merit but as *significance* of some purposive action, intervention or aspects thereof (see also Madaus and Stufflebeam 2002). The formation of the evaluand as systems of meanings implies, first and foremost, that each system has its singularity. Systems cannot be ordered along a scale or a hierarchy. Value, then, cannot be defined in terms of adherence/matching of external standards or in terms of competitive comparison. Moreover, within an epistemic region where reality is contingent and unpredictable or there is the recurrence of 'the claim that there is no one objective reality' (Christie and Alkin 2008: 134), valuing assumes a quite different trait from the type of valuing as determination of the objective merit or worth of the evaluand.

Notably, when the issue of the evaluative criteria is at stake, the *Developmental Evaluation* approach recognises how 'highly volatile environments, dynamic social innovations, and emergent interventions may demand ongoing development rather than striving to arrive at a fixed, stable model for replication' (Patton 2011: 26). Here what allows the definition of the value of an evaluand is the discovery and articulation of 'principles of intervention and development'. It is established as an ethic of (a commitment to) continuous progress, ongoing adaptation, rapid responsiveness and exploration of possibilities. In defining the significance of an evaluand, developmental evaluations:

> don't value traditional characteristics of summative excellence such as standardization of inputs, consistency of treatment, uniformity of outcomes, fidelity of replication, and clarity of causal linkages. They assume a world of multiple causes, diversity of outcomes, inconsistency of interventions, interactive effects at every level—and they find such a world

stimulating and challenging. They never expect to conduct a summative evaluation because they don't expect the change initiative—or world—to hold still long enough for summative judgment. They expect to be forever developing and changing—and they want an evaluation approach that supports development and change. (Patton 2011: 41)

The significance of entities lies in their role in the raising of consciousness about the realities of real-world uncertainties and support change and development *per se*.

Constructivism defines value as bounded to contexts and identifies significance in relation to the context as the main criteria to be considered when determining value (Stake 2004). Thus, there are multiple value standards. Criteria to determine value are not taken as given or unique as in the case of rationalism (Guba and Lincoln 1989: 51). A plurality of subjects (called stakeholders) with diverse interests are established as 'legitimate players in formulating evaluation criteria' (Dahler-Larsen 2012: 116). Value relates to the recognition of the evaluand as valuable entities and actions (action plans, actions and policies), which is more important than the coordination between them or the functionality to an objective. As Vedung (2010: 268) observes, within this conceptual chain 'the claims, concerns and issues of the various stakeholders [...] serve as points of departure' for the formulation of the judgement on the value of an entity, which is the accommodating result of a confrontation with difference and a reconstruction of socially constructed claims, concerns and issues. Through this conceptual articulation, value itself becomes a construction of a participatory evaluative inquiry, something that comes into existence through the interaction between the evaluator and the evaluands. In both cases, value does not respond to functionality, neither effectiveness nor purposefulness, but to significance. This means that value ultimately lies in the values, norms and meanings connected to an educational entity. Value can be deciphered on the basis of a signifying system.

The empirical analysis of the evaluand

If value lies in the significance of the evaluand, then the evaluative endeavour becomes an act of understanding and, as such, it requires the employment of a whole set of interpretative strategies of inquiry to grasp its significance in its historicity as system or construction (Christie and Alkin 2008: 134).

When the empirical analysis of the evaluand as a developmental factor is at stake, system as a grid of specification and complexity as a method of characterisation make thinkable empirical analysis as the attempt 'to capture and map complex systems dynamics and interdependencies, and track emergent interconnections' (Patton 2011: 24). Observation, detection of patterns through retrospective construction and extrapolation are identified as context-and-intended-use-dependent methods in service to developmental use (ibid. 25). The evaluation of the context-bounded significance of a complex evaluand inhabiting an uncertain space and a contingent time is said to require methodological flexibility, eclecticism and adaptability. In *Developmental Evaluation*, the evaluative inquiry is defined as 'watching for things to percolate up from interactions, capturing those ideas and new relationships, and placing them in front of project staff as options for further development' (Patton 2011: 61). Possibilities of comparison are lateralised, through the concept of extrapolation, and defined as 'a modest speculation on the likely applicability of [evaluative] findings to other situations under similar, but not identical, conditions' (ibid. 165–66). As such, educational evaluation as empirical form of inquiry connects analysis, interpretation and action for the next stage of development, entering a complex situation in order to bring some focus, create a basic understanding of the situation and get everyone 'on the same page through learning' (Patton 2011: 261). It has a dual objective: inquiring into and tracking developments, and also facilitating the interpretation of developments and their significance in order to judge them.

> Developmental evaluation focuses on developmental questions: What is being developed? How is what's being developed (what's emerging) to be judged? Given what's been developed so far (what has emerged), what's next? The developmental evaluator inquires into developments, tracks developments, facilitates interpretation of developments and their significance, and engages with innovators, change agents, program staff, participants in the process, and funders around making judgments about what is being developed, what has been developed, and the next stages of development. [...] in a way that is matched to and congruent with the characteristics and dynamics of a particular situation and the perspectives and priorities of specific social innovators. (Patton 2011: 263)

The drift for an evaluation becomes the pointing out, through interpretation, of lessons learned and potential applications to future efforts.

Similar conceptual series and chains of derivation can be detected in those material forms of evaluative thought that refer to the *logic model* as heuristic to analyse empirically an educational evaluand (Alkin 2011: 72). The empirical analysis of the evaluand becomes the depiction or diagrammatic representation of the various activities, their progression and linkages, on the basis of an apprehension of the particular character of the evaluand in question, its unique context, the intentions of the individuals involved into the activities and the logic behind that sequence of activities. The point for evaluation becomes to assist individuals in making the rationale of their activities explicit (again a form of bringing to consciousness).

The aim to define the significance of constructions opens a different field of methodological possibilities for constructivist approaches, whose empirical posture can be portrayed as creative discovery rather than verification (see, for a radical example of that, Eisner 2003 and his conception of evaluation as art). Evaluative methodology is characterised as hermeneutic/dialectic, in so far as it tends towards the development of shared and improved constructions through the forced reconsideration of various positions (Vedung 2010: 269). Its aim is to understand, take into account and critique different constructions (claims, concerns and issues). Understanding of claims, concerns and issues has to be carried out within each group, as a cross-fertilising and reconstructive technique. It has to be brought from one group to another, in order to confront, deal with and reconstruct claims, concerns and issues (Guba and Lincoln 1989: 72). In those forms of evaluative thought the following conceptual series recur: (a) recognition of a variety of constructions; (b) their analysis as the making of their elements as plain and communicable to others; (c) dialogue, as the soliciting of critiques for each construction from the holders of others; (d) reconstruction, as reiteration of the constructions in light of new information or new levels of sophistication that may have been introduced and (e) consensus, as the objective to be reached (see Guba and Lincoln 1989: 89–90).

In sum, educational evaluation becomes the detailed and local study of socially and culturally shaped evaluands, which is sensitive to the uniqueness of each evaluand and of its contextual conditions and its processes of sense-making, whose value as significance is context-dependent in relation to the developmental imperative or the reaching of a form of socially constructed consensus. Empirical analysis centres on activities, sense-making, transactions and effects occurring within the situation. Generalisation and (lateral) comparison become possible only as lessons learned and transfer from one system/situation to another. As such they are left to the users (Stake 2004). The objective of the inquiry becomes to 'describe social variations across time and space and point to new [...] opportunities' (Dahler-Larsen 2012: 132), investigating the many perspectives of local stakeholders in contexts. Privileged foci for evaluative empirical analysis are the norms, values, scripts, procedures and rituals that constitute not only the fabric of organisational life but also their dynamics as translation, tension, loose coupling and contradiction as sources of change (Dahler-Larsen 2012: 93). As Madaus and Kellaghan (2002: 24) argue, those privileged foci are constantly connected to methods and techniques associated with disciplines such as anthropology and sociology: long-term, direct observation; open-ended interviews; document or artefact analysis and in-depth case studies. As Scriven (1980: 59) put it, these approaches 'minimize much of the paraphernalia of science' and 'focus on the use of metaphor, analogy, informal (but valid) inference, vividness of description, reasons, explanations, inter-activeness, meanings, multiple (legitimate) perspectives, tacit knowledge'.

Analysing the significance of the evaluand and the use of educational evaluation

Within this epistemic space, a further domain of conceptual coordination and coexistence articulates itself on the ending point of the chains of derivation evaluation-complex system-contingency-emergence-development/change-significance and evaluation-construction-claims-concerns-issues-values-consensus-significance. A dual characterisation of the *function of educational evaluation within the government of education* emerges.

In the case of the first conceptual chain, the function of evaluation is related to consciousness and the desirability of raising human beings' awareness of the realities of real-world uncertainties. Thus, *Developmental Evaluation* defines its purpose/use as developing innovation and adaptation, providing timely feedback for development, generating learning and supporting action in the development process (Patton 2011: 46). Through the production of knowledge on complex systems' dynamics, emergent processes and outcomes (documenting function), the scope of evaluation is to nurture individuals' 'hunger for learning', to build 'ongoing and long-term capacity to think and engage evaluatively' and enable them to stay in touch with and respond accordingly to what is unfolding in uncertain situations (development support function) (ibid. 24). At the end of the chain that links system of meanings as a grid of specification to this use of evaluation, comparison does not find any place. On the contrary, developmental evaluation is linked to the production of potentially scalable innovations, the adaptation of effective general principles to contexts and, more generally, to the horizontal scaling across systems or vertical scaling to broader systems (Patton 2011: 22–23).

The chain evaluation-construction-claims-concerns-issues-values-consensus-significance opens the possibility for a different conceptualisation of the function of evaluation. Here its purpose is articulated around the concepts of consensus and dialogue. Evaluation is intended to generate consensus within and between groups with respect to as many constructions, claims, concerns and issues as possible. Through dialogue and negotiation among stakeholders, evaluation intends to sustain a shared construction of the value and social significance of the evaluand according to a pluralist ethic (Rossi *et al.* 1999: 49). Its task is defined as the preparation of an agenda and a forum for negotiation in relation to issues where there is no or incomplete consensus, collecting data and information on those issues (Vedung 2010: 268–69). Guba and Lincoln (1989: 56) provide an exemplary articulation of the documenting and consensus-building functions of evaluation within the constructivist approach that well summarises this point:

> The involvement of stakeholders [...] implies more than simply identifying them and finding out what their claims, concerns and issues are. Each group is required to confront and take account of the inputs from other groups. It is not mandated that they accept the opinions and judgments of

others, of course, but it is required that they deal with points of difference or conflict, either reconstructing their own constructions sufficiently to accommodate the differences or devising meaningful arguments for why the others' propositions should not be entertained. [...] In this process a great deal of learning takes place.

Learning stands here for reconstruction, a process through which each entity gains a superior knowledge. This means coming 'to understand its own construction better, and to revise it in ways that make it more informed and sophisticated than it was prior to the evaluation experience' (Guba and Lincoln 1989: 56). It also requires becoming aware of others' constructions better than before. The same conceptual chains can be detected in those evaluative models and theories that mobilise labels such as deliberative, responsive, democratic, inclusive, emancipatory or transformative (Christie and Alkin 2008: 134–35; Stake 2004; Schwandt 2002; House and Howe 1999; Mertens 1999).

Notwithstanding the differences, in all cases the function of evaluation assumes a dual character: (a) giving a structure to and clarifying a system of meanings and (b) interpreting and discovering hidden meanings. Evaluation leads to a better understanding of a complex, uncertain and unpredictable situation and has the function to create an order or a shared vision/understanding, reducing difference and conflict. It offers the knowledge basis for making important changes. Both system thinking and constructivism create the opportunity for the emergence of a specific logic of learning through comparison, which is alternative and can interact with the evolutionary and hierarchical modes of ordering deriving from the transferences from biology and political economy. Both attribute themselves an *enlightenment function* (Weiss 1977), that is the role to illuminate and clarify what is actually going on and to enable a gradual development and diffusion of knowledge, creating debates and innovative thinking where new meanings replace old ones (Eisner 2003).

The study of language, sociology and educational evaluation as fields of concomitance

As Dahler-Larsen has observed, the ways in which evaluation is demanded, formatted and shaped in contemporary society, together with its paradoxes, can be understood if we relate evaluation to 'society' as one of the 'great principles of social order in modernity' (Dahler-Larsen 2012: 29). In fact, there are clear relations of articulation between the section of the tree of derivation presented in this chapter and some of the key concepts and conceptual chains which can be identified in the enunciative fields of system-oriented or constructivist sociological approaches.

Based on Dahler-Larsen (2012) and Foucault's archaeological analysis of the study of language in *The Order of Things* (2002a), here I deepen the analysis of the enunciative tree of derivation of educational evaluation showing how the regularities I have identified so far present significant points of analogy (and somehow enter in a complex play of difference) with the field of the study of language through the mediation of sociology.

Through a lateral rapprochement, I map a further field of coordination and subordination (Figure 6.1), showing how educational evaluation imports from systemic thinking, constructivism and the related enunciative series: (a) the problem of meaning; (b) the understanding of individual behaviours/conducts as signifying something and (c) the idea that everything the

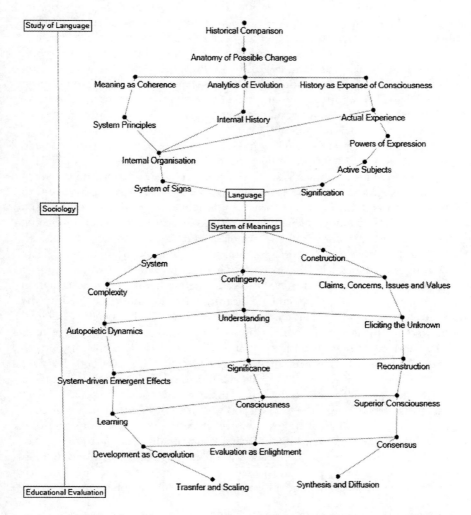

Figure 6.1 The study of language, sociology and educational evaluation as fields of concomitance.

individual arranges around him forms a coherent system of signification. I relate this to the epistemic figure of language as *grid of specification*, which in the field of educational evaluation makes it possible to think about the evaluand as historical *systems of meanings*.

In fact, all the evaluative approaches I have discussed in this chapter address the evaluand as an entity able to constitute a historically depth symbolic universe through language. Here, the evaluand is constituted as an entity or a subject that produces representations by means of which she carries on her activities and represents them to herself and others, establishing a relation to time, things and others (Foucault 2002a: 384–85). As such, these approaches oppose the techniques of comprehension to explanation, differing radically from those that mainly find their conditions of possibility in the transferences of the figures of living system or production. As it happens in the case of the study of language and cultural sociology, here educational evaluation becomes a knowing endeavour whose aim is to decipher a historical meaning on the basis of a signifying system, rather than to give an account of a historicised reality to be characterised in terms of conflict and its consequences, or function and its organs (ibid. 391).

Mirroring Chapters 4 and 5, I present two sets of *archaeological isotopias*, with the aim to show how some concepts occupy a similar position in the ramification of the enunciative fields of educational evaluation and the study of language via the mediation of sociology. A first set of isotopias relates to the formation of the evaluand, the establishment of the evaluative criteria and the nature of the empirical analysis. A second set concerns the developmental or consensus-building use of educational evaluation.

First, the pair signification/system occupies a symmetrical position. They delimit and characterise the space of what can be known about the object of analysis. It is possible to detect the idea that systems under examination (languages, societies or systems of meaning) are not unities formed by the simple combination of their elements, but are governed by specific principles that relate to the way in which those elements are connected. They have an internal organisation with its own principles, that differ from system to system. Despite the existing analogies with biology, the concept of system appears here in a different conceptual chain. It is synonymous of a situation, a border-less and self-referential set of relations which operate in a space where the distinction between the internal and external loses significance. The concept of signification identifies the scope of the analysis in the comprehension of individual behaviour, which in turn is conceptualised as an attempt to say something. As in the case of the analysis of language or society, both behaviours and involuntary mechanisms have a meaning on the projected surface of language/society/evaluand and, as such, constitute 'a coherent whole and a system' (ibid. 390).

Second, such a mode of conceiving the entities to be analysed has some important consequences that concern the ways in which entities can be characterised from within and distinguished from other entities. It implies the idea that each of them has its singularity, which derives from the distinctive internal principles that govern it. Thus, the singularity of a system can be defined on the basis of the regularities that can be detected in their governing principles. Systems cannot be ordered along a scale or a hierarchy and cannot, in particular, be the object of standard or competitive comparison.

Consistently, as it happens for the word in the modern study of language, value/significance is no longer constitutive of an entity in its very being or architecture. An entity is meaningful and valuable in so far as in its empirical manifestation, performing function and changes over time, 'it obeys a certain number of strict laws which regulate, in a similar way, all the other elements' of the same system (Foucault 2002a: 305). The value/significance of the evaluand derives from its belonging to a systemic organisation and its coherence within this totality. As the meaning of the word is determined by its belonging to a grammatical totality, the relation between the value of the evaluand and a social totality is 'primary, fundamental, and determining' (ibid. 306).

Third, the method to study the internal variations of systems constitutes a further area of archaeological isotopia. This understanding of the evaluand as systems opens the way for analytical strategies to study their internal variations that develop along three directions and are in analogy with the ways in which modern study of language addresses the analysis of language as totality (Foucault 2002a: 312): (a) the historical analysis of the evolution of systems, in order to identify changes, transformations and constants; (b) the analysis of the conditions that can determine a change in the system as a set of relationship and (c) a typological study of the internal principles which govern systems. In all the three fields, the combination of these three paths of analysis permits the identification of sets of relationships and historical paths which reveal a 'principle of evolution' that is internal to and distinctive of each system and somehow 'determines its fate' (ibid. 313).

Fourth, the anatomy of systems (languages, societies or systems if meanings) is 'an anatomy of possible changes', which outlines the potential for change or, to put it with Foucault (ibid. 320), the 'direction in which mutations will or will not be able to occur'. Systems have, then, a historicity that does not need the correlate of a history of the environment to emerge. On the contrary, systems reveal their historicity immediately, without intermediaries. In this respect, the study of language and system-oriented/constructivist evaluation establish for themselves the task to untie the relations between language/society/evaluand and external history 'in order to define an internal history' (ibid. 321).

Fifth, the transference of the figure of language/system of meanings creates the opportunity for the emergence of a specific logic of direct and lateral comparison, which in the enunciative field of educational evaluation coexists with the hierarchical and evolutionary modes of ordering deriving from the transferences from economy and biology. Accepting the principle of the irreducible heterogeneity of each system and the analytical need to study its proper anatomy and historical transformations have, in fact, important implications for what concerns the kind of comparison between systems that can be carried on. The typological analysis of the governing principles of a system, the study of the conditions that produce a change and the historical study of the system's transformations open up the possibility to identify forms of kinship between evaluands as systems. This allows the clustering of systems into groups which are discontinuous in relation to: (a) the types of principles that govern them; (b) the kind of interrelation between them; (c) the kind of conditions that determine a change or (d) the historical paths of change or principle of evolution. It is through such a kind of analysis that it becomes possible to compare or confront directly or laterally two systems without passing through a third term of comparison: what is sufficient is to study the typology of elements, their modifications and inflections. What emerges is a comparison between the entities/objects that is not based on the absence or presence of common elements but on the formal proximity, on the comparability of their internal structures and their evolutions. Again, as in the case of the transferences from political economy and biology, this epistemic figure allows the emergence of a logic of comparative evaluation that is intrinsically historical, in so far as it looks for similarities and differences in the modalities of systems' formation: evaluative empiricity is placed in the order of time (ibid. 319).

There is also a second set of isotopias where it is possible to observe similar chains of derivation between the enunciative fields. They relate to the characterisation of the knowing endeavour as analysis of actual experience with the aim to uncover an unthought. As in the case of modern study of language, societies or systems of meanings are established as rooted not in the materiality of the world, but in the active subject. As such they are the products of will and energy and express a profound will to something. As Foucault observes (ibid. 316), this discloses a paradoxical space of possibilities. If a system is defined through its belonging to a totality and its principled internal organisation, at the same time it is attributed profound powers of expression and is seen as the manifestation of the will of those who speak/act. This has some implications for the conceptualisation of the historicity of systems, whose mutations occur through a ceaseless and obscure human activity. This implication is mirrored by the centrality of the concept of actual experience (construction or complex system) in the three fields and its election as a privileged focus of analysis. Here actual experience indicates a set of entities concrete enough to be described, but also sufficiently removed from the positivity of things to become the object of an act of unveiling for a superior consciousness. As Foucault puts it (ibid. 350), the chain of derivation that links the concepts of language/system and those of signification/construction opens the way for further conceptual chains where what is at stake is the articulation of 'the possible history of a [cultural system] upon the semantic density which is both hidden and revealed in actual experience'. The space is disclosed to think of the knowing endeavour as the development of thought, an act of consciousness that is at the same time 'knowledge and a modification of what it knows, reflection and a transformation of the mode of being of that on which it reflects' (ibid. 357).

At the end of the chains, the objects of inquiry find themselves located within a paradoxical time made of discontinuity and continuity. On the one hand, they are systems, established as discontinuous entities that cannot be positioned within a continuum in time and space, compared through intermediary forms or reduced to one another. Here, 'signification is never primary and contemporaneous with itself, but always secondary and as it were derived in relation to a system that precedes it, constitutes its positive origin, and posits itself, little by little, in fragments and outlines through signification' (ibid. 394). On the other hand, objects of inquiry are processes of meaning production. Even if they are not brought to a consciousness, they can be given to a representation. They are linked up with one another within a fabric of significations where what is at stake is 'the continuous expanse of a discourse' (ibid. 392).

Conclusion

The analysis carried on in this chapter outlines a third archaeological quadrilateral (Figure 6.2). The quadrilateral visualises the relations of concomitance between the enunciative fields of educational evaluation, system-thinking

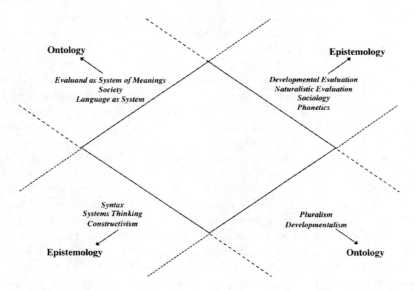

Figure 6.2 The archaeological quadrilateral of educational evaluation, sociology and the study of language.

and constructivist sociology and the study of language and shows how educational evaluation forms its objects, concepts and strategies through transferences from the latters.

The ontological formation of the evaluand through the transference of the figure of system of meanings as a grid of specification and complexity and construction as method of characterisation make it visible a contingent but patterned world. It functions and can be understood in terms of interrelations, autopoietic dynamics and emergent effects or socially constructed meanings to be elicited and reconstructed. Emergent effects can be mapped and recognised in order to generate learning and development. Reconstructions can be produced through dialogue in order to increase the level of consensus. In both cases, such a world is populated by active subjects, whose actual experience can and has to be made more and more transparent to consciousness. The time of educational entities is reframed as a dialectic history of syntheses, coevolutions and possible changes in the systems of meanings. Those changes can allow active subjects to win the struggle against uncertainty, unpredictability and the chaos of conflict. Evaluation as knowledge production on the significance of an entity plays here an enlightening function, becoming a key technique of an utopia: the race towards a superior consciousness to be reached through a dialectical analysis and a hermeneutic unveiling. This is a further shape assumed by the educational evaluation double I have already signalled in the previous chapters: whereas an empirical techne makes visible the anthropological finitude of the human being, or his perennial confrontation with uncertainty, unpredictability and risk, the utopia of development through superior consciousness promises a never-ending route towards a fulfilment (consensus through reconstruction or development through learning).

As it happens with the figure of living system or production, the formation of this specific space-time nexus is linked to the establishment of a particular kind of norm, which again acts as a basis for: (a) the judgement on the value/merit of the entities inhabiting such a space-time through their system and constructivist analysis and (b) the classification/management of the educational entities as entities to be supported and/or empowered in a process of self-development/synthesis through the acquisition of a superior consciousness of their own functioning, internal principles or diversity and the enlightenment of the possibilities for change.

An epistemological and governmental double emerges here in relation to educational evaluation as a governing tool to confront uncertainty and risk through a form of reflexive (self)-government. Here the primary locus on inquiry and intervention is not the educational process in itself, but the reflexive folding of the active subject on the process (Dean 2010: 205). Educational evaluation as empirical mode of characterisation of educational processes acts as a technique for the regulation, management and shaping of human conduct in service of a pluralist but developmental risk rationality (ibid. 207).

Although in a different form, evaluation becomes again functional to the promotion of autonomy, reflexivity and freedom to evaluate, manage and organise of responsible developmental entities. As it is the case of the study of language, system or constructivist evaluation act as possible points of integration between education as a moment of meaning production, the educational environment as an uncertain, unpredictable and potentially risky situation and finally the conduct of self-governing educational active subjects.

This is a further epistemic terrain where evaluation articulates itself to liberalism and neoliberalism as a technique to secure education 'in the face of processes that are deemed beyond governmental control' (ibid. 208). Will, choice, knowledgeability and development relate again to the 'metaphysic of individualism' (Olssen 2014: 217) I have discussed in the cases of the transferences from biology and political economy. In a more sophisticated way, evaluation turns again itself into an instrument of the (neo)liberal 'attempt to rationalize and justify a market society which […] organized on the principle of freedom of choice' (House 1978: 5). It stands as a social mechanism capable of rationally connecting the imperfect and fragmentary actors' knowledge in service of a developmental political and ethical project (see Hayek 1948).

There is an epistemological point of articulation here between the neoliberal adversity to scientism and epistemological preference for methods that 'constitute wholes by connecting together individual elements that can then take the form of a model' (Gane 2014: 1098) and the subjectivist epistemology of system thinking and constructivist evaluation. They share the assumption that the empirical world is so complex that human knowledge about it is, by definition, imperfect. They have in common the project of understanding how the independent action of multiple autonomous subjects 'can produce coherent wholes, persistent structures of relationships which serve important human purposes without having been designed for that end' (Hayek 1952: 141; quoted in Gane 2014: 1098). They adopt a subjectivist epistemology that starts from the sensory experience of actors and the interactions of individual efforts not to arrive to propositions that are 'true' (in the generalisable sense), but to identify what resources are at disposal or what is the relative importance of different needs, working through specific causal statements for a particular time and place (House 1978: 9). Finally, they substitute the problem of truth with that of coordination, significance, consensus and the like.

Also the relation between neoliberal politics and educational evaluation finds here a further point of connection. As a technique for self-government in risky and uncertain situations, in fact, evaluation offers itself as a viable governmental method that opposes itself to government through centralised planning or engineering based on scientifically detected objective facts. On the contrary, it provides a solution to those who argue against the integration of individual activities into an underlying social order and want to question any collectivist approach or form of 'intellectual government' under which 'only the competent scientists will be allowed to decide on the difficult social questions' (Hayek 1952: 168). This solution can be legitimated through the mobilisation of discursive powerful watchwords like reflexivity, autonomy, dialogue, self-determination, consensus and development.

Finally, on the terrain of ethics, two points can be remarked. First, evaluation assumes the role of a practice that shows how individual and collective entities are in line with moral expectations in society and adopt 'a reflexively modern mentality' (Dahler-Larsen 2012: 144). Evaluation becomes a tool for empowerment as self-determination and self-development through reflexivity. On the other hand, the *homo of evaluation* (HoE) is established again and through different pathways as a version of the liberal individual who is proprietor of her own capacities, fate and destiny. In a different fashion, it is possible to observe the re-emergence of the neoliberal project of autonomisation and responsibilisation of the individual chooser. In an ethical world characterised by local, qualitative knowledge and a plurality of criteria, viewpoints and forms of experience, rationalism, utilitarianism, developmentalism and technocracy coexist and enter in a relation of mutual reinforcement with dialogue, consensus and negotiated reconstruction of social constructions.

Chapter 7

Educational evaluation and its epistemic and political paradoxes

In this chapter I build on the previous archaeological analyses to locate educational evaluation within the epistemic space where it finds its conditions of possibility as a mode of inquiry, governmental practice and ethics. Moreover, I re-connect the archaeological terrain to the problem of government, showing how the configuration of this epistemic space produces political paradoxes and makes it possible to understand the complexities of the relationships between educational evaluation and a distinct set of political rationalities.

The *homo* of educational evaluation

In Chapters 4 to 6 I have discussed how educational evaluation constitutes itself as a differentiated enunciative field through the transference of the epistemic figures of living system, production and language from the fields of biology, political economy and the study of language, via organisational theory, management theory and sociology as concomitant fields. At the same time, the archaeological analysis has also highlighted how educational evaluation differs from those fields of concomitance, insofar as its ultimate objects of analysis are not modes of living, forms of production or systems of meanings in themselves. Rather, educational evaluation addresses education through those strata of conducts and behaviours within which education has already been given as effective, productive or significant to those who educate, are educated, think and govern education. Thus, educational evaluation elects as its object a particular kind of educational being, the HoE. My concern here is that such a being can be interpreted as a peculiar transposition of the figure of modern man, the figure that in *The Order of Things* Foucault locates at the heart of modernity (Foucault 2002a: 384).

The HoE entirely belongs to a form of educational life, is governed by a form of educational production and is surrounded by educational language. From within life, production and language it constitutes representations/evaluations and, through that, lives, satisfies its needs and represents to himself the sense of what it says and does. Finally, on this basis, he is capable to represent to himself precisely the value of that educational life, production and language (ibid. 384–85). The epistemic transferences from biology, political economy and the study of language constitute the grid of thought through which a being with the above characteristics (and its educational activity) offer himself to and is the subject of a possible evaluative knowledge.

If we take for good the archaeological analysis I have conducted so far, it is possible to locate the enunciative field of educational evaluation within an archaeological quadrilateral that delimits its epistemic conditions of possibility as a mode of inquiry, governmental practice and ethics (see Figure 7.1).

As object of inquiry and government, the HoE is constituted as a determined subject. His determination comes from positivities that are external and pre-existent to him. Those positivities relate to the nexus environment-organisation, the forms of production or the systems of meanings through which the HoE activity unfolds. He is a being living a condition of finitude, which in turn is the condition that makes any true knowledge about him and his activity to emerge. In educational evaluation his finitude takes the form of his (in)effectiveness, (under)performance or (un)consciousness.

Nevertheless, such a finitude is unstable. The HoE is also the reflexive subject of evaluation. This promises in the future the 'infinite capacity' which is denied to him in the present. In ontological terms, the HoE appears as a paradoxical figure of knowledge, a peculiar form of *empirical-transcendental doublet* (Foucault 2002a: 347), which is at the same time an externally determined object of knowledge (a being that can be appraised and as such governed), but also an unlimited knower, an agent who is able to know and control his fate (Dahler-Larsen 2012: 104). He can register all reality, collect data and

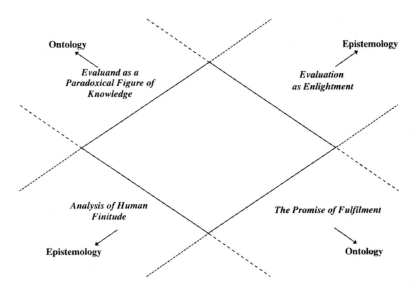

Figure 7.1 The epistemic quadrilateral of educational evaluation.

evidence, make interpretations, look for impact (by intervention, interaction and emergence) and seek social validations to be able to make warranted assertions (Bhola 2002: 390).

This creates an oscillation where what is given to evaluative experience is also what makes it possible. Educational evaluation presupposes an individual who acts according to the laws of educational life, production and significance, but who is also capable of an internal folding on itself, of knowing such laws and bring them to light. This ambiguous figure is simultaneously the object and the subject of evaluative knowledge and the subject who evaluates (Webb 2003: 8). As in the case of modern man, its designation is thus apparently imperious. He is provided with agency, he is the master of his destiny and he is the origin of any process of production and meaning. At the same time the HoE is 'a being who is already, in a necessarily subjacent density, in an irreducible anteriority, a living being, an instrument of production, a vehicle for words which exist before him' (Foucault 2002a: 341). If his existence finds a determination in life, production and language, as object of knowledge, he can be accessed only through its organisation, what he produces and the meanings he creates (Dahler-Larsen 2012: 101).

Relatedly, the epistemology of educational evaluation presupposes the existence of an unthought which needs and is waiting to be brought back to a *cogito* that is in the condition to unveil it. The process of valuing (worth, merit or significance) which underlies any process of educational evaluation consists exactly in an enlightenment process that is the unveiling of something which is unthought and hidden to the consciousness of the knower. Educational evaluation is a mode of inquiry that extends from what educational beings are in their positivity (their life, work and meanings) to what enables this same being to know what educational activity is, in what the essence of educational work and its laws consist and in what way it is able to produce significant meanings about education (see Foucault 2002a: 386).

Living system, form of production and system of meanings as grids of specifications connect the empirical positivities of the HoE to the forms of finitude that characterise his mode of being (Webb 2003: 8). In doing so, they create the conditions of possibility for evaluative knowledge and its inherent enlightening ambition. As categories, they make it possible to dissociate consciousness and representation and define the ways 'in which the empiricities can be given to representation but in a form that is not present to the consciousness' (Foucault 2002a: 395). At the same time, however, those categories designate the way in which the finitude of the HoE can be represented in a form which is positive and empirical but is not transparent to consciousness. What emerges here is a paradoxical trait of educational evaluation, as a mode of inquiry that treats of and produces representations, but at the same time attempts to shed light on an order of educational reality alternatively in terms of norms, rules or systems.

This paradoxical positioning of the HoE in relation to knowledge and fate is also paralleled looking at his historical ontology. He inhabits a developmental and teleological time, within which educational evaluation gains its sense of existence as a judgement on the value of an entity by the promise of improvement, the promise of a completion which can assume the forms of effectiveness, improvement, achievement, development, consensus and the like. Systems, forms of production and meanings undergo a continuous change. This creates the possibility, located in an undetermined future, for liberation from the limits imposed by the HoE finitude on himself. The HoE can evolve. Its finitude is outlined in the paradoxical form of the endless. It is limited, ineffective, unproductive and unconscious depending on the cases. However, educational evaluation with its search for value, worth, merit or significance and the related imperative of improvement, outlines not so much the rigour of limits, but rather the 'monotony of a journey which, though it probably has no end, is nevertheless perhaps not without hope' (Foucault 2002a: 342).

Notably, within this epistemic space, educational evaluation establishes a particular kind of relationship with history, which is fundamental to understand how its subjects and objects are constituted. In the previous chapters, I have already discussed to what extent the empiricities of evaluation are positioned in the order of time. But there is more. Educational evaluation cannot escape the movement of history. Its object is a historical being and it aims at defining 'synchronic sections' within the historicity of such a being. At the same time, the forms assumed by educational evaluation as a field of knowledge and a governing technology are historically determined. Here it comes another oscillation that entraps educational evaluation: the one between the temporal limits that define the particular forms of the objects to be evaluated and the historical positivity of the evaluating subject, 'which, by means of knowledge, gains access to them' (Foucault 2002a: 406). Evaluation is therefore caught in the paradox of a relativity that is impossible to escape, but that stands in itself as an absolute. In this light, it is possible to understand those processes of appropriation of its own objects according to the models of interpretation, comprehension or hermeneutics. They manifest the attempt to both unveil the hidden meanings of the HoE activities, and face the awareness that such an hermeneutic act will never be universal neither definitive. As in the case of the HoE finitude, this stands as another dangerous terrain that evaluation has to inhabit, a terrain where evaluation confronts with the perennial affirmation of its limits (Dahler-Larsen 2012: 226). In sum, the HoE enters the scene as both an evaluating subject and as an object that is evaluated. As evaluating subject, the HoE represents the very conditions of possibility of evaluation about the object HoE. In educational evaluation the transcendental and the empirical are not and cannot be so divided (Marshall 1996: 120). The problem of history for the HoE and educational evaluation becomes a matter of determining, 'according to the symbolic systems employed, according to the prescribed rules, according to the functional norms chosen and laid down, what sort of historical development each (HoE) is susceptible of' (Foucault 2002a: 411).

Epistemic and ethical paradoxes

The inhabiting of such an epistemic quadrilateral has some fundamental implications concerning the form that educational evaluation assumes as a rationality, techne and ethics. In particular, I argue that educational evaluation stands as: (a) a *paradoxical science of truth*, entrapped in a perennial oscillation between an ingenuous reduction of truth to the empirical and a prophetical promise; (b) a form of *modern ethic*, that does not formulate explicitly a morality of effectiveness, improvement or development, insofar as the imperative is located within the evaluative thought and its movement towards the apprehension of the unthought and (c) a *dialectical and teleological techne* that assumes (and is based on) a conception of time as fulfilment that can be known as a succession and has an inherently teleological nature.

Evaluation as a paradoxical science of truth

The first implication concerns the presumption that educational evaluation has to 'tell the truth' on the value of educational things, persons and activities. Such a truth has an ambiguous nature, which corresponds to a paradoxical face of educational evaluation. This seems transversal to apparently very different approaches to evaluation. In fact, the archaeological analysis has highlighted the coexistence in the epistemic space of educational evaluation of the positivist presumption to root the truth of the evaluative judgement into the empirical and the eschatological displacement of a truth that preexists the empirical and designs the paths of its future. Educational evaluation presents itself at the same time as empirical and critical (Webb 2003: 8). Through evaluation the HoE is simultaneously *reduced* to external positivities as a determined being and *promised* to a future of fulfilment, as a being capable to exceed his imperfection and reach a true state of completion somewhere in the future. Moved from the prophetical promise in the field of experience of a man of value, worth, merit or significance, educational evaluations represent acts of 'continuous support and threaten to existing institutions, policies, programs, and personnel [...] in the interface between science and politics' (Dahler-Larsen 2012: 14–15). They deliberately attempt to create an 'extra space for the new and different interpretations', attempting paradoxically to tell what is true about the evaluand and what the evaluand should desire and attempt to pursue. As such educational evaluation is a dangerous science of truth that intentionally creates a tension between 'objective' knowledge of facts and a regulated educational will. In this respect, educational evaluation as enlightenment stands as an impossible, as a particular kind of 'modern undertaking' (Schwandt 2002) that deliberately pursues 'a form of assisted sense-making as distinct as possible from what is believed to be the partisan, prejudicial, and unreflected viewpoints of everyday life' (Dahler-Larsen 2012: 13). In doing so, it statutorily produces a state of permanent insecurity and anxiety about facts, what one should expect from their enlightenment and the adequacy of what is being evaluated or assessed in relation to the ethical norm. Notably, it is this paradox that opens the way to the emergence of evaluative approaches that focus on the analysis of the actual experience, contesting both the reduction of truth to the empirical, and the eschatological promise of a future, but eventual attainment. Nevertheless, as discussed, those approaches find themselves to reproduce, in a different guise, the same paradoxical relation between truth, the empirical and the transcendental, articulating the possible history of a system of meanings upon the semantic density, which is both hidden and revealed in actual experience (Foucault 2002a: 350).

Educational evaluation as a face of the ethic of modernity

Educational evaluation has a clear ethical dimension and is inherently linked to the imperative of progress (Dahler-Larsen 2012: 100). Evaluative knowledge is established as naturally having the power to enlighten on the value of the evaluand. Further, it is conceived as naturally providing with the sufficient (and necessary) knowledge to improve that is to free the HoE from the empirically enlightened determinants of his being and action. As such, evaluation is intended to give the HoE the possibility to become something else. Here we find in the figure of educational evaluation a translation of what Foucault has called the 'modern ethic' (Foucault 2002a: 356), which in turn is again related to the appearance of the modern figure of man as an *empirical-transcendental doublet*. As modern man, in fact, the HoE is ethically determined by 'an imperative that haunts thought from within' where thought is called to be 'both knowledge and a modification of what it knows, reflection and a transformation of the mode of being of that on which it reflects' (Foucault 2002a: 357). Educational evaluation mobilises a logic of interrogation that problematises the educational being (Bouchet 2007: 7), leading to 'a whole series of questions concerned with being: What must I be, I who think and who am my thought, in order to be what I do not think, in order for my thought to be what I am not?' (Foucault 2002a: 354).

This is what creates the conditions of possibility for the apparent non-normative or value-free nature of educational evaluation. As a particular form of the modern ethic, it does not formulate explicitly a developmental morality. Its powerful and indisputable imperative is located within the evaluative thought and its movement 'towards the apprehension of the unthought' (Foucault 2002a: 357). Contents and forms of educational evaluation are those of making possible reflexivity, unveiling, consciousness, superior knowledge, the understanding of the hidden causes of imperfection and the facilitation of a new view of a practice that breaks with existing habits and convictions (Dahler-Larsen 2012: 14). In sum, educational evaluation is 'a mode of action' since its origins. It is inherently linked to the transformative ethic of modern thought and to politics with diverse value-orientations. Fundamentally, it is a form of thought that advances 'towards that region where man's Other must become the Same as himself' (Foucault 2002a: 358). Educational evaluation is about who we are and who we might become. It is profoundly rooted in a governmental paradox, being a practice of domination and production, of liberation and normalisation. Through it, the HoE is subjected to a norm and invited to produce his own identity, acquiring conscience and self-knowledge. Through it the HoE desires, hopes, self-esteem acquisitions, empowerment and awareness become artefacts of power (Ball 2012: 125).

Educational evaluation as dialectical and teleological

A third implication concerns the relation between educational evaluation and time. I have already discussed how the objects and subjects of evaluation are paradoxically placed in the order of time and history. Here I want to further develop this point, highlighting how educational evaluation, its transformative ethic and the related silent imperatives of effectiveness, improvement and significance assume and are based on a conception of *time as fulfilment*, that can be known as a succession and has an inherently teleological nature (Foucault 2002a: 371).

Educational evaluation is a frustrating form of rationality, techne and ethic that entraps the HoE in a never-ending struggle against his imperfection, attempting to distance a subject that it defines as determined and imperfect from his imperfection and promising him the possibility to reach a state of perfection. In addition to that, another constitutive trait of educational evaluation is its inherent dialectical mode of reasoning and its link to a dialectical scheme. Such a scheme reflects the HoE being in his finitude and moves towards a form of 'ever-to-be-accomplished unveiling of the Same' (ibid). As it happens for the whole modern thought, then, in educational evaluation:

> what is revealed at the foundation of the history of things and of the historicity proper to man is the distance creating a vacuum within the Same, it is the hiatus that disperses and regroups it at the two ends of itself. It is this profound spatiality that makes it possible for modern thought still to conceive of time – to know it as succession, to promise it to itself as fulfilment (Foucault 2002a: 371).

At the same time, the HoE as a determined and imperfect being can think what counts for himself as fulfilment only on the background of what already exists and has a proper, independent historicity. This is an educational time and space that is already institutionalised and dominated by a societal order that is external to him. At this point educational evaluation emerges as a dialectical and enlightening mode of knowing that attributes to itself the task to show how educational things and entities are generally given to representation, at what conditions and on what terrain, but also within what limits they can be enlightened and unveiled. In its different inflections, educational evaluation advances the presumption to be a *science of the 'unthought'* (Foucault 2002a: 367). Depending on the diverse approaches and the processes of translation from biology, political economy and the study of language, it has the objective to determine what historical development a subject or a social organisation is able to pursue, on the basis of the use of historically and socially determined symbolic systems, the establishment of rules or the choice of functional norms (Foucault 2002a: 412). As Dahler-Larsen (2012: 20) insightfully notes, if the ideal of evaluation is a responsive, reflexive, adaptable to change and learning-oriented subject, then 'what should one be after having been all these things?' Educational evaluation implies the production of an ethical paradox, that is the routinisation of the unusual and the making of an endless task. Relatedly it creates permanent insecurity and instability, the continuing imperative of accelerating evaluation and subsequent educational restructuring.

Political paradoxes

The fundamental articulation of educational evaluation on the figure of modern man, together with the related epistemic and ethical paradoxes, makes of it a chameleonic rationality, techne and ethics of government which is constantly at the centre of multiple tensions and attempts of co-option. As paradoxical science of truth and inflection of the modern ethic of action within a teleological and dialectical historical time of progress, educational evaluation assumes on the surface of the same historical ground many different faces, acting as a necessary, inevitable and indisputable instrument latched onto different political rationalities and the related purposive ethico-political and scientific action.

In particular, through the diverse articulations with the epistemic figures of living system, production and system of meanings, the HoE constitutes himself as a specific figure within the multiple rationalities of government and governmental practices of liberty that characterise contemporary advanced liberal democracies (Barry *et al.* 1996). The general point I want to make here is that, as a particular inflection of modern man in service of government in advanced liberal democracies, layer upon layer, the HoE is always the result of an unstable attempt 'to operate through and to adjust the competing demands of the social subject with its needs, the prudential subject with its responsibilities, the economic subject with its interests, [...] the juridical subject with its rights' and the reflexive subject with its capacity and will to know himself and master his fate (Dean 2010: 177). He always inhabits a realm made of ways of governing constituted by various assemblages of political rationalities, technologies and agencies. In different forms and with different emphasis, the HoE is constantly activated as agent, free chooser, consumer, professional stakeholder and, at the same time, monitored, calculated, controlled and reduced to a norm, standard or benchmark (O'Malley 1996). He is a free subject, but socially, institutionally or organisationally situated. His free choice is sovereign, but at the same time, he is object of evaluation. Importantly, he is at the centre of the main political paradox of contemporary advanced liberal democracies: the attempt to construct a world of autonomous and free subjects deploying multiple technologies that produce freedom through regulation and subjectification (Rose 1996: 33). In the rest of the chapter I attempt to show how, caught in this paradox, the HoE can alternatively assume different traits and emphasis, depending on the political rationality which attempts to co-opt him.

The homo of evaluation and liberalism

I have already discussed the direct link existing between evaluation and the foundations of modernity, the rise of the modern liberal state and the related problems of government, rationality and autonomy. I want to further enrich this argument, showing how some of the emergences of the HoE share key distinctive features with the liberal individual.

The current evaluative approaches, models and techniques where it is possible to observe the transferences from biology and political economy, in fact, are ontologically, culturally and methodologically individualist and share the biologising naturalism of liberalism (Olssen 2014: 217). As tools to make government more scientific (Vedung 2010), they assume a rational, autonomous and utilitarian individual who exists prior to society, in a uniform but evolutionary time and space. Such an individual is thought as a *homo economicus*, a unitary rational and free-choosing unit living in a market space. He belongs to a collection of independent 'centres of consciousness', each pursuing their own private goals and confronting others as alien objects, but bound by common interests (House 1978: 10). At the same time, the HoE is assumed to be a *responsible, disciplined and prudential subject* (Dean 2010: 137), who should be governed and should self-govern himself as a calculative and responsible individual, being enmeshed within an unstable relation with his environment, and living a perennial disequilibrium between his needs and the possibilities to fulfil them with the existing resources (an ontology of scarcity).

As the liberal individual, the HoE is affected by environmental factors, but his derivation and development is determined by internally shaped drives. Development is assumed to be a consequence of inner mechanisms and capacities that are logically distinct from social processes. As in the case of liberalism, the individuals of evaluation are conceived as the bearers of an array of problematic conducts and capacities. On the ethical ground, the HoE is committed to maximise a state of mind like satisfaction and, in doing so, to pursue progress against external threats through scientific knowledge. Progress is, for such an individual, the single standard of social utility against which to compare things and conducts. Through evaluation, he attempts to master nature and the social order, maximising happiness and guaranteeing to himself welfare against the threats of life and market. Evaluation is functional to the production of individuals who will govern and care for themselves, that is of free individuals committed to make the most of their own existence by conducting their life responsibly and searching for enlightenment, in a situation where social institutions act as misleading forces.

The political duality of the liberal individual as a normalised subject and a citizen with rights and liberties is paralleled by the dual character of the HoE as object and subject of evaluative knowledge. In fact, in the evaluative rationality, the individual is the primary locus and actor of the evaluation-based government, whose intrinsic rational capacity must serve as the regulating principle of the rationality of government. In the evaluative approaches and techniques based on means–ends rationality, the HoE has subjective goals, but the means to reach those goals are ascertained in an objective/scientific way (Vedung 2010: 275). As the liberal individual, the HoE is a subject who constantly monitors and evaluates his own and others' conduct, according to an objective epistemology. In a frame bounded by rationalism and instrumentalism, he is in search of truth through scientific methods, experimentation and the discovery of causal connections and general laws within a linear time made of antecedent conditions and consequences. At the same time, he recognises the authority of the evaluative expertise and the related expert figures, entitled to deploy a range of scientific and technical knowledge that allow the exercise of rule over time and space. In both the cases, evaluation stands as a diagnostic and engineering mode of inquiry, whose function is to render possible specific modes of government, making up as intelligible, delimited, calculable and practicable their domain of objects. Evaluative information has the pretension to establish itself as scientifically objective. Objectivity is achieved by using preferably measuring and experimental methods that allow a calculative and inductive reasoning and a temporally linear cause-effect and means-end representation of the world (Gane 2014).

In this respect, educational evaluation as form of expertise and a utilitarian mode of regulation is a correlative of liberal freedom. As a paradoxical science of truth, it offers a positive knowledge of a problematic human conduct and provides the true basis for its management (Deere 2014: 519). Given its diagnostic power, it stands as the privileged way to disclose for external scrutiny the inner worlds of human conduct and render it controllable. It rationalises and justifies a market society organised on the principle of freedom of choice. As a face of the ethic of modernity, it provides to liberalism and the liberal individual a rational and utilitarian mode of self-regulation, which is compatible with the liberal principle that action is to be direct action by the individuals and groups concerned and not action by the government. Thus, educational evaluation assumes the character of an effective governmental technique in *the constitution of society as a governable domain*, through the administration of life at a distance. It offers a scientific method to understand what is the right thing to do, translating into a mode of action the liberal dissatisfaction with government. But it also offers a kind of knowledge that renders judgeable modes of government in themselves.

In this respect, educational evaluation stands as a valuable liberal pedagogical machine for governing, leading and controlling individuals (Lemke 2007), and makes them autonomous and responsible subjects that constantly think about, calculate about, predict and judge their own activities and those of others. In parallel with the political duality of the liberal individual, evaluation is a form of intervention which is compatible with the rights and liberties of the individuals, and which allows the aggregation of their diverse interests. At the same time, it is a way to shape liberty and ensure that the individual exercises freedom responsibly. In doing so it is also a key governmental technique for the maintenance of security (Dean 2010: 146).

Finally, the teleological and dialectical character of educational evaluation assumes, in the marriage with liberalism, the shape of the promise of a future of satisfaction and happiness for the liberal rational free-chooser and maximiser, within an ethical frame where maximising happiness is the 'right' thing to do (House 1978). In doing so, it contributes to settle the norms of good government. In particular, educational evaluation attempts 'to establish norms of government derived from the [educational] population in its concrete [living, economic and cultural] relations with the processes that will lead to the production of the resources necessary for its sustenance and prosperity' and use these norms 'to criticise earlier forms of detailed regulation' and create optimal conditions for life (Dean 2010: 144).

The homo of evaluation and welfare state liberalism

Nevertheless, when co-opted within a liberal political rationality, the HoE as empirical-transcendental doublet is not only the rational, utilitarian and autonomous chooser. This is a subjectivity which is one relative moment of a double which relates to the opposition between classical liberalism and welfare state liberalism (House 1978). As I have highlighted in the case of transferences from biology and political economy, the HoE inhabits an environment whose shape shifts constantly from market to society, and vice versa. This space is thought along the opposition between conflict and consensus. When co-opted within a welfare state liberal rationality, the HoE alternatively becomes the economic subject of rational choice and an individual acting within a society, that is a culturally thick space (Dean 2010: 147). Society stands here for a natural-historical space where the problems of the exercise of economic rational choice co-exist and combine with those arising from the institutional and political character of social life (Foucault 2008: 299), and in particular with the problem of order. The mutual processes of co-option between educational evaluation and welfare state liberalism find their conditions of possibility exactly in these analogies between the *homines* they assume, as two relative moments of a double. The HoE has the potential to turn himself into a peculiar version of the liberal individual, which is at the same time an economic rational chooser living in a market and a *homo sociologicus*, a norm-following and role-playing actor who has social needs and whose actions can be explained and governed through collective norms and rules which express a social 'ought' (Reckwitz 2002: 246). The world of the *homo sociologicus* 'is first and foremost a system of normative rules and expectations, to which agents/actors as rule-following figures conform (or become 'deviant')' (Reckwitz 2002: 256). He has an ethics of duties. Cultural aspects, styles of conduct, organisational forms and relationships are identified as a new grid of intelligibility within which the success and failure of the HoE could be located (Ball 2012: 91). The lack of discipline and aspiration are identified as two key elements explaining failure. What is established is 'a sociological norm' that operates through the 'interplay of measurement and morality' (Ball 2012: 92). This is a mode of thought that results in a new iteration of performance measurement, with the educational subjects becoming 'objects of knowledge and subjects of intervention' (Ball 2012: 98).

Through this double, the liberal *homo economicus* is located in a social whole and becomes manageable. Here the principle of utility requires that the government takes strong action, in order to find out what works, but respecting the inviolability of the private sphere. Within this problematic, evaluation becomes one of the multiple means to intervene into the individual sphere through the building of a normative consensus, implanting in the individuals the aspiration to pursue their own educational and professional welfare and advancement (Rose 1996: 40). The HoE is a figure emerging within the historical process of formation of a vocabulary to translate the particular into the general, and to locate 'the juridical subject of right and responsibility, as but one region within the wider [...] evolution of society' (Dean 2010: 153). This guarantees social order against the threats of conflict. Within welfare state liberalism, educational evaluation plays the role of 'a dialogical partner' for liberalism in education and its process of self-review and self-renewal on the basis of the recognition of the rational and autonomous (economic) subject's finitude (Dean 2010: 152).

The homo of evaluation and neoliberalism

I have already discussed the processes of co-option that is possible to recognise in the contemporary global scenario between educational evaluation and the neoliberal project to rewrite the state as a market-maker and produce enterprising and entrepreneurial individuals (Peters 2001; Carlson 2009). Again, the terrain of the encounter between the two can be identified, primarily in the analogies of the kind of subjectivity they produce. Whereas in the case of liberalism and welfare state liberalism, the HoE encounters the *homo economicus* as a naturally free and autonomous, but externally determined and empirically knowable subject, in the case of neoliberalism it is another face of the *empirical-transcendental doublet* which is emphasised and constitutes the initial point of articulation. The HoE, as unlimited knower, meets with the neoliberal *homo economicus* as the free and enterprising individual (I refer here mainly to Hayek conception of the *homo economicus* – 1979) on the ground of the political problem of man's imperfection and irrationality. This is a problem shared by both neoliberalism and educational evaluation: 'how to govern through the autonomy of the governed when they are no longer virtuous' (Dean 2010: 190). The HoE and the neoliberal *homo economicus* are both autonomous actors, capable of strategic conduct and association, and as such they are the source of energy for any societal function, as in the case of education. They are again both free choosers. Nevertheless, the choice of the HoE, as in the case of the neoliberal *homo economicus*, assumes the form of a human faculty/behaviour that can be manipulated through a governmentality which intervenes on the space within which choice is exercised (Foucault 2008: 270). Thus, in such a perspective, the conditions for freedom or completion cannot be found in humankind *in se*, but rather have to be created. Both the HoE and the neoliberal *homo economicus* have to be facilitated and cultivated, or better crafted and valued as self-actualising subjects. But they are limited, and this is the distinctive point of neoliberalism and neoliberal evaluation. As the HoE is a subject always hunted by the risk to fail (in terms of adaptiveness, production and consciousness), the *homo economicus* is the subject that needs to be taught how to behave as free, enterprising, active and agile (Miller and Rose 2008: 39).

Thus, as the main character of a modern ethic of action based on the search for a true knowledge on the forms of finitude, the HoE becomes a central figure in the neoliberal project and its attempt to shift the problem of government in education from the security of the educational processes to the security of the governmental mechanisms of education in themselves (Dean 2010: 180). When co-opted within a neoliberal rationality, evaluation becomes the driver of a cultural transformation (or evolution in Hayek's terms) that attempts to overcome the sociological problematic of the fragile order and work through the will and voluntary associations of responsible and autonomous free subjects. The HoE becomes one of the many faces of the neoliberal *homo economicus*, and vice versa. Learning is a key point of articulation between the two (Simons 2002: 260). Within the neoliberal project, educational evaluation stands as the privileged governmental means to select rules of conduct that will help individuals and groups to adapt to their educational environment and develop. The cultural evolution of the neoliberal *homo economicus* is fundamentally an ongoing learning process which, as in the case of evaluation, is rooted in the apprehension of the dynamics of the 'spontaneous social orders' of life, market, production or language (Dean 2010: 183). For the neoliberal *homo economicus*, evaluation becomes a moral imperative and a key instrument of an institutional framework aimed at recognising the rules of just conduct from the process of cultural evolution and reinforcing them. It is a form of self-discipline that makes of the individual a subject of reason through learning. The cultural project of evaluation to make of the individual learner an evaluator of himself/the others becomes here part of the neoliberal project to make of the individual an entrepreneur of himself, who acquires the skills to apprehend his economic finitude and tries to overcome it through the ethos of enterprise. In sum, the encounter between evaluation (and its apparently pluralist emphasis) and neoliberalism flourishes in the space opened by neoliberal mistrust in central planning and its assumption that 'the spontaneous order of the market can only properly operate if individuals are free in the sense that they are permitted to use their knowledge for their own purposes (Hayek 1976: 8)' (Dean 2010: 186).

The homo of evaluation and risk rationality

In advanced liberal democracies the HoE finds a space of emergence and further characterisation as epistemic figure also within the 'polymorphous rationality of risk' (Dean 2010: 202). In particular, risk rationality encounters neoliberalism and complexity or constructivist oriented evaluation models on the common ground of the opposition to government through centralised planning or engineering based on scientifically detected objective facts, and the emphasis posed on the paradoxical figure of the autonomous agent to be culturally reformed. The HoE stands here as the reflexive modern subject who confront with an uncertain and unpredictable world and, given this form of ontological determination, attempts and is asked to regain control against individualised, desocialised and privatised risk, uncertainty and unpredictability. As I have discussed in the case of the transference of the figure of system of meaning, complexity, uncertainty and all the connected risk vocabulary play a role in the enunciative field of educational evaluation as drivers for the ontological characterisation of the HoE as a human being permanently facing/concerned with risks in his various educational activities (learning, teaching, managing, administering, governing and so on). Those risks are related to the effects and the side-effects of human action (another individualising version of man's finitude and imperfection), which constantly create problems, often in changing and surprising forms (Dahler-Larsen 2012: 123). The HoE finitude takes the form of its vulnerability.

Yet, risks are multiple and polymorphous and require different forms of intervention. They can be related to observable empirical events or to hidden and invisible correlations. The HoE has to confront with risks that can assume the form of rates of ineffectiveness and unproductivity within a given population that are subject to calculation and, through evaluation, can be screened, pre-detected and intervened on to minimise future occurrence (Castel 1991). He can also be thought as facing with symptoms that indicate/predict an imminent danger (Dean 2010: 218). Here evaluation becomes the observational formulation of a judgement on the value of individuals and groups, in order to identify their falling into a risk-category (underperforming, ineffective, unproductive and the like). It acts as a functional knowing endeavour which is propaedeutic to therapeutic and disciplinary practices of improvement, development and capacity building. Within this discursive construction, educational evaluation as the necessary, but also ritualistic endeavour of the reflexive modern subject finds its condition of possibility in the need to avoid, minimise, counterbalance, manage and allocate an unavoidable risk of failure, ineffectiveness or underperformance. The ineffectiveness of the HoE is the manifestation of a level of risk and it must be prevented or eliminated before it manifests itself.

Again, development and improvement become social necessities and an ethical and practical imperative. As Dahler-Larsen (2012: 124) observes, educational evaluation can be considered as one of the forms in which reflexive modernisation turns 'the modern desire for constant improvement' against modern institutions, organisations and primarily individuals. Yet, risk and vulnerability never vanishes, they can be minimised but never completely eliminated.

The distinctive trait of this further inflection of the HoE-at-risk is that he becomes a central figure within a governmental project that, with Dean (2010: 202), it is possible to call a *reflexive government of performance*. Individual and collective action is stimulated and mobilised in order to make of it a field of intervention, calculation, comparison and optimisation. Here the problem of security becomes that of 'constructing centres of agency and activity, of making them durable, and of implanting continuous relations of authority' through discrete and indirect control at a distance (Dean 2010: 202). The fallibility of the HoE-at-risk and his perennial confrontation with danger act as stimulus rather than impediment. The empirical discovery of the HoE transcendental fallibility functions as an incitement to continuous action, cultural reformation, therapeutic intervention, development and improvement (Miller and Rose 1990). Educational evaluation establishes itself as a powerful governmental technique in a scenario of 'new prudentialism' (Dean 2010: 194), a form of government based on the responsibilisation of the HoE for his own risks of poor educational performance or ineffectiveness within competitive environments.

A reflexive government of performance

Educational evaluation constitutes something like a milieu of life, existence and work for ourselves as educational subjects. It is a practice of production and calculation, an act of confession and instrumentalism, a remoralisation of our relations to the state, to ourselves, to the others and to our future (Ball 2012: 132). There is no space or time which is not evaluated. We are all asked to think, behave and feel like the HoE. And yet there is some 'schizophrenia' in the polymorphous demands bearing on us as educational subjects. We are asked to think about ourselves and act as: (a) economic actors naturally free to pursue our interests; (b) socialised actors who are asked to follow norms and play roles to guarantee individual and collective welfare and (c) malleable substances willing to self-constitute themselves as entrepreneurial, responsible, autonomous and prudential subjects according to modalities established through technologies of indirect regulation. We are caught in the paradoxical attempt to construct a world of autonomous and responsible subjects through the deployment of technologies that produce freedom through regulation and subjectification.

The archaeological analysis carried on so far shows how educational evaluation can be intended as a complete and peculiar form of government, whose object is the educational individual and whose intervention is 'totalitarian' insofar as it attends to every aspect of educational lives which concerns happiness, needs satisfaction, self-realisation and significance. It establishes a particular object for the art of government, the 'evaluand', understood as 'a live, active, productive man' (Foucault 1988: 79). Through a reconceptualisation of life and continuous pedagogic reformation, a productive and flexible population is produced, with a commitment to endless learning and de-learning (Ball 2012: 133).

However, as I have discussed throughout the chapter, educational evaluation participates in a paradoxical modernist ontology that both establishes and excludes the possibility that the living, productive and active individual could be understood in terms of the externality of the structures of the social world. Through educational evaluation, the security of education as a domain external to government is made possible. Categories and classificatory systems are inscribed in the practices and organisational structures of educational daily life. Concepts like performance, production, results, merit, worth, effectiveness, efficiency, comparison and the like are deeply implicated in producing the very reality that they claimed to evaluate. Hence educational evaluation acts as a 'way of organising the [educational] world, and in doing so it positions people in relation to the categories and classifications it constructs' (Olssen 1993: 165). It determines a segment, concentrates, focuses and encloses, isolating a space in which the mechanisms of its power can function.

At the same time, educational evaluation stands as a central pillar of a mode of government which is reflexive, folds on itself and makes of the instrument of government themselves a governmental domain (Dean 2010: 201). In its multiple and possible political inflections, the HoE as a limited but promethean *empirical-transcendental doublet* is a key figure in reflexive educational government, that is in a project of educational transformation through the government of the mechanisms, techniques and agencies of educational government. The rationale for the contemporary reflexive government in the field of education and the centrality assumed by educational evaluation lies in the idea that education itself can be changed 'no longer via a conscious design based on the rational knowledge of social processes but through the transformation of the mechanisms by which it had previously been governed' or to put it another way, 'a knowledge and indirect regulation of the conducts of individuals and groups' (Dean 2010: 226–27).

Within these dynamics the HoE is caught as a central subject of two distinct technologies of government in contemporary advanced liberal societies. Through contemporary models and techniques of educational evaluation, education is no longer 'inscribed within a centralised and coordinating state', but rather it is 'reconfigured as a set of constructed markets in service provision and expertise, made operable through heterogeneous technologies of agency and rendered calculable by technologies of performance' whose function is to govern at a distance (Dean 2010: 223). On the one hand, educational evaluation stands as a set of techniques to govern through indigenous mechanisms of government, the active participation of individual HoEs and primarily the aspirations and choices of individuals and groups. It enhances and deploys possibilities of agency. It constructs local sites of self-government that can be indirectly managed through the logic of contractualism or modalities of intervention that culturally shape individuals as active, informed or self-governing educational subjects able to confront their finitude and overcome or minimise it. On the other hand, through educational evaluation, the government of educational processes is being displaced by the governmental mechanisms through performance criteria that regulate educational subjects and their educational activities. In a cultural milieu of distrust, educational expertise enclosures are blurred and subsumed by performance-oriented calculative regimes (Rose and Miller 1992). This is a cascade-process that occurs at the different scales of educational life. Educational security becomes a problem of securing system, policy, program and school evaluation, self-evaluation, monitoring, staff appraisal and students assessment and makes all these processes functional to the cultural reformation of individual and institutional conduct and an endless race towards the gaining of competitive advantage within a zero-sum competitive game.

The HoE is a figure suspended in a perennial oscillation between the poles of a fluid continuum between the active subject, which is master of his destiny and capable to maximise his welfare or minimise his own risks, and the target subject who requires to be controlled, managed, culturally reformed, educated or secured, preferably in a preventive form. It is caught in a politics of education that rests upon the production of a permanent state of insecurity and inequality. Inequality is the basis for striving and competition. Insecurity is the basis for responsibility – for our own well-being, adaptiveness, productivity of effectiveness and capacity to deal with risk – and enterprise, intended as a permanent and anxious mobilisation and activation to reach success, to protect from risk and insecurity, calculating and measuring ourselves in relation to an uncertain and risky future. As Ball (2012: 139) argues, 'collective conditions of experience' are rendered 'into personal problems' and 'political and economic decisions' are displaced 'into individual failings and responsibilities'.

Chapter 8

Epistemological ruptures and the invention of other evaluations in education

This book is not an apology for radical freedom, neither it promises a once and for all liberation from educational evaluation and its tyranny. I entirely take here Foucault's point that freedom is never ethical if it is thought and lived as the effect of the erasure of codes and the displacement of the interdictions and restrictions (Foucault 1994: 674). Thus, to think about the possibility of not being evaluated (as part of the activity of government) would represent a theoretical and philosophical paroxysm. Relatedly, my aim here is not an attempt to fix once and for all a substantive critique of this or that evaluative theory, epistemological underpinning, technology or more or less desirable or perverse effect, or to propose an alternative set of evaluative principles or how-to-do methodologies. Rather, the book aims at proposing an exemplary experiment of reasoning. The strength and emancipatory capacity of this kind of reasoning lie in the theoretical and analytical attitude and the ethical effects it produces. To quote Faubion (1998: xv), this experiment of reasoning has been a projection on educational evaluation of an affirmative 'critique of the strictures, the exclusions, and the [paradoxes] of what [Foucault] often calls "humanism" – the doctrine that, behind history or beyond it, looms the singular nature or the singular essence of the human subject'. The aim of such an exercise of practical critique was to produce and mobilise concepts to multiply possibilities of analysis and, ultimately, possibilities of crossing over [*franchissement*]' (Foucault 1997a: 315) for public thinking and acting in the present-ness of educational evaluation. As Dean (2010: 14) argues, there are 'a multiplicity of presents, and a multiplicity of who we are in them' and this relates also to educational evaluation. In this respect, this attempt of conceptual production and mobilisation has the aim to make the present-ness of educational evaluation open and revisable. As analytics of the conditions for truth, the archaeological analysis was intended to make intelligible the limits and potentials of who we are and how we have become subjects and objects of educational evaluation, and to make possible modifications of the 'pre-existing relation linking will, authority, and the use of reason' (Foucault 1997a: 305). It was thus preparatory for a critical ontology of ourselves as an ethical experience, as a labour on the paradoxical intertwining between evaluative government and liberation. With experience, I intend a practice which is capable of introducing a vertical cut in the horizontal quiet of time, of the present as repetition of antecedent events (Foucault 2006: xxix). Importantly, there is an intimate relation between our capacity to critically understand how we are made subjects and governed through forms of knowledge which stands to us as truths assumed by authoritative voices, and our potentials in experimenting ways to govern ourselves and the others differently, accepting, transgressing or rejecting the limits imposed on ourselves.

Epistemological ruptures: Space, time and norm

Throughout the book, I have discussed what appear to be the archaeological conditions of possibility for the emergence across political, academic and public arenas of discursive struggle of that set of dispersed and heterogeneous political and scientific statements that constitute the enunciative field of educational evaluation.

I have identified these conditions of possibility in a specific set of epistemic processes of transference from biology, political economy and the study of language. Moving from that, the archaeological analysis pointed out how a peculiar figure of the modern *homo*, whose nature is inherently ambiguous and paradoxical, has made educational evaluation thinkable as a mode of inquiry and as a practice of government. I have discussed the traits of this *Homo of Evaluation* (HoE), a man that is fallible and socially determined, but also a reflexive knower. The HoE stands in a paradoxical relation with its powers of knowing and acting, and is forced to an ethic of action that is inherently linked to the mission of Enlightenment and the promise of ever to be accomplished fulfilment. The characterisation of the HoE as empirical-transcendental doublet seems to be the condition and the common epistemic ground for most of the dualisms and oppositions that characterise educational evaluation as enunciative field. This common ground produces most of the paradoxical oscillations in educational evaluation: between quantitative and qualitative, positivist and phenomenological, explanation and comprehension, rationalistic and naturalistic and reductionist and holistic. I have also shown how the HoE is a chameleonic figure, which is potentially and actually co-opted and enrolled by different and somehow conflicting political rationalities and governmental projects.

Now, it is legitimate to raise the always dangerous and challenging 'so what' question. The archaeological analysis leaves us with a different understanding of the epistemic relations through which educational evaluation constitutes itself as an enunciative field. But to what extent it offers us the possibility to think otherwise educational evaluation? The legitimate question would be how to avoid the shortcuts, reductionisms, paradoxes and frustrations that educational evaluation produces in the scholarly debate, in the professional world and more generally in the policy and public debate. A first reasonable answer could point out to the enemy of reductionism and causal thinking. This is for sure a tough argument and is a key part of the answer. As Love (2002) puts it:

> Saying 'yes' to the fullness of the human means pronouncing a resolute 'no' to each of the various form of reductionism, which would constrict or deny the reality of human freedom. The most obvious instance of such reductionism is the scientific positivism, the advocate of a narrow empiricism; but the reductionist label applies to any method who seeks to explain away the fullness of our experience by dismissing that experience as 'nothing but' the effect of this or that underlying cause. (p. viii)

Nevertheless, this is not the full answer, if a full answer could ever be offered. Besides, most of the phenomenological explorations in the field of evaluation have frequently faced the same paradoxes as described in Chapter 7.

The archaeological analysis invites us to focus on a different stratum of the conditions of possibility for educational evaluation as a mode of inquiry and a technology of government. It pushes us to think within the interstices of the empirical/transcendental paradox, exploring the possibilities opened by the deconstruction of the quadrilateral of the HoE (Figure 7.1). This means to challenge the paradoxical figure of HoE as it is assumed by educational evaluation: an evaluand that is limited and fallible, but forced to aspire to a fulfilment; totally determined, but forced to forge his destiny and entrapped in a teleological dialectic, limited in his knowing capacity, but in the need to aspire to a truth which is external to him and can be reached through the techne of the empirical (being it positivist or interpretative).

Challenging the paradoxical figure of HoE discloses in front of us a distinct set of experimental spaces. The first one is probably the most obvious and less problematic. We should attempt to challenge the contours of the epistemic space of knowledge within which educational evaluation finds its conditions of possibility and structures itself through a confrontation (a mutual nurturing) between a historicity that promises a potentially never-ending progress through value production and an anthropology that affirms the finitude and limitation of the HoE in relation to his capacity to produce value. What one should free the HoE from is the *utopia of fulfilment* that obsesses educational evaluation.

I would suggest the need to question the aspirations of educational evaluation to produce an educational change that is directional and appraisable, being located in a stabilised space and a time sequence. The idea is to reinforce those evaluative paths 'that have recently resisted the hegemonic pressures of the evidence-based epistemology and pay close attention to the potentials involved in the practising of those epistemological ruptures that revise the rules in which we understand educational reality and by which we think about educational change and progress' (Grimaldi 2015: 53). With Popkewitz (1997: 23–24), one could summarise as follows the epistemological ruptures implied by such a questioning:

- rethinking the spatial dimension in the practice of educational evaluation, focusing on the construction of identities through the formation of social spaces;
- thinking of time as a multiplicity of strands moving with an uneven flow, understanding change as ruptures or breaks and looking at continuities as conditional and relational;
- escaping from the enduring evolutionary principle that, implicitly or explicitly, continues to inform educational evaluation and results in the centrality of the logic of comparison and the tendency to create differentiation drawing on 'some norms of unity' (Popkewitz 1997: 25).

Such an evaluative questioning implies to acknowledge that educational reality 'happens in sequences of actions located within constraining or enabling structures' and it is a matter of particular educational subjects/actors, in particular educational places, at particular educational times (Abbott 2001: 183).

Space and a politics of educational evaluation beyond subjects

The first epistemological rupture consists of an invitation for educational evaluation to refocus itself on the 'rules and standards of reason' through which subjects are formed and valued through their locations within 'historicizing [educational] spaces in a variegated [educational] time frame' (Popkewitz 1997: 23). This implies to fully embrace a relational view of space and, relatedly, a relational politics of the spatial in education (Massey 2005: 147). The adoption of such a politics invites to interrogate the working of space and subjectivity in the mundane functioning of the everyday of schooling and the production of educational value. Such a politics of evaluation would fully assume that educational entities, identities and values are collectively produced through practices which form relations. It would focus on those relations, questioning: (a) the places from which the educational subjects speak, act and judge; (b) the construction of the educational objects that shape their practice and pursuit of knowledge and (c) the emergence of the concepts that structure the educational subject's speech and action, and define their value.

In such a perspective, human beings are understood as heterogeneous and situationally emerging within assemblages of meanings, representations, practices and subjectivation. The HoE, as portrayed in Chapter 7, dissolves into the amalgam of the education assemblage (Hunter 1996), which is machinic, strategic and overcoded with meaning. He/she is conceived as resulting from the coming together of trajectories of 'economy and politics, policy, organizational arrangements, knowledge, subjectivity, pedagogy, everyday practices, and feelings' (Youdell and Armstrong 2011: 145) in a materially and discursively situated location.

Educational evaluation then becomes not an endeavour to discover and disclose the true value of individuated educational entities (a demonstrative and self-evident value). Rather it reframes the judgement on educational value, restoring the status of value as events (Deere 2014: 526), that is 'incorporeal entities expressed in language but attributed to configurations of bodies in the transition from one state of affairs to another' (Patton 2014: 106). In this perspective, value as event can be understood as singular and fortuitous appearances of truths on educational value that could only have arisen given the confluence of particular knowledge and power relations (Gilson 2014: 144). As such, those truths can be arranged and followed in their lineages, series and effects. This means to examine the shifting assumptions of educational value, worth and merit, the enacted practical technologies of educational government, the changes in systems of recognition and objects examined and the ways in which people are 'invited' to recognise themselves and their practices as 'of value' (Popkewitz 1997: 23).

This 'eventalisation' (Dean 1994: 41) of educational evaluation is 'paired with a disruption of the conventional understanding of causal relations' and pursues 'a shift from thinking of causality as a linear relation between cause and effect' (Gilson 2014: 144). In this view, educational value is not 'capturable as a slice through time in the sense of an essential section', it is not something 'intrinsically coherent' (Massey 2005: 141). Instead, evaluation as an act of knowing challenges education's continuous teleological development, the unity of the educational knowing subject, the objectivity of evaluative analysis conducted by that educational subject and the fixity of stable categories of evaluative analysis.

As knowing endeavour, an educational evaluation inspired by a relational politics of the spatial in education attempts to open the possibilities and locate the points for constructing otherwise the rules of the game of truth within which the evaluand emerges as a particular kind of valuable entity. Evaluation practice stands as a moment and site of possibility when and where the education assemblage and its material and discursive situatedness might be challenged, interrogating educational practice in order to scrutiny not so much 'who tells the truth' but rather 'the rules on which that truth is based and the conditions in which that truth is told' (Popkewitz 1997: 27).

More positively, the point of such a perspective is to make educational evaluation becoming a way to engage in a performative politics of reinscription (Butler 1997), interrogating (a) the ways in which educational subjects are constituted through social spaces and (b) the ways in which educational subjects are unsettled both through the practices of subjectivated subjects and through relations of power. It would be a practice of denaturalisation and negotiation of the spaces in which educational individuals are placed (Massey 2005: 141), that makes 'the rules for telling the truth contingent, historical, and susceptible to critique' and disturbs 'the narratives of progress and reconciliation' (Popkewitz 1997: 26). As a practice of resignification, it would not focus on the individual subject, but foreground multiplicity, collectivities and the event, making possible 'the emergence of smooth spaces that unsettle the education assemblage' (Youdell and Armstrong 2011: 150). Such an educational evaluation would open up new possibilities for a *politics of becoming*, disrupting the forms of reason and the spatial configurations that prevent educational subjects from thinking and practicing alternative types of educational reasoning. It would be an educational evaluation which 'lays an emphasis on [...] practices of relationality, a recognition of implication, and a modesty of judgement in the face of the inevitability of specificity' (Massey 2005: 147).

Time as multiplicity and a non-teleological educational evaluation

The evaluative space of the HoE is underwritten by a notion of uniform, non-reversible and evolutionary time (Massey 2005: 141). As Ball (2012: 49) highlights, this is a cumulative, serial and tyrannical time, linearly oriented towards a terminal point which is mythologised through the promise of fulfilment and realisation. It is the time of one, single, pre-given and uniform thought (Foucault 2002b: 21). In contrast to that, the second epistemological rupture I advocate here consists in thinking the time of educational value as a multiplicity of strands moving with an uneven flow. Every educational space has its own historicity as a milieu of identity and value formation. The 'here and now' of educational value is where the meeting up of spatial dynamics forms a configuration, that is an encounter of trajectories which have their own temporalities and, through their successions and accumulations, make a history of educational value. Education can be thus thought as an intertwining of formations of educational value histories which are inescapably entangled with their spatiality. Such a temporality 'is not linear, nor singular, nor pre-given, but it is integral to the spatial' (Massey 2005: 148).

Adopting such a perspective means to abandon the idea to conceive of the educational value in dialectical and teleological terms. It implies a non-causal and non-linear mode of reasoning that abandons the objective to recover an origin or to identify agents and factors of change that move 'in a continuum from the past to the present and the future'. The time of educational value becomes a temporal dispersion. It is 'highly local, [...] proper to a particular place and moment, with larger inclusive presents reaching beyond it topologically and temporally' (Abbott 2001: 295).

Such an understanding of the time of educational value has several implications for educational evaluation. It turns into a practice that attempts 'to insert difference into the continuum of time' putting into play a principle of:

(a) dissipation of the claimed unity of educational value and its origin; (b) dispersion and singularisation of educational value as event and c) differentiation of different educational values through evaluation (Revel 2014: 195). The first implication relates to the abandonment of the causal, fast and anxiety time of the order of variables and the related attempt to constitute a different temporality, the uneven time of life world. As for space, such a time is relational and locally produced, ultimately shaped by its locality. As a 'Chinese box' time, it can be thought as 'a series of overlapping presents of various sizes, each organised around a particular location and overlapping across the whole social process' (Abbott 2001: 295). The second one is that educational evaluation becomes a mode of establishing a problematising relation to educational time and the historicity of value-telling forms. The time of value for such an educational evaluation is not 'an idealized temporal space that is completely freed from the material conditions of its unfolding or a realist time reduced to the infinite and continuous accumulation of its different moments' (Revel 2014: 191). It is a temporal dispersion that has to be explored in the attempt to understand the temporally different modalities in which the true and the false on educational value 'enter into a relation and mutually define one another on the basis of norms and limits that are constantly being redefined, rearticulated, and readjusted' (Revel 2014: 192). Finally, such a perspective calls to an understanding of change and progress that is strictly bounded to 'breaking the chains of reason that bind and limit alternatives for action' (Popkewitz 1997: 24) in a situated space-time configuration. It invites to think change as ruptures or breaks and look at continuities as conditional and relational. Educational evaluation is asked to reveal the multiplicity, the plurality of times, experiences and values. It becomes the attempt to recognise the values of education in the plural. The temporal dispersion that arises through different educational configurations makes evaluative work a matter of mapping diverse, diverging, intersecting and overlapping temporalities of educational value. Educational evaluation becomes an endeavour to produce whole stories, where complex educational events involve complex subjects. This involvement occurs through differently flowing modes of ordering and forms of relationality (Abbott 2001: 181). As for the relational politics of the spatial in education, such a perspective calls educational evaluation to expose educational 'thought' to an unpredictable becoming and to the negotiation of value. In such a perspective, the present of educational value turns into a connection between something educational subjects know and something they cannot yet discern. Evaluating represents a means to pursue a critical ontology of educational value, a knowledge endeavour focused on the making of the educational present into an actuality that is concerned primarily with the situatedness of educational value (and the judgement on it) 'in a certain place in the world and in a certain moment of history of thought, and in a type of specific [evaluative] exercise' (Revel 2014: 188).

Norm and non-normative educational evaluation: A limit-attitude beyond value

As already argued, educational evaluation as a governmental technology is articulated on the establishment of norms. It creates a space of equivalence, where all educational entities become comparable in relation to a norm, but also an individualising space of differences and inequalities which can be visualised through hierarchical ordering (Ball 2012: 51). Interestingly, norm here does not stand for a certain specific value, but rather is 'a rule of judgement and a means of producing that rule' (Dean 2010: 141). It does not need any recourse to a point of externality (Ewald 1990) and operates as if there were an average and normalised fictional entity that serves as self-referential common denominator. The normalised HoE stands as a paradoxical figure that is always asked to surpass himself, thinking in terms of development, understanding himself in terms of developmental categories and deviant identities and knowing education as a series of temporally structured, normable occurrences. Both the epistemic terrain where the HoE emerges and the political rationalities that co-opt him define his agency by ignoring difference in educational ways of life (Normand 2016: 89). As empirical-transcendental doublet, the HoE oscillates along the paradoxical ethical continuum between a fictionalised should-be and an objectified reality which requires a work of transformation. Through educational evaluation, HoE 'differences are constructed from a universal sameness', that is from principles about educational value that establish a norm-based demarcation between valuable entities and those who need remediation on a continuum of values (Popkewitz 1997: 25).

The perspective I advocate here invites to question contemporary normalising educational evaluation in the light of the already-mentioned ideas of difference and multiplicity. In the face of an educational evaluation that diagnoses the HoE to subject his singularity to a form of identity, a single continuum of values and the obsessive relation to the sameness, the challenge here becomes to rethink evaluation as a neither axiomatic, nor typological but topological 'project of liberating difference through the invention of an acategorical [evaluative] thought' (Patton 2014: 589). As Patton (2014) puts it, this requires:

> abandoning the subordination of both difference and repetition to figures of the same in favour of a thought without contradiction, without dialectics and without negation, one that embraces divergence and multiplicity [...]. It requires an acategorical thought and a conception of being as univocal that revolves around the different rather than the same. (p. 590)

An acategorical evaluative thought does not conform to existing categories and concepts on educational value, but rather denaturalises the spaces of educational value in which individualities are placed and fully explores its affirmative potential to invent different horizons and modes of educational value, turning discursively and materially situated educational practice 'into the density within which the investigation of difference and the disquietude of the [educational] present play out' (Revel 2014: 199). Educational value becomes something pertaining to spatio-temporal multiplicities, that is so-far histories of educational value. In an anti-foundationalist perspective, evaluation becomes non-normative, not rooted into a value *archè* or into a foundational truth. It subtracts itself to the game of establishing value definitions and identities, as effects and sings of power positions (Bazzicalupo 2018: 27). Educational value is conceived as always relational, open and being made. Marked by a constitutive interrelatedness (Massey 2005: 189), it is projected in the openness of the educational future.

Such a non-normative educational evaluation would be experimental, a way to intensify the exploration of alternative discursive practices to construct educational values that do not result in the formation of oppositional norms. This would be coupled with the attempt to position difference within a discourse that takes into account the hybridity, multiplicity and the performative effects of any form of classification and positioning, rather than establishing a single continuum of values. Evaluation would turn into a work of freedom that does not point endlessly towards an impossible state of being, but rather separates out, from the contingency that has made educational subjects what they are as valuable educational entities, the possibility for them of no longer being, doing or thinking what they are, do or think. This would be a practice of differentiation that requires that educational subjects question themselves about the way they belong to some history of educational value in order to contribute to construct within their own present and to introduce discontinuity within their present (Revel 2014: 196–97). The matter of educational evaluation would be not to elaborate a judgement on the universal value of an educational entity, but rather to work on the situated nexus between power, knowledge and subjects, to catch discontinuities and the possibility to practice and think about educational value differently.

To recall the Foucault's question that opens this chapter, educational evaluation can contribute to a growth of capabilities that is disconnected from the intensification of power relations if it disconnects itself from and discard any promethean politics of the subject, any notion of teleological progress and any attempt to establish an evolutionary moral space that creates differentiation drawing on some norms of unity (Osberg 2010). Rather, it can act as a limit-attitude beyond value at the singular, making the rules for 'telling the value' of education contingent, historical and susceptible to critique and participating to the 'historico-practical test of the limits that we may cross over' (Foucault 1997a: 316) in relation to the production of education and educational value.

Other evaluations in education: Contesting the anthropological postulate

The epistemic ruptures outlined so far open the way for a further experimental space. It appears dangerous and contested as the previous ones. It suggests that we need to engage with the contestation of the anthropological postulate that constitutes the fundamental condition of possibility for educational evaluation (Han 2006). This means to lay down a question: does it exists something like the HoE, that is an empirical/transcendental doublet which is empirically knowable as a limited, determined and fallible being but is at the same time able of a reflexive torsion and overlapping on its fallibility and determinations?

Recalling Foucault (2002a: 371), this would probably require to go through the wakening of educational evaluation from what he termed as the 'anthropological sleep', that is to stop to talk about an omnipotent, almighty but limited HoE, 'about his reign or his liberation' and fulfilment. This would also mean avoiding to take the HoE as the starting-point to reach the truth about value, merit and worth about himself and his educational activity, and refusing any form of mythologisation of human activity or of human being's monopoly of thought (an exhaustion of the cogito, in Canguilhem 2006 terms).

It is understandable how and to what extent this could be said to be a dangerous experimental space. As Popkewitz and Brennan (1997) put it:

> To remove people from history, it is argued, is to make the world seem deterministic and beyond the possibility of intervention. In fact, efforts to remove the actor have been viewed as reactionary [...]. Not to have a visible actor – groupings of people and individuals – in narratives of social affairs is asserted as anti-humanistic (and even anti-democratic). [...] The assumption is of a world in which salvation can be found through positing prior universal actors who will bring the good works, and in which potential is not prevented through the schemas of theorists who 'decenter' the subject. (p. 309)

Nonetheless, looked carefully, the decentering of the HoE that I advocate here is nothing more than a 'historicisation' of the HoE and more specifically, a problematisation of its constitution as an agent as a core feature of modern evaluative thought. It is moved by a suspicion of the humanist values that underpin the celebration of the rule of the autonomous, self-identifying and self-realising subject (Rose 1989). It would imply for the promoters of educational evaluation to abandon 'the tranquil assurance' with which they take for granted as a given and independent object for evaluation, what is 'initially only the project of constituting that object' (Canguilhem 2006: 93). This means to give attention to the social construction of true knowledge on educational value. Such a 'turn to knowledge' as the problematic in educational evaluation 'entails a rethinking of the "humanism" that is tied to the a priori identification of agents and the idea of progress as an evolutionary concept', but is not intended at all to 'forego social change' (Popkewitz 1997: 24). On the contrary, its aim is to 'relocate the rules on which change and social possibilities are understood'. This decentering of the HoE:

> does not prevent the subject from acting and does not abandon the Enlightenment project. The strategy of decentering the subject is itself a product of the very self-reflectivity produced through an Enlightenment ethos. The decentering of the subject has its own sense of irony: there is an acceptance of the need to construct knowledge that can enable people to act intentionally. The subject is made into a dimension of the questionable and of "insistent contest and resignification," not as a foundation of research that is taken as the unquestionable. (Popkewitz and Brennan 1997: 310)

In such a perspective, educational evaluation can aspire at becoming a way of constructing histories about how our subjectivities are formed (making the agendas and categories of the subject problematic), providing a space for alternative acting and thinking. It would be a means to substitute the (neo) liberal HoE as pre-given, free, responsible and functional subject with an educational subject which, within the nexus truth-power, is codified and identified through a process of subjectivation which is never saturated and always open to forms of re-inscription (Bazzicalupo 2018). In such a way, the HoE is re-inserted but in a different location than that argued in those evaluative approaches rooted in the epistemology of consciousness. Instead, 'humanism is reinserted into [evaluative] analysis by questioning the givenness of the subject as historically constructed and thus reasserting an individuality that can challenge' the forms of determination that limit the HoE and his possibility for acting and thinking (Popkewitz and Brennan 1997: 311). The eventalisation of educational evaluation means here the recovery and re-launch of the contingency of the educational actuality (Dean 1994), which is in turn the presupposition of its political contestability and changeability. Evaluating stands as a practice of productive imagination that makes to emerge the contingency and fragility of the given truth on educational value, the possible crossing points to change it and the discontinuities that it is possible to discover within educational practice (Bazzicalupo 2018: 35).

I suggest that these are the privileged paths of epistemological reflection if we want to overcome the forms of reductionism and over-determination that underlie contemporary educational evaluation in education and produce those discomforts that are at the basis of many criticisms. As subjects of educational evaluation, we are revocable and a critical ontology of ourselves can be considered 'as a means of confronting our own revocability' (Ball 2012: 126).

Those outlined above are among the experimental spaces we could and should come across in order to open up in front of a revocable HoE who reflects on his educational activity a truly free space where his confrontation with his own revocability and his search for a mode of being, acting and thinking is not over-determined by the tyranny of what is defined as an impossible but unavoidable task. These are among the experimental spaces that we should inhabit to work towards the collective outlining of a different evaluative practice and the design of other evaluative spaces in education. Within those spaces, evaluation could be reframed as an ethical exercise of freedom (Bevir 1999: 76), that is a never-ending exercise in the art of not being governed too much and at that costs, or a questioning activity that resists normalising pressures, putting under scrutiny the limits of the traditions and practices we inherit.

References

Abbott, A. (2001) *Time Matters: On Theory and Method*, Chicago, IL: University of Chicago Press.
Alkin, M.C. (2011) *Evaluation Essentials. From A to Z*, New York: The Guilford Press.
Aronowitz, S. and Giroux, H. (1991) *Postmodern Education: Politics, Culture, and Social Criticism*, Minneapolis, MN: University of Minnesota Press.
Bacchi, C. (2012) Why study problematizations? Making politics visible, *Open Journal of Political Science*, 2 (1), 1–8.
Ball, S.J. (2003) The teacher's soul and the terrors of performativity, *Journal of Education Policy*, 18 (2), 215–228.
Ball, S.J. (2006) *Education Policy and Social Class. The Selected Works of Stephen Ball*, London and New York: Routledge.
Ball, S.J. (2012) *Foucault, Power, and Education*, London and New York: Routledge.
Ball, S.J. (2015) Education, governance and the tyranny of numbers, *Journal of Education Policy*, 30 (3), 299–301.
Ball, S.J. (2016) Subjectivity as a site of struggle: Refusing neoliberalism? *British Journal of Sociology of Education*, 37 (8), 1129–1146.
Ball, S.J. (2017) *Foucault as Educator*, Cham: Springer.
Ball, S.J., Junemann, C. and Santori, D. (2017) *Edu.Net: Globalisation and Education Policy Mobility*, London: Routledge.
Barad, K. (2003) Posthumanist performativity: Toward an understanding of how matter comes to matter, *Signs: Journal of Women in Culture and Society*, 28 (3), 801–831.
Barry, A., Osborne, T. and Rose, N. (eds) (1996) *Foucault and Political Reason: Liberalism, Neo-Liberalism, and Rationalities of Government*, Chicago, IL: University of Chicago Press.
Bazzicalupo, L. (2018) La Critica non normativa nel pensiero francese contemporaneo, *I Castelli di Yale*, 6 (1), 19–38.
Bevir, M. (1999) Foucault and critique: Deploying agency against autonomy, *Political Theory*, 27 (1), 65–84.
Bhola, H.S. (2002) Developing discourses on evaluation. In Stufflebeam, D.L., Madaus, G.F. and Kellaghan, T. (eds) *Evaluation Models: Viewpoints on Educational and Human Services Evaluation* (second edn), Boston, MA: Kluwer Academic Publishers, 383–394.
Bhola, H.S. (2003) Social and cultural contexts of educational evaluation: A global perspective. In Kellaghan, T., Stufflebeam, D.L. and Wingate, L. (eds) *International Handbook of Educational Evaluation*, Dordrecht: Kluwer Academic Publishers, 397–415.
Biesta, G. (2007) Why "what works" won't work: Evidence-based practice and the democratic deficit in educational research, *Educational Theory*, 57 (1), 1–22.

Boltanski, L. (2011) *On Critique: A Sociology of Emancipation*, Cambridge: Polity Press.
Borer, V.L. and Lawn, M. (2013) Governing education systems by shaping data: From the past to the present, from national to international perspectives, *European Educational Research Journal*, 12 (1), 48–52.
Bouchet, D. (2007) The ambiguity of the modern conception of autonomy and the paradox of culture, *Thesis Eleven*, 88 (1), 31–54.
Brisolara, S. and Seigart, D. (2012) Feminist evaluation research. In Hesse-Biber, S.N. (ed) *Handbook of Feminist Research: Theory and Praxis*, London: Sage, 290–312.
Brown, W. (2015) *Undoing the Demos: Neoliberalism's Stealth Revolution*, Cambridge, MA: MIT Press.
Burchell, G., Gordon, C. and Miller, P. (eds) (1991) *The Foucault Effect: Studies in Governmentality*, Chicago, IL: The University of Chicago Press.
Butler, J. (1997) *Excitable Speech: A Politics of the Performative*, London: Routledge.
Campbell, D.T. (1969) Reforms as experiments, *American Psychologist*, 24 (4), 409–429.
Campbell, D.T. and Stanley, J. (1963) *Experimental and Quasi Experimental Designs for Research*, Chicago, IL: Rand-McNally.
Canguilhem, G. (2006) The death of man, or exhaustion of the cogito? In Gutting, G. (ed) *The Cambridge Companion to Foucault* (second edn), Cambridge: Cambridge University Press, 74–94.
Carlson, D.L. (2009) Producing entrepreneurial subjects: Neoliberal rationalities and portfolio assessment. In Peters, M.A., Besley, A.C., Olssen, M., Maurer, S. and Weber, S. (eds) *Governmentality Studies in Education*, Rotterdam: Sense Publishers, 257–270.
Castel, R. (1991) From dangerousness to risk. In Burchell, G., Gordon, C. and Miller, P. (eds) *The Foucault Effect: Studies in Governmentality*, Chicago, IL: Chicago University Press, 281–298.
Christie, C.A. and Alkin, M.C. (2008) Evaluation theory tree re-examined, *Studies in Educational Evaluation*, 34 (3), 131–135.
Clarke, J. (2008) Performance paradoxes: The politics of evaluation in public services, In Davis, H. and Martin, S. (eds) *Public Services Inspection in the UK. Research Highlights in Social Work (50)*, London: Jessica Kingsley Publishers, 120–134.
Clarke, J. (2009) Governance puzzles. In Budd, L. and Harris, L. (eds) *eGovernance: Managing or Governing?* London: Routledge, 29–52.
Cook, T.D. (2002) Randomized experiments in educational policy research: A critical examination of the reasons the educational evaluation community has offered for not doing them, *Educational Evaluation and Policy Analysis*, 24 (3), 175–199.
Cronbach, L.J. (1982) *Designing Evaluations of Educational and Social Programs*, San Francisco, CA: Jossey-Bass.
Cronbach, L.J., Ambron, S.R., Dornbusch, S.M., Hess, R.D., Hornik, R.C., Phillips, D.C., Walker, D.F. and Weiner, S.S. (1980) *Toward a Reform of Program Evaluation: Aims, Methods, and Institutional Arrangements*, San Francisco, CA: Jossey-Bass.
Dahler-Larsen, P. (2005) Evaluation and public management. In Ferlie, E., Lynn L.E. and Pollitt, C. (eds) *The Oxford Handbook of Public Management*, Oxford/New York: Oxford University Press.
Dahler-Larsen, P. (2012) *The Evaluation Society*, Stanford, CA: Stanford University Press.
Davidson, A. (1997) *Foucault and His Interlocutors*, Chicago and London: University of Chicago Press.
Davidson, E.J. (2005) *Evaluation Methodology Basics: The Nuts and Bolts of Sound Evaluation*, Thousand Oaks, CA: Sage.

De Lima, I.V. (2010) *Foucault's Archaeology of Political Economy*, New York: Palgrave-Macmillan.
Dean, M. (1994) *Critical and Effective Histories Foucault's Methods and Historical Sociology*, London and New York: Routledge.
Dean, M. (2007) *Governing Societies: Political Perspectives on Domestic and International Rule*, London: McGraw-Hill Education.
Dean, M. (2010) *Governmentality. Power and Rule in Modern Societies* (second edn), London: Sage.
Deere, D.T. (2014) Truth. In Lawlor, L. and Nale, J. (eds) *The Cambridge Foucault Lexicon*, New York: Cambridge University Press, 517–527.
Defert, D. and Ewald, F. (eds) (2001) *Dits et Écrits 1954–1988. Vol. II, 1976–1988 Michel Foucault*, Paris: Gallimard.
Deleuze, G. (1988) *Foucault*, Minnesota, MN: University of Minnesota Press.
Deleuze, G. (1992) What is a dispositif? In *Michel Foucault: Philosopher* (translated by Armstrong, T.J.), New York: Harvester Wheatsheaf, 159–168.
Desrosieres, A. (2010) A politics of knowledge-tools: The case of statistics. In Sangolt, L. (ed) *Between Enlightenment and Disaster: Dimensions of the Political Use of Knowledge*, Brussels: Peter Lang, 111–129.
Desrosieres, A. (2011) The economics of convention and statistics: The paradox of origins, *Historical Social Research*, 36 (4), 64–81.
Dreyfus, H.L. and Rabinow, P. (1982) *Michel Foucault. Beyond Structuralism and Hermeneutics* (second edn), Chicago, IL: The University of Chicago Press.
Eisner, E.W. (1994) *The Educational Imagination* (third edn), Upper Saddle River, NJ: Prentice-Hall.
Eisner, E.W. (2003) Educational connoisseurship and educational criticism: An arts-based approach to educational evaluation. In Kellaghan, T., Stufflebeam, D.L. and Wingate, L. (eds) *International Handbook of Educational Evaluation*, Dordrecht: Kluwer Academic Publishers, 153–166.
Espeland, W.N. and Sauder, M. (2012) The dynamics of indicators. In Davis, K.E., Fisher, A., Kingsbury, B. and Merry, S.E. (eds) *Governance by Indicators*, Oxford: Oxford University Press, 86–109.
European Commission/EACEA/Eurydice, (2015) *Assuring Quality in Education: Policies and Approaches to School Evaluation in Europe. Eurydice Report*, Luxembourg: Publications Office of the European Union.
Ewald, F. (1990) Norms, discipline and the law, *Representations*, 30, 138–161.
Faubert, V. (2009) *School Evaluation: Current Practices in OECD Countries and a Literature Review*, Education Working Paper 42, Paris: OECD.
Faubion, J.D. (ed) (1998) Introduction. In Foucault, M., *Aesthetics, Method, and Epistemology. Essential Works of Foucault, 1954–1984, Volume Two*, New York: New Press.
Felouzis, G. and Hanhart, S. (2011) Politiques éducatives et évaluation: nouvelles tendances, nouveaux acteurs. In Felouzis, G. and Hanhart, S. (eds) *Gouverner l'Education par les Nombres? Usages, Débats et Controversies*, Brussels: De Boeck, 7–31.
Fimiani, M. (1997) *Foucault e Kant: Critica, Clinica, Etica*, Napoli: La città del sole.
Finger, G. and Russell, N. (1994) School evaluation using fourth generation evaluation: A case study, *Evaluation Journal of Australasia*, 6 (1), 43–54.
Foucault, M. (1970) Theatrum philosophicum, *Critique*, 282, 885–908.
Foucault, M. (1970/1994) *The Order of Things: An Archaeology of the Human Sciences* (a translation of *Les mots et le choses*), New York: Vintage Books.
Foucault, M. (1971) Orders of discourse, *Social Science Information*, 10 (2), 7–30.

References

Foucault, M. (1977a) Nietzsche, Genealogy, History. In Bouchard, D.F. and Simon, S. (eds) *Language, Counter-Meaning, Practice: Selected Essays and Interviews*, Ithaca, NY: Cornell University Press, 139–164.

Foucault, M. (1977b) Revolutionary action: 'Until now'. In Bouchard, D.F. (ed) *Language, Counter-Memory, Practice. Selected Essays and Interviews*, New York: Cornell University Press, 221–234.

Foucault, M. (1980) *Power/Knowledge: Selected Interviews and Other Writings by Michel Foucault, 1972–1977* (edited by Gordon C.), New York: Pantheon Books.

Foucault, M. (1981) Questions of method: An interview with Michel Foucault, *Ideology&Consciousness*, 8, 3–14.

Foucault, M. (1982a) On the genealogy of ethics. In Dreyfus, H.L. and Rabinow, P. *Michel Foucault. Beyond Structuralism and Hermeneutics* (second edn), Chicago, IL: The University of Chicago Press, 229–252.

Foucault, M. (1982b) The subject and power, *Critical Inquiry*, 8 (4), 777–795.

Foucault, M. (1983) Afterword: The subject and power. In Dreyfus, H. and Rabinow, P. (eds) *Michel Foucault: Beyond Structuralism and Hermeneutics* (second edn), Chicago, IL: Chicago University Press, 208–226.

Foucault, M. (1984) *The Foucault Reader* (edited by Rabinow P.), New York: Pantheon Books.

Foucault, M. (1985) *The History of Sexuality, Vol. 2: The Use of Pleasure*, New York: Pantheon Books.

Foucault, M. (1988) Politics and reason. In Kritzman L.D. (ed) *Politics, Philosophy, Culture: Interviews and Other Writings 1977–1984*, New York: Routledge.

Foucault, M. (1988) Truth, power, self: An interview with Michel Foucault. In Martin, L.H., Gutman, H. and Hutton, P. (eds) *Technologies of the Self: A Seminar with Michel Foucault*, London: Tavistock, 9–15.

Foucault, M. (1991) Governmentality. In Burchell, G., Gordon, C. and Miller, P. (eds) *The Foucault Effect: Studies in Governmentality*, Chicago, IL: The University of Chicago Press, 87–104.

Foucault, M. (1994) Le souci de la vérité. In *Dits et Écrits 1954–1988: IV 1980–1988*, Paris: Gallimard.

Foucault, M. (1995) *Discipline and Punish: the Birth of the Prison*, New York: Vintage Books.

Foucault, M. (1997a) What is enlightenment? In Rabinow P. (ed) *Ethics: Subjectivity and Truth. Essential Works 1956–1984, Vol. 1*, New York: New Press, 303–319.

Foucault, M. (1997b) Polemics, politics, and problematizations. An Interview with Michel Foucault. In Rabinow P. (ed) *Ethics: Subjectivity and Truth. Essential Works 1956–1984, Vol. 1*, New York: New Press, 111–119.

Foucault, M. (1997c) The ethics of the concern for self as a practice of freedom. In Rabinow P. (ed) *Ethics: Subjectivity and Truth. Essential Works 1956–1984, Vol. 1*, New York: New Press, 281–301.

Foucault, M. (1997d) Candidacy presentation: College de France, 1969. In Rabinow P. (ed) *Ethics: Subjectivity and Truth. Essential Works 1956–1984, Vol. 1*, New York: New Press, 5–10.

Foucault, M. (1998) What is an author? In Foucault, M., *Aesthetics, Method, and Epistemology. Essential Works of Foucault, 1954–1984, Volume Two* (edited by Faubion J.D.), New York: New Press, 205–222.

Foucault, M. (2001) *Power. Essential Works of Foucault 1954–1984, Vol. 3* (edited by Faubion J.D.), New York: New Press.

Foucault, M. (2002a) *The Order of Things. An Archaeology of the Human Sciences*, London: Routledge.

Foucault, M. (2002b) *The Archaeology of Knowledge*, London: Routledge.
Foucault, M. (2003) *Society Must Be Defended. Lectures at the Collège de France 1975–76*, New York: Picador.
Foucault, M. (2006) *History of Madness*, Abingdon: Routledge.
Foucault, M. (2007) What is critique? In *The Politics of Truth*, New York: Semiotext(e), 41–81.
Foucault, M. (2008) *The Birth of Biopolitics. Lectures at the Collège de France 1978–79*, Basingstoke: Palgrave Macmillan.
Foucault, M. (2009) *Security, Territory and Population. Lectures at the College de France 1977–1978*, New York: Palgrave Macmillan.
Friedman, M. (1953) *Essays in Positive Economics*, Chicago, IL: University of Chicago Press.
Gambardella, D. and Lumino, R. (2015) *Evaluative Knowledge and Policy Making: Beyond the Intellectual Virtus of Téchne*, Milano: McGraw-Hill education.
Gane, N. (2014) Sociology and neoliberalism: A missing history, *Sociology*, 48 (6), 1092–1106.
Gannon, S. (2013) My school redux: Re-storying schooling with the My School website, *Discourse: Studies in the Cultural Politics of Education*, 34 (1), 17–30.
Gilson, E. (2014) Event. In Lawlor, L. and Nale, J. (eds) *The Cambridge Foucault Lexicon*, Cambridge: Cambridge University Press, 143–146.
Goldstein, H. and Moss, G. (2014) Knowledge and numbers in education, *Comparative Education*, 50 (3), 259–265.
Gorur, R. and Koyama, J.P. (2013) The struggle to technicise in education policy, *The Australian Educational Researcher*, 40 (5), 633–648.
Grek, S. (2009) Governing by numbers: The PISA 'effect' in Europe, *Journal of Education Policy*, 24 (1), 23–37.
Grek, S., Lawn, M., Lingard, B. and Varjo, J. (2009) North by northwest: Quality assurance and evaluation processes in European schooling, *Journal of Education Policy*, 24 (2), 121–133.
Grimaldi, E. (2015) What future for educational research in Europe? Political, epistemological and ethical challenges, *European Educational Research Journal*, 14 (1), 49–55.
Grimaldi, E. and Barzanò, G. (2014) Making Sense of the Educational Present: Problematising the merit turn in the Italian eduscape, *European Educational Research Journal*, 13 (1), 26–46.
Guba, E. (1969) The failure of educational evaluation, *Educational Technology*, 9 (5), 29–38.
Guba, E. and Lincoln, Y.S. (1989) *Fourth Generation Evaluation*, London: Sage.
Guba, E. and Lincoln, Y.S. (2004) The roots of fourth generation evaluation: Theoretical and methodological origins. In Alkin, M. (ed) *Evaluation Roots: Tracing Theorists' Views and Influences*, Thousand Oaks, CA: Sage, 225–242.
Gunter, H.M., Grimaldi, E., Hall, D. and Serpieri, R. (eds) (2016) *New Public Management and the Reform of Education: European Lessons for Policy and Practice*, London: Routledge.
Gutting, G. (1989) *Michel Foucault's Archaeology of Scientific Reason: Science and the History of Reason*, Cambridge: Cambridge University Press.
Gutting, G. (2014) Archaeology. In Lawlor, L. and Nale, J. (eds) *The Cambridge Foucault Lexicon*, Cambridge: Cambridge University Press, 13–19.
Hacking, I. (1975) *The Emergence of Probability*, Cambridge: Cambridge University Press.
Hacking, I. (1986) The archaeology of Foucault. In Couzens Hoy, D. (ed) *Foucault: A Critical Reader*, Cambridge, MA: Basil Blackwell, 27–40.
Hacking, I. (1992) "Style" for historians and philosophers, *Studies in the History and Philosophy of Science*, 23 (1), 1–20.
Hammersley, M. (2013) *The Myth of Research-Based Policy and Practice*, London: Sage.

Han, B. (2006) The analytic of finitude and the history of subjectivity. In Gutting, G. (ed) *The Cambridge Companion to Foucault* (second edn), Cambridge: Cambridge University Press, 176–209.

Harvey, C. (2010) Making hollow men, *Educational Theory*, 60 (2), 189–201.

Hayek, F. (1948) *Individualism and Economic Order*, Chicago: University of Chicago Press.

Hayek, F. (1952) *The Counter-Revolution of Science*, Indianapolis, IN: Liberty Fund.

Hayek, F. (1976) *Law, Legislation and Liberty, Vol. 2: The Mirage of Social Justice*, London: Routledge and Kegan Paul.

Hayek, F. (1979) *Law, Legislation and Liberty, Vol. 3: The Political Order of a Free People*, London: Routledge and Kegan Paul.

Henriques, J., Hollway, W., Urwin, C., Venn, C. and Walkerdine, V. (1984) *Changing the Subject: Psychology, Social Regulation, and Subjectivity*, London: Methuen.

Hopkins, D. and West, M. (2002) Evaluation as school improvement: A developmental perspective from England. In Nevo, D. (ed) *School-Based Evaluation: An International Perspective (Advances in Program Evaluation, Vol. 8)*, Bingley: Emerald Group Publishing Limited, 89–112.

House, E.R. (1978) Assumptions underlying evaluation models, *Educational Researcher*, 7 (3), 4–12.

House, E.R. and Howe, K. (1999) *Values in Evaluation and Social Research*, Thousand Oaks, CA: Sage.

Hunter, I. (1994) *Rethinking the School: Subjectivity, Bureaucracy, Criticism*, New York: Allen & Unwin.

Hunter, I. (1996) Assembling the school. In Barry, A., Osborne, T. and Rose, N. (eds) *Foucault and Political Reason: Liberalism, Neo-Liberalism, and Rationalities of Government*, Chicago, IL: University of Chicago Press, 143–166.

ILO (2011) *A Skilled Workforce for Strong, Sustainable and Balanced Growth: A G20 Training Strategy*, Geneva: International Labour Office.

Johnson, P. (2006) Unravelling Foucault's 'different spaces', *History of the Human Sciences*, 19 (4), 75–90.

Joint Committee on Standards for Educational Evaluation (1994) *The Program Evaluation Standards. How to Assess Evaluations of Educational Programs*, Thousand Oaks, CA: Sage.

Kellaghan, T., Stufflebeam, D.L. and Wingate, L. (eds) (2003) *International Handbook of Educational Evaluation*, Dordrecht: Kluwer Academic Publishers.

King, J., Morris, L. and Fitzgibbon, C. (1987) *How to Assess Program Implementation*, Thousand Oaks, CA: Sage.

Kitchin, R., Lauriault, T. and McArdle, G. (2015) Knowing and governing cities through urban indicators, city benchmarking and real-time dashboards, *Regional Studies, Regional Science*, 2 (1), 6–28.

Kologlugil, S. (2010) Michel Foucault's archaeology of knowledge and economic discourse, *Erasmus Journal for Philosophy and Economics*, 3 (2), 1–25.

Koopman, C. (2013) *Genealogy as Critique: Problematization and Transformation in Foucault and Others*, Bloomington, IN: Indiana University Press.

Koopman, C. (2014) Problematization. In Lawlor, L. and Nale, J. (eds) *The Cambridge Foucault Lexicon*, New York: Cambridge University Press, 517–527.

Kuji-Shikatani, K., Gallagher, M.J., Franz, R., and Börner, M. (2015) Leadership's role in building the education sector's capacity to use evaluative thinking. In Patton, M.Q., McKegg, K. and Wehipeihana, N. (eds) *Developmental Evaluation Exemplars: Principles in Practice*, New York: Guilford Publications, 252–270.

References

Landri, P. (2014) Governing by standards: The fabrication of austerity in the Italian education system, *Education Inquiry*, 5 (1), 24–57.

Landri, P. (2018) *Digital Governance of Education: Technology, Standards and Europeanization of Education*, London: Bloomsbury Publishing.

Lascoumes, P. and Le Galès, P. (2007) Introduction: Understanding public policy through its instruments—From the nature of instruments to the sociology of public policy instrumentation, *Governance*, 20 (1), 1–21.

Latour, B. (1986) Visualization and cognition. Thinking with eyes and hands, *Knowledge and Society*, 6 (6), 1–40.

Lawn, M. (2013a) The rise of data in education. In Lawn, M. (ed) *The Rise of Data in Education Systems: Collection, Visualization and Use*, Oxford: Symposium Books, 7–25.

Lawn, M. (2013b) The internationalization of education data: Exhibitions, tests, standards and associations. In Lawn, M. (ed) *The Rise of Data in Education Systems: Collection, Visualization and Use*, Oxford: Symposium Books, 11–25.

Lawn, M. and Segerholm, C. (2011) Europe through experts and technologies. In Ozga J., Dahler-Larsen, P., Segerholm, C. and Simola, H. (eds) *Fabricating Quality in Education: Data and Governance in Europe*, London: Routledge, 32–46.

Legg, S. (2005) Foucault's population geographies: Classifications, biopolitics and governmental spaces, *Population Space and Place*, 11 (3), 137–156.

Lemke, T. (2007) An indigestible meal? Foucault, governmentality and state theory, *Distinktion: Scandinavian Journal of Social Theory*, 8 (2), 43–64.

Leonard, S.N., Fitzgerald, R.N. and Riordan, G. (2016) Using developmental evaluation as a design thinking tool for curriculum innovation in professional higher education, *Higher Education Research & Development*, 35 (2), 309–321.

Lincoln, Y.S. (2002) Constructivist knowing, participatory ethics and responsive evaluation: A model for the 21st century. In Stufflebeam, D.L., Madaus, G.F. and Kellaghan, T. (eds) *Evaluation Models: Viewpoints on Educational and Human Services Evaluation* (second edn), Boston, MA: Kluwer Academic Publishers, 69–78.

Lingard, B. (2011) Policy as numbers: Ac/counting for educational research, *Australian Educational Researcher*, 38 (3), 355–382.

Lingard, B., Creagh, S. and Vass, G. (2012) Education policy as numbers: Data categories and two Australian cases of misrecognition, *Journal of Education Policy*, 27 (3), 315–333.

Lingard, B. and Sellar, S. (2013) Catalyst data: Pervasive systemic effects of audit and accountability in Australian schooling, *Journal of Education Policy*, 28 (5), 634–656.

Love, W.J. (2002) Introduction. In Ricouer, P. (ed) *Fallible Man*, New York: Fordham University Press.

Lynch, R.A. (2014) Archive. In Lawlor, L. and Nale, J. (eds) *The Cambridge Foucault Lexicon*, Cambridge: Cambridge University Press, 20–23.

Machado, R. (1992) Archaeology and epistemology. In Armstrong T.J. (ed) *Michel Foucault: Philosopher*, New York: Harvester Wheatsheaf, 3–19.

Madaus, G.F. and Kellaghan, T. (2002) Models, metaphors, and definitions in evaluation. In Stufflebeam, D.L., Madaus, G.F. and Kellaghan, T. (eds) *Evaluation Models: Viewpoints on Educational and Human Services Evaluation* (Vol. 6), Dordrecht: Kluwer Academic Publishers, 19–31.

Madaus, G.F. and Stufflebeam, D.L. (2002) Program evaluation: A historical overview. In Stufflebeam, D.L., Madaus, G.F., and Kellaghan, T. (eds) *Evaluation Models: Viewpoints on Educational and Human Services Evaluation* (Vol. 6), Dordrecht: Kluwer Academic Publishers, 3–18.

Major-Poetzl, P. (1983) *Michel Foucault's Archaeology of Western Culture*, Brighton: Harvester.

Marshall, J. (1996) Personal autonomy and liberal education: A Foucauldian critique. In Peters M., Hope W., Marshall J. and Webster S. (eds) *Critical Theory, Post-Structuralism and the Social Context*, Palmerston North: The Dunmore Press, 106–126.

Massey, D. (2005) *For Space*, London: Sage.

McLaughlin, M.W. (1975) *Evaluation and Reform*, Cambridge, MA: Ballinger Publishing.

Mertens, D. (1999) Inclusive evaluation: Implications of transformative theory for evaluation, *American Journal of Evaluation*, 20 (1), 1–14.

Meyer, H. and Benavot, A. (eds) (2013) *PISA, Power, and Policy: The Emergence of Global Educational Governance*, Oxford: Symposium Books.

Miller, P. and Rose, N. (1990) Governing economic life, *Economy and Society*, 19 (1), 1–31.

Miller, P. and Rose, N. (2008) *Governing the Present: Administering Economic, Social and Personal Life*, Cambridge: Polity Press.

Mills, S. (1997) *Discourse*, London & New York: Routledge.

Nealon, J.T. (2014) Historical a priori. In Lawlor, L. and Nale, J. (eds) *The Cambridge Foucault Lexicon*, Cambridge: Cambridge University Press, 200–206.

Nicoli, M. (2015) Un uomo che valuta, *Im@go. A Journal of the Social Imaginary*, 4, 92–109.

Normand, R. (2016) *The Changing Epistemic Governance of European Education: The Fabrication of the Homo Academicus Europeanus?* Switzerland: Springer Academic Publishing.

Novoa, A. and Yariv-Mashal, T. (2003) Comparative research in education: A mode of governance or a historical journey?, *Comparative Education*, 39 (4), 423–438.

O'Malley, P. (1996) Risk and responsibility. In Barry, A., Osborne, T. and Rose, N. (eds) *Foucault and Political Reason: Liberalism, Neo-Liberalism, and Rationalities of Government*, London: UCL Press, 189–207.

Ocean, J. and Skourdoumbis, A. (2016) Who's counting? Legitimating measurement in the audit culture, *Discourse: Studies in the Cultural Politics of Education*, 37 (3), 442–456.

OECD (2002) *Glossary of Key Terms in Evaluation and Results Based Management*, Paris: OECD Publishing.

OECD (2007) *Human Capital: How What You Know Shapes Your Life*, Paris: OECD Publishing.

OECD (2011) *Evaluation and Assessment Frameworks for Improving School Outcomes. Common Policy Challenges*, Paris: OECD Publishing.

OECD (2013) *Synergies for Better Learning: An International Perspective on Evaluation and Assessment*, Paris: OECD Publishing.

Oksala, J. (2012) *Foucault, Politics, and Violence*, Evanston, IL: Northwestern University Press.

O'leary, T. (2006) *Foucault and the Art of Ethics*, London/New York: Continuum.

Olssen, M. (1999) *Michel Foucault: Materialism and Education*, Westport: Bergin and Garvey.

Olssen, M. (2014) Framing and analysing educational research: A recent history of transactions from a foucauldian perspective. In Reid, A.D., Hart E.P. and Peters M.A. (eds) *A Companion to Research in Education*, Dordrecht: Springer, 215–228.

Olssen, M., Codd, J.A. and O'Neill, A.M. (2004) *Education Policy: Globalization, Citizenship and Democracy*, London: Sage.

Osberg, D. (2010) Editorial. Knowledge is not made for understanding; it is made for cutting, *Complicity: An International Journal of Complexity and Education*, 7 (2), iii–viii.

Ozga, J. (2009) Governing education through data in England: From regulation to self-evaluation, *Journal of Education Policy*, 24 (2), 149–162.

Ozga, J. (2016) Trust in numbers? Digital education governance and the inspection process, *European Educational Research Journal*, 15 (1), 69–81.

References

Ozga J., Dahler-Larsen, P., Segerholm, C. and Simola, H. (eds) (2011) *Fabricating Quality in Education: Data and Governance in Europe*, London: Routledge.

Ozga, J. and Jones, R. (2006) Travelling and embedded policy: The case of knowledge transfer, *Journal of Education Policy*, 21 (1), 1–17.

Patton, M.Q. (1997) *Utilization-focused Evaluation: The New Century Text* (third edn), Thousand Oaks, CA: Sage.

Patton, M.Q. (2011) *Developmental Evaluation: Applying Complexity Concepts to Enhance Innovation and Use*, New York: Guildford.

Patton, P. (2014) Difference. In Lawlor, L. and Nale, J. (eds) *The Cambridge Foucault Lexicon*, Cambridge: Cambridge University Press, 102–109.

Peck, J. and Theodore, N. (2012) Follow the policy: A distended case approach, *Environment and Planning A*, 44 (1), 21–30.

Peters, M.A. (2001) Education, enterprise culture and the entrepreneurial self: A Foucauldian perspective, *Journal of Educational Enquiry*, 2 (2), 58–71.

Peters, M.A., Besley, A.C., Olssen, M., Maurer, S. and Weber, S. (eds) (2009) *Governmentality Studies in Education*, Dordrecht: Springer.

Pettersson, D., Popkewitz, T.S. and Lindblad, S. (2016) On the use of educational numbers: Comparative constructions of hierarchies by means of large-scale assessments, *Espacio, Tiempo y Educación*, 3 (1), 177–202.

Piattoeva N. (2015) Elastic numbers: National examinations data as a technology of government, *Journal of Education Policy*, 30 (3), 316–334.

Pinto, V. (2012) *Valutare e Punire*, Napoli: Cronopio.

Popkewitz T.S. (1997) A changing terrain of knowledge and power: A social epistemology of educational research, *Educational Researcher*, 26 (9), 18–29.

Popkewitz, T.S. (2000) The denial of change in educational change: Systems of ideas in the construction of national policy and evaluation, *Educational Researcher*, 29 (1), 17–29.

Popkewitz, T.S. and Brennan, M. (1997) Restructuring of social and political theory in education: Foucault and a social epistemology of school practices, *Educational Theory*, 47 (3), 287–313.

Popkewitz, T.S. and Pitman, A. (1986) The idea and ideology of progress in social and educational thought, *Curriculum and Teaching*, 1 (1/2), 11–24.

Porter, T.M. (1995) *Trust in Numbers. The Pursuit of Objectivity in Science and Public Life*, Princeton, NJ: Princeton University Press.

Porter, T.M. (1996) Making things quantitative. In Power, M. (ed) *Accounting and Science: Natural Inquiry and Commercial Reason*, New York: Cambridge University Press.

Power, M. (1994) *The Audit Explosion*, No. 7, London: Demos.

Power, M. (1997) *The Audit Society. Rituals of Verification*, Oxford: Oxford University Press.

Power, M. (2004) Counting, control and calculation: Reflection on measuring and management, *Human Relations*, 57 (6), 765–783.

Power, M. (2011) Foucault and sociology, *Annual Review of Sociology*, 37 (1), 35–56.

Rabinow, P. (1997) Introduction: The history of systems of thought. In Rabinow P. (ed) *Ethics: Subjectivity and Truth. The Essential Works of Michel Foucault 1954–1984, Vol. 1*, New York: New Press, xi–xlii.

Reckwitz, A. (2002) Toward a theory of social practices: A development in culturalist theorizing, *European Journal of Social Theory*, 5 (2), 243–263.

Revel, J. (2014) History. In Lawlor, L. and Nale, J. (eds) *The Cambridge Foucault Lexicon*, Cambridge: Cambridge University Press, 187–199.

References

Rivlin, A.M. (1971) *Systematic Thinking for Social Action*, Washington, DC: The Brookings Institution.

Rizvi, F. and Lingard, B. (2010) *Globalizing Education Policy*, London and New York: Routledge.

Rogers, P.J. (2002) Program theory: Not whether programs work but how they work. In Stufflebeam, D.L., Madaus, G.F. and Kellaghan, T. (eds) *Evaluation Models: Viewpoints on Educational and Human Services Evaluation* (second edn), Boston: Kluwer Academic Publishers, 209–232.

Rose, N. (1989) *Governing the Soul: The Shaping of the Private Self*, London: Routledge.

Rose, N. (1996) Governing advanced liberal democracies. In Barry, A., Osborne, T. and Rose, N. (eds) *Foucault and Political Reason: Liberalism, Neo-Liberalism, and Rationalities of Government*, Chicago, IL: University of Chicago Press, 37–64.

Rose, N. (1998) *Inventing Our Selves. Psychology, Power, and Personhood*, Cambridge: Cambridge University Press.

Rose, N. (1999) *Powers of Freedom. Reframing Political Thought*, Cambridge: Cambridge University Press.

Rossi, P.H., Lipsey, M.W. and Freeman, H.E. (1999) *Evaluation: A Systematic Approach*, Thousand Oaks, CA: Sage.

Roth, M.S. (1981) Foucault's history of the present, *History and Theory*, 20 (1), 32–46.

Russell, N. and Willinsky, J. (1997) Fourth generation educational evaluation: The impact of a post-modern paradigm on school based evaluation, *Studies in Educational Evaluation*, 23 (3), 187–199.

Ryan, K.E. and Cousins, J.B. (eds) (2009) *The SAGE International Handbook of Educational Evaluation*, Thousand Oaks, CA: Sage.

Ryan, K.E., Chandler, M. and Samuels, M. (2007) What should school-based evaluation look like?, *Studies in Educational Evaluation*, 33 (3–4), 197–212.

Sahlberg, P. (2014) *Finnish Lessons 2.0: What Can the World Learn from Educational Change in Finland?* New York: Teachers College Press.

Saltman, K. (2010) *The Gift of Education: Public Education and Venture Philanthrophy*, New York: Palgrave Macmillan.

Sanders, J. (1999) The development of standards for evaluations of students. Paper presented at the Annual Meeting of the National Council on Measurement in Education, Montreal, Canada (retrieved http://www.jcsee.org/wp-content/uploads/2009/09/JCGeneralBackground.pdf).

Sanderson, I. (2002) Evaluation, policy learning and evidence-based policy making, *Public Administration*, 80 (1), 1–22.

Sauder, M. and Espeland, W.N. (2009) The discipline of rankings: Tight coupling and organizational change, *American Sociological Review*, 74 (1), 63–82.

Scheerens, J. and Creemers, B.P.M. (1989) Conceptualizing school effectiveness, *International Journal of Educational Research*, 13 (7), 691–706.

Scheerens, J. and Demeuse, M. (2005) The theoretical basis of the effective school improvement model (ESI), *School Effectiveness and School Improvement*, 16 (4), 373–385.

Scheerens, J., Glas, C.A. and Thomas, S.M. (2003) *Educational Evaluation, Assessment, and Monitoring. A Systemic Approach*, Lisse, The Netherlands: Swets & Zeitlinger.

Scheurich, J.J. and Bell McKenzie, K. (2005) Foucault's methodologies. Archaeology and genealogy. In Denzin, N.K. and Lincoln, Y.S., (eds) *The Sage Handbook of Qualitative Research* (third edn), Thousand Oaks, CA: Sage, 841–868.

Schwandt, T.A. (2002) *Evaluation Practice Reconsidered*, New York: Peter Lang.

Scriven, M. (1980) *Evaluation Thesaurus* (first edn), Port Reyes, CA: Edgepress.
Scriven, M. (1991) *Evaluation Thesaurus* (fourth edn), Newbury Park, CA: Sage.
Scriven, M. (2002) Evaluation ideologies. In Stufflebeam, D.L., Madaus, G.F. and Kellaghan, T. (eds) *Evaluation Models: Viewpoints on Educational and Human Services Evaluation* (Vol. 6), Dordrecht: Kluwer Academic Publishers, 249–278.
Sellar, S., Thompson, G. and Rutkowski, D. (2017) *The Global Education Race: Taking the Measure of PISA and International Testing*, Edmonton, Alberta, Canada: Brush Education.
Selwyn, N. (2015) Data entry: Towards the critical study of digital data and education, *Learning, Media and Technology*, 40 (1), 64–82.
Shiner, L. (1982) Reading Foucault: Anti-method and the genealogy of power-knowledge, *History and Theory*, 21 (3), 382–98.
Shore, C. and Wright, S. (2015a) Governing by numbers: Audit culture, rankings and the new world order, *Social Anthropology*, 23 (1), 22–28.
Shore, C. and Wright, S. (2015b) Audit culture revisited: Rankings, ratings, and the reassembling of society, *Current Anthropology: A World Journal of the Sciences of Man*, 3, 421–444.
Simola H., Ozga, J., Segerholm, C., Varjo, J. and Normann Andersen, V. (2011) Governing by numbers. In Ozga, J., Dahler-Larsen, P., Segerholm, C. and Simola, H. (eds) *Fabricating Quality in Education: Data and Governance in Europe*, London: Routledge: 96–106.
Simons, M. (2002) Governmentality, education and quality management, *Zeitschrift für Erziehungswissenschaft*, 5 (4), 617–633.
Simons, M. and Masschelein, J. (2006) The learning society and governmentality: An introduction, *Educational Philosophy and Theory*, 38 (4), 417–430.
Stake, R.E. (1983) Program evaluation, particularly responsive evaluation. In Madaus, G.F., Scriven, M. and Stufflebeam, D.L. (eds) *Evaluation Models: Viewpoints on Educational and Social Services Evaluation*, Norwell, MA: Kluwer, 287–310.
Stake, R.E. (2003) Responsive evaluation. In Kellaghan, T., Stufflebeam, D.L. and Wingate, L. (eds) *International Handbook of Educational Evaluation*, Dordrecht: Kluwer Academic Publishers: 63–68.
Stake, R.E. (2004) Stake and responsive evaluation. In Alkin, M. (ed) *Evaluation Roots: Tracing Theorists' Views and Influences*, Thousand Oaks, CA: Sage, 203–217.
Stufflebeam, D.L. (1972) The relevance of the CIPP evaluation model for educational accountability, *SRIS Quarterly*, 5 (1), 1–30.
Stufflebeam, D.L. (1983) The CIPP model for program evaluation. In Madaus, G.F., Scriven, M. and Stufflebeam, D.L. (eds), *Evaluation Models: Viewpoints on Educational and Social Services Evaluation*, Norwell, MA: Kluwer, 117–141.
Stufflebeam, D.L. (2001) Evaluation models, *New Directions for Evaluation*, 89, 7–98.
Stufflebeam, D.L. (2003) The CIPP model for evaluation. In Kellaghan T. and Stufflebeam D.L. (eds) *International Handbook of Educational Evaluation*, Dordrecht: Springer, 31–62.
Stufflebeam, D.L. and Coryn, C.L.S. (2014) *Evaluation Theory, Models, and Applications* (second edn), San Francisco, CA: Jossey-Bass.
Stufflebeam, D.L., Madaus, G.F. and Kellaghan, T. (eds) (2002) *Evaluation Models: Viewpoints on Educational and Social Services Evaluation* (second edn), Boston: Kluwer Academic Publishers.
Tamboukou, M. (1999) Writing genealogies: An exploration of Foucault's strategies for doing research, *Discourse: Studies in the Cultural Politics of Education*, 20 (2), 201–217.
Tanke, J.J. (2009) *Foucault's Philosophy of Art: A Genealogy of Modernity*, London and New York: Continuum Publishing.
Thévenot, L. (2009) Postscript to the special issue. Governing life by standards: A view from engagements, *Social Studies of Science*, 39 (5), 793–813.

UNESCO (2016) *Designing Effective Monitoring and Evaluation of Education Systems for 2030: A Global Synthesis of Policies and Practices* (retrieved http://www.unesco.org/new/fileadmin/MULTIMEDIA/HQ/ED/pdf/me-report.pdf).

UNICEF (2010) *Bridging the Gap 'The Role of Monitoring and Evaluation in Evidence-based Policy Making'*, New York: UNICEF Evaluation Office.

Van Dijck, J., Poell, T. and De Waal, M. (2018) *The Platform Society: Public Values in a Connective World*, Oxford: Oxford University Press.

Vedung, E. (1997) *Public Policy and Program Evaluation*, New Brunswick, NJ, and London: Transaction.

Vedung, E. (2010) Four waves of evaluation diffusion, *Evaluation*, 16 (3), 263–277.

Veyne, P. (1997) Foucault revolutionizes history. In Davidson, A. (ed) *Foucault and His Interlocutors*, Chicago and London: University of Chicago Press, 146–182.

Webb, D. (2003) *Foucault's Archaeology. Science and Transformation*, Edinburgh: Edinburgh University Press.

Weiss, C.H. (1977) Research for policy's sake: The enlightenment function of social research, *Policy Analysis*, 3 (4), 531–545.

Wickham, G. and Kendall, G. (1999) *Using Foucault's Methods*, London: Sage.

Williamson, B. (2016) Digital education governance: Data visualization, predictive analytics, and 'real-time' policy instruments, *Journal of Education Policy*, 31 (2), 123–141.

Williams, B. and Imam, I. (eds) (2007) *Systems Concepts in Evaluation: An Expert Anthology*, Point Reyes, CA: EdgePress.

World Bank (2011a) *The Changing Wealth of Nations: Measuring Sustainable Development in the New Millennium. Environment and Development*, World Bank (retrieved https://openknowledge.worldbank.org/handle/10986/2252).

World Bank (2011b) *Learning for All. Investing in People's Knowledge and Skills to Promote Development*, World Bank. (retrieved http://documents.worldbank.org/curated/en/685531468337836407/pdf/644870WP0Learn00Box0361538B0PUBLIC0.pdf).

Youdell, D. and Armstrong, F. (2011) A politics beyond subjects: The affective choreographies and smooth spaces of schooling, *Emotion, Space and Society*, 4 (3), 144–150.

Index

Note: **Bold** page numbers refer to figures, tables and boxes.

Abbott, Andrew 166–9
Actuality 5, 10, 52, 169, 173
Agonism 3, 10
Analytics 10, 50; of government 11, 16–20, 22, 25, **46–7**, 50, 53
Anatomy 82, 101, 139–40
Anthropological postulate 13, 145–9, 172–4
Archaeological quadrilateral 12, 102, 122, 141, 146
Archaeology: of educational evaluation 3, 45–9, 80–5; of human sciences 50–1, 79–80; of knowledge 26, 31–2, 34, 36, 42, 51; as method 2, 7–8, 10–11, 22–45, **46**, 50
Archive 30–2
Assessment 2, 56–66, **67**, 68–70, 74, 78, 85, 88, 90–6, 110–4, 161

Ball, S. J. xiv–xv, 52, 54, 57, 74–7, 95, 103–4, 123–5, 156, 160, 162, 168, 170, 173
Biology 2, 11–2, 51, 54, 72, 81–2, **84**, 97–101, **102**

Canguilhem, Georges 172
Clinique 3, 6–8
Comparison 2, 3, 60, 65–7, 75, 77–8, 89, 92–7, 103, 111, 131, 133–136, 139–140, 159–160, 166
Conditions of possibility 1–2, 11, 25, 35–36, 80, 86, 92–93, 97, 100, 119, 127, 138, 145–150, 156, 164–165
Critical ontology of ourselves 2–5, 8, 11, 14, 19, 45, 163, 173
Critique 3–5, 13, 19, 25, 50, 163, 168, 171

Dahler-Larsen, Peter 1, 54, 57, 73, 86, 89, 97–98, 108, 118–119, 129–131, 134, 136–137, 144, 149–151, 159
Dean, Mitchell 2, 4, 8, 14–18, 21–25, 49, 50, 142, 153, 155–162, 163, 167, 170
Deleuze, Gilles 25
Desrosières, Alain 73–74, 114,
Development 57, 91, 95, 102–104, 114–117, 122–125, 128, 131–136, 142–144, 148–150, 152–153, 159, 167, 170
Diagnosis 12, 94, 96–97, 100, 103–105
Difference 30, 43–44, 75–76, 85, 92–93, 95, 97, 119, 123, 132, 136, 140, 166–171
Discursive practice xiv, 23–28, 31, **46–47**, 49, 51–52
Discursive regularities 27–30

Educational evaluation 1–3, 6–10, 54–61, 163; as a dialectical and teleological techne 149, 151–152; as an enunciative field 53–61, 70–71, 80–85, 86, 105, 126, 164; epistemological space of 7, 49, 72, 78–80, **81**; as a form of modern ethic 149, 150–151; as a form of rationality 61–64; as a form of truth production 20–22, 24–25, 48; as a governmental practice 14–20, 49; globalised space of 59–61; as a governmental techne 66–68; as identity formation 68–70; as a paradoxical science of truth 149–150; politics of 166–174; and the project of a mathematical formalisation 73–78; as a regime of practice 7, 48, 53, 163–164; as a way of seeing and perceiving 64–66
Effectiveness 12–13, 57, 62, **83–84**, 90–97, 100–101, 103, 108, 119–122, 129, 132, 146, 149–151, 159–161

Index

Empirical–transcendental doublet 12, 146, 150, 155–157, 160, 164–170
Enlightenment 4–7, 12–13, 58, 74, 142, 147–150, 154, 164, 173; function 136
Environment 34, 52, 81, 88–91, 94–95, 97, 101–105, 108, 119, 123–126, 128, 139, 143, 153–155, 159, 164
Episteme 51
Epistemological ruptures 13–14, 163–173
Epistemology: of consciousness 173; constructivist 55, 143; of educational evaluation 101–103, 121–123, 140–142, 145–147; evidence-based 77, 165; liberal **102**, 118, **122**, **141**, 153–155; neoliberal **102**, 124, **122**, **141**, 156–158; positivist 128, 154; realist 65; social 77; subjectivist 127, 143
Ethics 3, 8–10, 125, 144, 145–146, 149, 152, 156
Evaluation 1–6, 10, 20–22, 45–49, 53–57, 73–78
Event 3–4, 22, 25–28, 30–31, 43–44, 48, 50, 164, 167–169, 173

Field: of concomitance 12, **38**–39, 51, 97–102, 118–122, 136–141, 145; enunciative 3, 11, 25–32, 42–43, 51, 53, 61, 80–85; of memory **38**–39, 51; of non-discursive practices **40**–42, **47**–48; of presence **38**–39, 51; of stabilisation 29–30; of use 29–31, 51; of visibility 11, 17–19, 45–**46**, 60, 66, 75, 86–89, 107, 119, 128–129
Formation: of concepts 21, 32, 38–39, 42, **46**, 49, 86, 105, 126; of enunciative modalities 32, 35–37, 42, **47**, 49; of the evaluand 87–89, 102–103, 106–109, 122–125, 128–131, 141–144; identity 11, 17–19, 45–**47**, 61, 66, 68–70, 84; of objects 21, 32–35, 42, **46**, 47, 49, 86, 105, 126; of strategies 32, 40–42, **47**, 48–49, 51
Forms of articulation 42–45
Foucault, Michel 2–10, 14–52, 72–74, 79–82, 97, 119, 136, 145–152, 163–164, 171–173
Freedom 8–9, 21, 35, 48, 54, 70, 123–125, 143, 153–157, 160, 163–165, 171, 174
Fulfilment 6, 12–13, 92, 142, 149–151, 164–165, 168, 172

Gane, Nicholas 143, 154
Genealogy 14, 22–24, 50–51

GERM 58, **67**
Government 11–13, 15, 20, 45, 56, 96, 125, 135, 145–146, 152–164; by numbers 73–78; of performance 159–162; of population 11, 53–55, 57, 72–73; reflexive 159–162; regimes of 11, 15–19, 22, 30, 45–50
Governmentality 11, 14–22, 53–55, 57, 72–78, 94, 103, 123, 142–143, 152–164
Grid of specification 12, **33**–34, 45–**46**, 49, 86–88, 90–91, 105–108, 114–115, 127–130, 147
Gutting, G. M. 25, 33–34, 38–39, 41, 48–49, 51

Hacking, Ian 74, 79
Hayek, Friedrich von 143–144, 157–158
Historical a priori 32, 51, 72, 79–82
History 89–91, 95, 102–104, 108–111, 121–122, 139–142, 148, 151–152, 168–174
Homo of educational evaluation 145–149, 164–166; and liberalism 153–155; and neoliberalism 156–158; and risk rationality 158–159; and welfare state liberalism 155–156
Hunter, Ian 54, 60, 166

Improvement 60–62, 65–**67**, 83–84, 94–95, 113–115, 123, 129, 148–151, 159
Indicator 66–**68**, 76–77, 91–92, 100, 114
Interdiscursive configuration 12, 42–45, 86

Kant, Immanuel 6–7, 50

Labour 12, 72, 80–82, 84–85, 108, 111, 117–125, 163–164
Liberalism 4, 13, 54–55, 123–124, 143, 153–156

Major-Poetzl, Pamela 30, 50
Man: figure of 78–80, 150, 153–159
Management theory 12, 105, 118–123, 145
Massey, Doreen 166–168, 171
Mathematical formalisation 72–80
Meaning 12, 82, 85, 126–144, 147–148, 158
Merit 82, 90–92, 102, 109–111, 119–123, 131, 142, 147–149, 160, 167, 172

Method of characterisation 12, 38–39, 85, 89, 93, 97–99, 100, 105, 108–112, 114, 121–122, 128–130, 132, 140–142
Miller, Peter 16, 54, 64, 157–159
Modernity 6–7, 54–57, 79–82, 136, 145, 150–153

Neoliberalism 2, 4, 13, 21, 54, 56–58, 71, 73–74, 78, 103, 123–125, 143–144, 156–158
Norm 13, 15–16, 35, 58, 74–75, 81–82, 92–95, 103–104, 117, 123, 132, 142, 147, 150–153, 164–172

Olssen, Mark 6, 15, 24, 26–28, 74, 104, 123–124, 143, 153, 160
Ontology 102–104, 122–125, 141–143, 145–149, 153, 160
Organisation 12, 56, 75, 82–**83**, 86, 89–96, 98–99, 102–105, 108–109, 111–121, 128–130, 134, 138–140, 146
Organisational theory 12, 86, 97–104, 145–146

Paradoxes: epistemic and ethical 3, 6–7, 12–13, 80, 125, 127, 140–141, 149–152, 160, 163–165, 170; political 3, 13–14, 54, 117, 124–125, 145, 152–160, 163–165
Peters, M. A. 4, 14, 58, 157
Political economy 2, 11–12, 72, 81–82, 105, 118–125, 145–146, 153–158
Popkewitz, T. S. 116–117, 166–173
Power, Michael 4, 56, 66
Present 1–5, 7–8, 13, 23, 31, 35, 84, 163–164, 168–171
Problematisation 5–8
Production 12, 81–85, 105–118, 122–125; forms of 105, 119–122
Prudentialism 159

Rabinow, Paul 24–27, 30–31, 48, 50–51
Rationality: forms of 11, 16–20, 23, 45–50; political 4, 13, 21, 54, 145, 152–159, 164, 170
Repetition 3, 7–8, 26, 29–30, 39, 164, 170
Revel, Judith 169–171

Risk rationality 142, 158–162
Rose, Nikolas 15–16, 54–58, 70, 73–80, 117–118, 156–161, 172

Same 151–152, 170–171
Sociology 12, 51, 54, 63–64, 127, 134, 136–142, 145
Space 103, 123, 142, 153–155, 164–168; epistemic 1–3, 6, 72, 78–**81**, 145, 148–152, 165; experimental 171–174; other 8–10
Statement 11, 23–32, **46**, 50–51; governing 42, 87–88, 105–106, 127–128
Study of language 2, 11–12, 72, 81–82, 127, 136–144, 146, 152, 164
Subject: historicization of 50, 166, 168–169
Subjectivity: forms of 5–7, 14, 22, 36, 43, 49–50, 155–157, 166–167
System 86–104, 107, 118, 126–127, 136–139; evaluation **67**; living 12, 82, 86–**87**, 97–104; of meanings 12, 82, 85, 127–136, 138–144

Techne 11, 16–20, 66–67
Thought 4–5, 7, 13–15; material forms of 20, 22, 30–32, **46**, 53, 61, 66, 68, 149–152, 169–172
Time 3–4, 8, 12–13, 103, 123, 142, 148–151, 153–155, 163–164, 166–169
Tree of conceptual derivation 42–45, **98**, **120**, **137**
Truth 2–10, 16–22, **46**, 50; game of 10, 22, 24, 48, 167; historicity of 24–26, 48; regime of 2, 8, 10–11, 16, 22

Value 86, 90–93, 97–98, 100, 102–103, 108–111, 117–122, 125–127, 131–132, 135, 139, 142, 148–151, 159, 165, 170; of education 22, 82, 105, 145, 149–150, 166–174

Webb, David 24–27, 30, 35, 39–40, 49–50, 147, 149
Worth 22, 82, 90–93, 97–103, 109–111, 127, 131, 147–149, 160, 167, 172